The Play Theory of Mass Communication

The Play Theory
of Mass
Communication

William Stephenson

The University
of Chicago Press
Chicago and London

Library of Congress Catalog Card Number: 66–23700
THE UNIVERSITY OF CHICAGO PRESS, CHICAGO 60637
The University of Chicago Press, Ltd., London, W.C. 1
© *1967 by The University of Chicago. All rights reserved*
Published 1967. Second Impression 1968
Printed in the United States of America

Spero meliora

In remembrance of
Lewis F. Richardson, F. R. S.

and dedicated to
M. B. S.

Acknowledgments

The chapters of this book are a selection from studies worked at during the past six years. One cannot be so involved without owing much to many people. I am indebted to the Dean and Faculty of the School of Journalism of the University of Missouri for welcoming so happily a psychologist into their fold. Thanks are due, too, to the Research Council of the University, and to Dr. Roy Keller and his assistants of the Computer Center, for computer time and assistance with programming, to which Mr. Thomas Danbury also contributed.

In the background I have been much encouraged by the keen interest in Q-method of Professor Malcolm McLean, Gallup Professor of Journalism at the State University of Iowa. I owe much to the late Lewis F. Richardson F.R.S. for personal friendliness and inspiration from his brilliant studies of foreign politics. Reflections of my years at the University of Chicago will be seen in the chapter on David Riesman's famous theory, and it is a pleasure to express here my admiration for his writings and insights. We enjoy a kind of second-cousin friendship, and I feel that he won't regret the methodological liberties I have taken with his concepts. My thinking owes much to the scholarly work of Johan Huizinga. I give my deep thanks, too, to the President and Directors of the D'Arcy Advertising Company of St. Louis, New York, and Chicago, whose generosity made possible the Distinguished Research Professorship I hold at the University of Missouri.

To Miss Tena Cummings, Ph.D., for her long labors and critical appraisals, I wish to express my deepest thanks: the book owes a great deal to her.

We have an obligation in communication research, Wilbur Schramm has written, to face the great problems. One of the greatest, surely, must lie in international communication. My efforts to define a problem in this area would have pleased Lewis Richardson — for he loved fun, and the irony of Play Theory as a counter to world conflict would have appealed to him.

Contents

1

Two New Theories of Mass Communication Research

From its beginnings, in 1924 or so, mass communication theory has concerned itself primarily with how the mass media influence the attitudes, beliefs, and actions of people. There was little evidence up to 1959, however, that the mass media had any significant effects on the deeper or more important beliefs of people. For a time it seemed that research in mass communication would "wither away," to quote one of its earliest advocates (9). It is now reviving, largely because of the urgent communication problems facing the newly developing nations of the world (109). The problem is still the same — how can the beliefs and attitudes of people be changed? — but the approach to it is now more circumspect.

What, then, can mass communication do? It is the thesis of this book that at its best mass communication allows people to become absorbed in *subjective play*. People read newspapers, magazines, and paperbacks in vast numbers, and there are ever increasing audiences for movies, radio, records, and television. All of this, it seems obvious, is enjoyable. But what exactly is this enjoyment? There are some who look with an uneasy eye at these mass pleasures; behind them they see the lurkings of "hidden persuasion" and "tyranny over the mind" (a view expressed by Aldous Huxley). Mankind, these critics feel, is being painlessly put to sleep, hypnotized by the cunning of advertisers and purveyors of mass pap for the public. This, it seems to me, is a jaundiced view. I suggest, instead, that often it is the very beliefs that mass communication cannot change that keep mankind out of step with the times. Careful regard of what mass communication is achieving shows that it is not only allowing people to enjoy themselves but is doing so in a distinctive way, the significance of which has been overlooked up to now. In order to see what this is we have to distinguish between two principles of great importance, one of *social control* and the other of *convergent selectivity*.

The principle of social control is made manifest in our inner beliefs and values. It gives us our religious belief, our political faith, our status and place in life. Depending upon the region in which we live, each of us follows the same customs, worships the same God, and has the same basic way of life. These are all subject to social control. The principle of convergent selectivity is very different. It concerns new or non-customary modes of behavior, our fads and fancies, which allow us opportunities to exist for ourselves, to please ourselves, free to a degree from social control. It is here that mass communication is important, and, as will be shown, in a fundamental way.

Typical of social control is the formation of public opinion. The object in a democratic system of government is to reach a consensus after due debate of the pros and cons of a public issue. The hope is that a large majority of the public will agree to the same conclusion. Allied to it is propaganda, which seeks through bias to sway public opinion. Different, however, is convergent selectivity, in which the object is to let each person choose something different for himself. Typical of convergency is the bargain sale, the rush of settlers for land, and much else — including our reactions to the entertainment poured out endlessly by the mass media. All these are characterized by a special excitement, by individuality, by wishes and wants. Advertising is based on the principle of convergent selectivity and not, as is widely believed, on the propagandist or public opinion principle of one for all. When one buys this or that toothpaste, car, or cookie, one has a certain freedom to decide for himself, under conditions not available to him before, conditions which have never been properly studied. We shall see that the conditions tend to be self-developing and self-enhancing — an enrichment of individual aspects of self rather than the reverse.

I was puzzled, when I first looked seriously at mass communication research in 1958, to find that little was being done in it to study the connection with entertainment. Writing later, Katz and Foulkes (59) had the same to say: "It is a most intriguing fact in the intellectual history of social research that the choice was made to study the mass media as agents of persuasion rather than agents of entertainment" (p. 378). The reason is to be found, in part, in the heavy load of conscience carried by these earlier theorists, who were bent on doing good in terms of their own values instead of being good scientists in universal terms. It is because I look at things as they are that I accept entertainment and the enjoyment of mass communication as worth serious scientific study. Most important here is the distinction to be made between social control and convergent selectivity, a distinction which opens the way to much of importance and interest in mass communication research and which has bearings upon what mass communication can and cannot do about people.

What is missing altogether in all earlier research on mass communication is any consideration of its *play* elements. I propose that neither social control nor convergent selectivity can be understood without attending to the play they enjoin. We are therefore to consider a play theory and not an information theory of mass communication.

The main idea is very simple, for in what does a person find greater enjoyment than in playing games? Not all playing is in the form of a game, however, with set rules and developed skills. We shall find that *subjective play*, which reaches into myth and fantasy, takes complicated forms of its own. We shall see that it is related to self-psychological considerations and not to instinctive or gross impulses of the human being. Here we shall consider a new concept of *communication-pleasure* (153), which holds that play has little gain for the player except in self-enhancement. Play theory is a cultural-anthropological concept with roots in history, and anything that is novel in my treatment of mass communication research stems from this cultural viewpoint, following the source work of the Dutch scholar Johan Huizinga (52).

My concern is to introduce these concepts of convergent selectivity and play theory as they apply to mass communication. They are of great interest and near to the heart of matters concerning what can and what should not be changed in human behavior by mass communication.

THE RESEARCH FIELD

Communication theory began with Lasswell (70), about whom there will be more to say later. Its scope is better understood, however, by looking first at the endeavors of a committee of professors of University College, London, who in 1955 set about the study of communication. Every department of the university collaborated, including zoologists, economists, mathematicians, linguistic experts, historians, physiologists, and electronics engineers (5). They were deeply concerned about the seriousness of communication problems in every part of life — in law courts, parliaments, news-gathering agencies, and newspapers, in relation to radio, television, and movies, in national and international affairs and within every large organization, business or otherwise. Vast complications of communication are everywhere of crucial importance, and yet, the committee argued, there is little or no scientific guidance for any of it. Millions of words are printed; advertisers bombard the public's eyes and ears; ideological leaders speak hortatively in constant floods of speeches, reports, and documentaries; and thousands of journalists, with or without training, are employed in modern industry editing and writing house magazines and information brochures — all, like a billion ants, informing or being informed by one another. Is any scientific order discernible, the committee inquired, in this interminable intercourse?

Some of the professors argued that the time was not ripe for its study because so little is known about the key to it all, the human brain. Others wondered whether there is need for a separate discipline for its study on the ground that everything possible is being done in the separate fields of psychology, engineering, and art to foster communication research. It was with misgivings that the committee recommended a separate place for communication research with its own scientists, pursuing its own theories. I would regard myself as such a scientist.

First among the theoretical matters, the committee argued, would be the study of stable systems of communication in which transmitters and receivers are mutually interactive — as happens, for example, in a conversation between two people. This means that one must study the human brain, how memory is developed and stored, how speech develops; it means the study as well of all the other tools of communication for transmitting, storing, and reacting to information, as in printing, painting, telephoning, movies, television, and so on. It becomes apparent, indeed, that the general body of principles upon which one has to proceed in this proposed new discipline consists of almost everything in the field of human intercourse. Languages have to be studied (both natural and artificial), as well as legal communication, music, movements and gestures, and even the dance of bees — for this, too, is communication: all concern the discipline. The sensory organs, and even stammering, have to be specially studied from a communication standpoint. Every sort of group and national organization, different nationalities, rumor, propaganda, and semantics, all come within its purview — as do automatic calculators, mechanical transmitters, and every manner of technical advance from the simplest telephone to Telstar. All of this, a "Compleat Angler of Communication" (as one might describe it) was seriously presented by the committee as a basic body of principles in relation to which the infant field of communication research must proceed!

One might wait for the millennium before giving birth to a theory of communication this way. Dr. Colin Cherry (16), one of the original collaborators on the committee, pursues his studies following a very simple concept of "bits of information," by which modern information theory, computers, and brain machines operate. Scientists are apt to abstract simple ideas with which to work rather than to become involved in every possible aspect of a domain; so Volta studied a tiny cell and not thunder and lightning. I do not accept the thesis that for communication research to prosper we have to study everything in the animal, insect, and human kingdoms having to do with communication.

INFORMATION THEORY VERSUS Q-METHODOLOGY

One of my preoccupations is with methodological matters, and we should compare what is here proposed with what is currently more popular under the rubric of information theory. Q-methodology and Q-sorting (147) is known well enough in psychological circles. Fundamentally it is a method by which an individual can model for himself what his attitude of mind is about complicated topics, issues, or situations. Its primary concern therefore is with a person's subjectivity as *he* describes it, not as *we* (psychologists or onlookers) infer it. All measurements in Q are central to the person — the scales, so to speak, are in the person's own mind. The method begins with data for a single case and then proceeds by comparing it with data from others. It begins with what one person models about himself and compares this with models provided by others. These models are then subjected to factor analysis. This method is to be used throughout these chapters.

Information theory is something quite different. Its language is that of electronics and telephony, of "information loss," "feedback," "directional flow," "networks," "bits of information," and the like; as this is in wide current use and seems to appear more scientific than my use of factor analysis, it is of importance to say at the outset why I have adopted Q–self-models and not the models of information theory.

A basis for comparison is available in the work of Ruesch and Bateson (124), who were among the first to adopt the language of information theory to communication problems. They recognized the special functions in communication of *evaluation* (such as editors undertake), *transmission* (by the various media or by word of mouth), and *reception* (by the public, by audiences, or by consumers). The principle of "feedback" was mentioned — as when consumers write to a manufacturer complaining about a product.

The total communication matrix at issue for any situation includes four different levels or systems, called the *intrapersonal, interpersonal, group,* and *cultural.*

The first is the "little black box" concept. The individual, X, can observe what goes on in his own mind (in respect to which he is a self-observer and totally and exclusively participant in what goes on), it seems, but no one can step into this black box to see what is in it — or so Ruesch and Bateson appear to say. What goes on, they suppose, can never be examined or codified, and discussion of it has to be carried out only in terms of neurological concepts of reception, transmission, central storage and the like. In short, brain theory is at issue; otherwise the consciousness involved is regarded as completely inaccessible to observation. It is admitted, however, that X can perhaps predict his own reactions — and better in some respects, maybe, than can anyone else. He cannot, of course, tell his own blood pressure or temperature unaided by instruments.

Ruesch and Bateson's second level is that of interpersonal networks. The typical situation involves equivalent parts in closed circuits, as when two persons, X and Y, enter into a conversation. This is discussed theoretically as having "no directional flow": what goes on is contained within X and Y. When X is talking, Y has to listen and understand at the same time, so that there is always "information loss" in such networks. It follows, therefore, that X can never grasp all of what Y communicates and vice versa. For the same theoretical reason there is always a discrepancy between X's (inner) view of himself and the knowledge he gets about himself from others such as Y. This is a level of language study and of non-verbal communication.

The third level of organization recommended by Ruesch and Bateson is the group network. In this there is specialization of function, and unequal division of receiving and transmission. One television transmitter may communicate to vast audiences, to millions of people simultaneously across the world. Or millions of people vote in an election to come to one decision. For the former it is from one to many, and for the latter from many to one. In the latter there is a progressive abstraction of communication — a presidential candidate could not possibly comprehend the myriads of thoughts and feelings cast in his direction during an election even if all could reach him. He has instead to grasp the "pulse of the public" to extract its major preoccupations. The assessment of public opinion is thus of great importance in communication research.

The fourth level of Ruesch and Bateson's schema is the cultural network. In this, innumerable influences communicate to innumerable people — from many to many. Each person living in a culture is conceived of as bombarded by countless messages, the sources of which he is quite unable to recognize; what is transmitted, and what received, cannot be ascribed; and "correction of information" is impossible. This is the network way of saying that the customary aspects of people's behavior are acquired under complex cultural conditions in which the printed word, monuments, myth, primary group, and similar conditions influence the individual without his awareness. Customary behavior is natural to him. Ruesch and Bateson regard this as an infinitesimal part of a person's total network of communication. There is in it no "atomism," that is, no symbolism of the basic effects so that research in the area is extremely difficult. Prediction and observation, we are told, are alike difficult; the influences are all beyond the reach of observation by the ordinary person.

DISCUSSION

Given a welter of facts such as confronted the University College committee, a good scientist certainly turns to abstractions and to simplification. Using formal models (118) he can record his beliefs about the facts and regularities in symbolic terms which makes it easier for him to think about the facts. Mathematical formulations especially lend themselves to scientific rigor. But one has always to ask whether the abstraction is really relevant to the facts. It is easy to be analogical and purely descriptive without being scientific at all. Insofar as information theory merely models a "constructive model," a network is like a radio set with resistances, capacities, conductors, and so on; it can never reveal new principles but can merely feed back what human ingenuity puts into it. Such a model may give a false sense of security, as though it were explaining something. Ruesch and Bateson, however, thought of their information model as more hypothetical (though not abstract in a mathematical sense) than purely "constructive," and this is of considerable scientific importance. The two authors made use of their theory in deductive respects.

One of their deductions was (*a*) that in interpersonal communication there is always "information loss." Another, at the group network level, was (*b*) that completeness of any information obtained by person X decreases with every increase in complexity and differentiation of the system. Another, in the cultural network, was (*c*) that correction of information is impossible in that network. Altogether apart from lack of precision in the use of the various terms, however, these deductions do not in my view constitute genuine advances toward acceptable principles. Thus, to consider *b*, it is true that in the modern world it is impossible for anyone to know everything about everything; but a process of proliferation, which runs in a direction opposite to *b*, is far more important. In advertising, for example, or in political propaganda, a simple slogan can induce new conceptions and attitudes, new "images" in the public mind. Communication is not just the passing of information from a source to the public; it is better conceived as a re-creation of information ideas by the public, given a hint by way of a key symbol, slogan, or theme.

It happens that Q-method is applicable to all four of the Ruesch and Bateson systems. The first, the *intrapersonal*, is basic to all else in Q. Ruesch and Bateson place this outside the realm of observation; I put it inside and give it precedence over all else. For me it is fallacious to seek to distinguish a region of consciousness which is outside the framework of systematic scientific observation. To do so is apt to make us overlook everything a person can observe and say about himself. Q-method is also readily applicable to the interpersonal level. X can describe himself, as can Y, and each can describe the other, as Q-sorts. Ruesch and Bateson had little to offer from information theory at the group level of communication, but again Q-method has much to say about it. It solves some perplexing methodological problems in the measurement of public opinion (139) and offers political science a primary tool for sampling political opinion to determine what opinions exist in the first place before attempts are made to count their incidence in the public.

The same is true for the cultural level; there are many ways in which Q-method applies to the study of cultures. The method of the cultural anthropologist, as described, for example, by Kluckhohn (65), is particularly interesting. The anthropologist is described as a "participant observer," "dispassionate," one who tries to "feel with" the culture he is observing, "to see things their way." He has to try to be objective in the process and not to be sentimental or to romanticize, as so many anthropologists and historians have done in the past. But he has to be subjective, to use his own feelings as an instrument of research. Kluckhohn's methodology fits that of Q-method almost completely. In particular, *social* character is an important concept in this area (a bit of "atomism" that belies the arbitrary deduction by Ruesch and Bateson that nothing of the kind can be found in the network). We shall see that social character is very easy to measure along Q-method lines. Riesman's (116) concept of social character is one of the easiest of cultural parameters to measure by Q.

In view of Q's comprehensive coverage of the whole communication field, therefore, I prefer to stay with it. Moreover, it is my view, born of long experience with attempts to apply formal models to subjective behavior, that one does better to proceed cautiously by analogy with other systems. As a wise student of science has said, if one can tend to the phenomenon itself, clearly defining it and shrewdly speculating about it, the models will build themselves.

THE SUBJECTIVE STANDPOINT

We shall begin, therefore, with the lowest level of Ruesch and Bateson's schema, that concerning intrapersonal communication. What, indeed, does a person say to himself; what conversations does he carry on in his own mind? This is likely to be crucial in any consideration of the effects of mass communication upon him from whatever source.

Focusing upon this subjectivity has wider consequences than appear on the surface. Our concern is to be with inner experience. Though in one sense this merely reflects the outer behavior of a person, the refusal of social scientists and psychologists to begin from this standpoint has seriously militated against progress in understanding human behavior. The movie critic and essayist Robert Warshow (162) in his work *The Immediate Experience* makes this clear for us in the field of communication. Warshow does not like the way people discuss "high" and "mass" cultures; in the arts, cultures are examined from the standpoint of what they represent in the world. Matters of paramount interest are dealt with by movie directors, for example, with emphasis on the "truth," or the "aesthetic" character of things. The sociologist or psychologist examines the cultures, instead, in terms of sociological or psychoanalytical interpretations — the gun play of Westerns is examined as an expression of latent homosexuality or of "phallic" adoration in the mass male audience of the country, all thinly covered over and made palatable by the dress of mythological cowboys and Indians. Warshow wanted to weave a way between the aesthetic preoccupations of "high" art and the crudities of "mass" psychology to consider instead the ordinary man or woman enjoying a movie, a newspaper, or a television program. It was an enjoyment he knew very well because he loved movies.

Thus, the focus has to be on the person looking, viewing, reading, listening — not as *we* observe him, but as he observes it all himself. His *self* makes all the observations from within. Warshow was a literary critic with formidable tasks of his own to make his points clear to his readers. Ours is a more difficult, a more laborious and tedious task — to succeed where there has been only literary perceptiveness such as his up to now.

A METHODOLOGICAL ADVANCE

There were good reasons why Ruesch and Bateson and information theory more generally could not model the intrapersonal level of communication. For over a century social scientists have been concerned with the fundamental problem of what should be the basis of measurement in their science. In physics there are units of weight and length, time and mass, and these suffice for all measurements. In the social sciences, when these units cannot be used, recourse is made to other devices either of an *ad hoc* nature (different therefore in every study) or else systematically constructed, as scales of intelligence, attitudes, personality, and the like. These scales are based on the large-sample theory and the *Theory of Error* (159). Psychologists understand this very well, for a branch of their work, called *differential psychology*, is fashioned upon this methodology. The principle is important: it supposes that if we wish to measure a person's intelligence (for example), a test is made and applied to a large sample of individuals from a parent population. According to the theory of errors, the scores gained by such a large sample, for a suitably constructed test, will tend to be normally distributed. The scores — whatever their units may be — can be transformed to *standard scores*, which are pure numbers whose mean for the test is 0 and whose standard deviation is 1.0. Being pure numbers, they involve nothing of the innumerable and even unknowable units involved in the tests. According to this, then, any test one cares to make for the parent population of individuals — however brief or long, whether about intelligence, attitudes, moods, temperament, opinions, or whatever — can be systematically reduced to standard scores, the same pure numbers for everything so measured. This, systematically, solves a very important problem of units; instead of length, time, or mass, the psychologist can use pure numbers, whose mean is 0 and standard deviation 1.0, for anything he cares to measure.

The elegance of this has long been overlooked even in the study of the psychology of individual differences; it is unlikely that the founders of this branch of psychology, Sir Francis Galton and Charles Spearman, would have been so remiss. The methodology suffers, however, from the limitation that all measurement in it is relative to the samples. The units for a sample of ten-year-old children would not necessarily be the same as those for a sample of adults, and it is difficult, if not impossible, to find any beginning point or absolute zero from which to begin to make measurements.

What I have done in Q-methodology is to discard these differential and parent person-population methods (called R-methodology [147]) in favor of a comparative one based on the single case. This miniscule procedure calls upon the individual to model his subjectivity (such as his attitude of mind about a matter) in the form of distributions of scores which are subjective to him but which again are subject to the law of error. A basis is provided in this way for measurement of anything *subjective* to the person. It looks at first sight as though it must be the antithesis of objective science and indeed for this reason the methodology has been slow to gain wide acceptance; yet it provides a basis for measurement of feelings, attitudes, opinions, thinking, fantasy, and all else of a subjective nature; and it does so in relation to the law of error. All scores are pure numbers; all are standard scores (mean 0, standard deviation 1.0). They are relative to a parent population of statements (and not individuals), whose nature will be described later. But, most important, the scores given to the statements by different individuals are comparable — the zero on all scales is the same absolute value for everyone.

Q-method is important in another way — every measurement made in the method is subjective and central-to-self of the person who performs a Q-sort. Every measurement involves the self explicitly, as a self-concept or the like (145). The importance of this becomes clear when it is realized that in all measurement along sampling (R) lines this self-reference is everywhere overlooked. The concern in Q-method is with a person's ideas, attitudes, opinions, beliefs, as these are modeled by the individual as such. A profound and basic error is made in R-method to achieve its objectivity: it measures *ideas, attitudes, beliefs, opinions*, and so on categorically — that is, as abstractions — oblivious of the self-reference which attaches to all such matters. In Q-method this mistake is remedied and all measurements retain self-reference. This will become clear later. We shall measure subjectivity and deal with subjective operations (Q-sorts) with all the rigor of science, using statistical and experimental methods to suit our needs. Information theory uses the objective units of science, of length, and of time, but it cannot operate at the intrapersonal level. I am confident that the intrapersonal is the most fundamental level upon which to make a beginning in social and psychological science in general and in communication theory in particular. With this beginning, as we shall see, we can probe into all four levels of the Ruesch-Bateson schema.

2

Methodology for
a Theory of
Mass Communication

Q-methodology is fully described elsewhere (147) and I shall here take much of it for granted. It is necessary, however, to restate some of the principles which are particular to these chapters. I am to approach mass communication theory entirely from the subjective standpoint, and this requires a radical realignment in methodology because all previous work has been from an objective standpoint.

DEFINITIONS

Certain prior definitions are required, two of particular importance. One concerns events that are to be scientifically modeled and the other what is selected to make their study possible.

Events. — An event, such as we are to study in communication, is always a tripartite interaction between a person (X), a medium or social mechanism (Y), and a "message" (Z). The event is an XYZ interaction.

By an event is meant a segment of behavior (147). Thus what people thought and felt about Khrushchev's visit to this country in 1959 constitutes an event. The visit (Z) was heard about, viewed on television, and so on by many of us (X), via the various mass media (Y).

It may seem a needless bit of formality to so designate events, but, as Wiebe (166) showed in his study of the difficulties in promoting a sense of civic responsibility compared with the ease of selling a soap, communication theorists have long made the mistake of discussing communication in terms of X and Z, forgetting the intervening mechanism Y. One can promote soap (Z) to women (X), knowing that supermarkets (Y) will make it easy for X to buy Z. One cannot sell "brotherhood" or safe driving or a sense of civic responsibility (Z) to anyone (X), because facilitating social mechanisms (Y) are missing. Promotion of safe driving $(Z$ to $X)$ has had little or no success. But if it became mandatory to cancel driving licenses for exceeding the speed limit, highways would no doubt become safer to drive along: canceling driving licenses is an example of a social mechanism.

The Selective Principle. — It is proposed that the basic elements in human communication in general, and mass communication in particular, are a person's self-referent opinions, discretely regarded, made in relation to events or situations as defined above, that is, as XYZ interactions.

Thus, about Khrushchev's visit to this country in 1959, a person may say: "I saw him on TV, and though I must say I admired the way he handled himself, I still would not believe a word he says." Such a statement is in the context of Khrushchev's visit and involves XYZ of the tripartite principle. A statement like this is self-referent, a matter of opinion, not a matter of *fact*, such as the remark, "I know Khrushchev is over fifty years old." Self-referent statements are subjective, involving "excess meaning"; it is the purpose of science, indeed, to determine what is fact and what is not. Thus, "self-referent statement" is a technical term, involving synthetic and not analytic propositions (60). The statements can be variously categorized as self-involving, self-reflective, self-justifying, self-denying, and the like. Clearly, not everything a person says about himself is a self-referent opinion.

Q-POPULATIONS AND Q-SAMPLES

A collection of self-referent statements made by a person (X) in an XYZ situation constitutes a Q-population.

There are many common-sense as well as technical ways of collecting self-referent statements from a person — by engaging him in discussion, getting him to write, using projective material, and so on, all in relation to the particular XYZ communication situation at issue. Thus, an intensive interview on the topic of Khrushchev's 1959 visit, or projective techniques focusing on Khrushchev's visit, would be technical ways to engage the person so that he provides self-referent statements unself-consciously.

These statements would provide a collection for the *one* person, but a more comprehensive collection can be made by taking statements from several persons. The law of diminishing returns applies to collections about any *XYZ* situation, however; statements from ten or twenty suitably chosen persons will provide a collection that can scarcely be bettered by choosing a hundred. About most events many statements are common to different persons, and almost every statement will mean something to many others, whether it was collected from one person or many. (Also, Q-method takes care of statements which mean nothing to a person, by scoring them zero in Q-sorting.)

Samples are taken from such a Q-population either at random or, more usually, in balanced block designs (147). Thus, in connection with a study undertaken by Stouffer (150) to test a theory about why some people prefer to get their "news" by radio and others from newspapers, we needed a Q-sample to fit the balanced design given later (Table 2). The design was replicated five times, resulting in the following Q-sample of size $n = 20$.

Q-SAMPLE (TRN)

1. Radio delivers the news first. (*ad*)
2. The newspaper delivers news more fully (at least the routine news). (*bd*)
3. Radio news costs next to nothing (once the overhead for the radio and current is paid). (*ad*)
4. Seeing is believing, and this makes television news fascinating. (*ac*)
5. Newspapers cater to minority interests, such as those who read the financial page, or society page, without losing the larger circulation among the general public. (*bd*)
6. Radio can be heard while you are doing other work, so that you are apt to hear the news without making any intention or special effort to do so. (*ad*)
7. You can read a newspaper when you like; it has not to be read at some specified hour, as happens for radio or TV. (*db*)
8. Listening to radio news requires a minimum of mental effort. (*ac*)
9. National and foreign news is particularly well reported on TV — more so than in metropolitan newspapers. (*ad*)
10. Newspapers permit the reader to select what he wants to read, and to skip uninteresting news. (*bd*)
11. You get a sense of intimate participation in looking at TV news. (*ac*)
12. In a newspaper the reader sets his own pace; he can reread anything he does not understand the first time. (*bd*)

13. Radio and TV do a good job of reporting local and community news. (*ad*)
14. I become more deeply involved in reading news in a newspaper — it is more absorbing than what you see or hear on radio or TV. (*bc*)
15. I miss hearing the news on TV — it is a habit with me, part of my day. (*ac*)
16. It is a habit — I miss hearing the news on radio if for some reason I cannot get near the radio to listen to it. (*ac*)
17. It is irritating to be interrupted while I am reading the news. (*bc*)
18. I get most of my solid news from the radio and TV: reading a news-paper is something different — it gives me more to think about. (*bc*)
19. The news on television is entertaining, but the news in a newspaper is more satisfying. (*bc*)
20. I often find myself waiting for the newspaper to arrive, but I rarely find myself waiting for radio or TV news. (*bc*)

The intention in each statement is that it is self-referent, but the "I" is frequently omitted for the sake of brevity. The symbols (*ac, ad*, etc.) refer to the design, a matter we shall consider in a moment.

It is important to notice that all of the statements are held to be synthetic; none is a statement of *fact*. It may be true that under certain circumstances radio can deliver the news first (1) but there are other times when it cannot.

Q-SORTS: BASIC OPERATIONS

X can give his impressions about an *XYZ* event, directly modeled as a Q-sort, in such a way that the self is central to it.

Thus, given the Q-sample of twenty statements about "news" X looks them over, grasps their meaning for him, and then sorts them first in three piles — those which he agrees with (+) are placed in one pile, those he disagrees with (−) in another, leaving those about which he is neutral (or indifferent, or unable or unwilling to express an opinion) in the middle (0). The piles are then further sorted into the form of a "forced" frequency distribution, say, on an 11-point scale from + 5 to − 5 with the following frequencies:

	Agree					Neutral	Disagree				
Score	+5	+4	+3	+2	+1	0	−1	−2	−3	−4	−5
Frequency	1	1	2	2	2	4	2	2	2	1	1

The Q-sample is chosen so that many statements *do not matter* to the subject, and so that there are as many for him to agree with as there are to disagree with.

Q-sorting is the basic operation of all work to be considered in the following pages. Q-sorts are correlated for set conditions of instruction for one person or for many, and subjected to factor analysis. The resulting factors are the basic classifications of our scientific work.

A Q-sort has the remarkable statistical properties noted in the first chapter. Reduced to standard scores the scores are pure numbers whose mean is zero and standard deviation is 1.0. This zero, because it is at a point of not mattering to the person, is necessarily at the same absolute level for all persons, for all Q-sorts, for all conditions of instruction for a given *XYZ* situation. Thus, all scores in the system are comparable, beginning from the same zero and all being pure numbers.

SMALL-SAMPLE DOCTRINE

Since Q-methodology makes use of relatively small samples (of both people and statements), it is necessary to say something here about this practice. As far as small samples are concerned, I follow Fisher's practices (32).

Social scientists use random sampling methods (whether probability, area, or quota) to select examples of people for their surveys. The practice depends upon the large-sample doctrine, which has a long history, stemming from Demoivre's discovery of the normal curve in 1721 to its rich development by Karl Pearson in the early 1900's. The law of error, upon which the doctrine depends, fascinated the early social scientists. Sir Francis Galton wrote:

> I know of scarcely anything so apt to impress the imagination as the wonderful form of cosmic order, expressed by the "Law of Error." The law would have been personified by the Greeks and deified, if they had known of it. It reigns with serenity and complete self-effacement amidst the wildest confusion. . . . whenever a large sample of chaotic elements are taken in hand and marshalled in the order of their magnitude, an unsuspected and most beautiful form of regularity proves to have been latent all the time [37, p. 86].

A parent population of persons is postulated, in the large-sample doctrine, as involving "chaotic elements"; people are so complex that it is considered better to start with the assumption that for anything one can consider about human beings and their behavior the law of error will apply. Thus, in current studies in the social sciences the endeavor is to reduce error to a minimum by using large numbers of cases — the larger the *n*, the smaller the error, and the clearer, therefore (or so it seems), will real facts appear. The law of error underlies all such thinking.

It is only in recent years, with Fisher (32), that a different logic has become acceptable. Fisher does not concern himself with reducing error to a minimum, but with measuring it in any given set of circumstances; one can then determine how far real facts occur in comparison with the measured error. This is achieved in relation to balanced designs (147) whose replication provides the necessary measurements of error in terms of which to measure the main "effects" of the design.

Thus, to study the over-all views of people about the relative merits of radio, television, newspapers, and news magazines as communicators, interviews would be undertaken with a small set of persons about the XYZ situation comprised of persons (X), media (Y), and incidental learning (Z). A collection of self-referent statements would be made of the kind, for example, "In my opinion, radio gets the news first."

A balanced block design for the situation is shown in Table 1. The design comprehensively covers all the major possibilities of media (A) and content (B), regarded as "effects," A with four "levels," and B with three. Every statement for the XYZ situation can be placed into one or

TABLE 1
BALANCED DESIGN FOR MASS COMMUNICATION

Effects	Levels				No.
A, Media	(a) Radio	(b) Television	(c) Newspapers	(d) News-magazines	4
B, Content	(e) News	(f) Features	(g) Advertisements		3

other of the twelve (4×3) combinations of these effects and levels, namely, into the following cells:

$$a\ a\ a \qquad b\ b\ b \qquad c\ c\ c \qquad d\ d\ d$$
$$e\ f\ g \qquad e\ f\ g \qquad e\ f\ g \qquad e\ f\ g$$

Thus, the following statement would be ae: "I like to listen to the news every hour on radio." The following is as certainly bf: "Jack Paar's program on TV is my favorite."

Five statements might be taken for each cell, providing a Q-sample of size $n = 60$. When this is quantified, as it is in a Q-sort, its variance, $\Sigma (d^2)$, is divisible into the following components (32, 147):

$$\Sigma(d^2) = \Sigma(A^2) + \Sigma(B^2) + \Sigma(A \times B) + \Sigma R^2$$
$$\text{d.f. } 59 = \quad 3 \quad + \quad 2 \quad + \quad 6 \quad + \quad 48.$$

Thus, hypotheses about either media (A) or content (B), or their inter-action $(A \times B)$, can be tested in terms of replication (R), which provides the basic estimate of error. Data for every Q-sort, or for every Q-factor, can be so examined. Thus, if $\Sigma(A^2)$ is statistically significant as judged by F-test for forty-eight degrees of freedom, $\Sigma(R^2)$, it means that one or other of the *media* matters more to the factor (or a Q-sort), for balanced conditions of *content*. If interaction is significant, it means that effects other than those specified (A, B) have mediated.

Since such analysis can be done on every Q-sort or Q-factor it is apparent that a method of testing is available in this manner which is not only versatile, but more logic-tight than large-sampling methods which deal only with single conditions. Here the concern is always with "effects" for balanced design, that is, A is proved significant or not when B is held constant, and vice versa.

The Q-statements for this same XYZ situation can be fitted into many different balanced designs. Thus, limiting the media to two levels instead of the four of Table 1 and introducing a theoretical effect instead of content, gives the design shown in Table 2.

TABLE 2
BALANCED DESIGN FOR MASS COMMUNICATION

Effects	Levels		No.
A, Media	(a) Radio-TV	(b) Newspapers	2
B, Play theory	(c) Ludenic	(d) Non-ludenic	2

The content is restricted to "news" and the new effect is a theoretical matter concerning play theory. There are four combinations for the design:

$$a \quad a \qquad b \quad b$$
$$c \quad d \qquad c \quad d$$

Q-sample TRN given earlier was based on this design, for five replications $(n = 20)$. The symbols in TRN refer to these cells *ac, ad, bc, bd*. The statements are postulated as ludenic or not on theoretical grounds; the logic otherwise is the same as for Table 1. Analysis of variance, for any Q-sort or Q-factor, would proceed as follows:

$$\Sigma(d^2) = \Sigma A^2 + \Sigma B^2 + \Sigma(A \times B) + \Sigma(R^2)$$
$$\text{d.f. } 19 = 1 + 1 + 1 + 16.$$

Q-samples are usually composed for balanced designs, but the Q-sort data are rarely subjected to variance analysis because usually we are not primarily interested in the specified effects. Thus, those for Table 1 would concern only known or logical possibilities, which we do not particularly wish to test. Those in Table 2 are more theoretical, but we are not ready to *test* these either (especially *B*). Rather, instead of *testing*, we wish to be inductive, that is, to make discoveries rather than to test specified hypotheses. The reasons for this are briefly as follows.

When individuals perform a Q-sort they are, of course, unaware of the structure; they merely offer a description of a condition. But in the process they are apt to project, to displace affect, to rationalize, and to do much else in a dynamic manner in relation to effects which are quite different from those of the Q-sample's structure. We want to be free, in analysis of Q-sorts, to make use of what the individual actually does in these respects. Again, I have argued elsewhere for the wider use of *abductive* inference (145), that is, for conditions which allow us to arrive at conclusions on other than *deductive* grounds. I therefore resort to factor analysis, an abductive and not a deductive method like variance analysis, to analyze Q-sort data. The structure of a Q-sample is nevertheless important; it helps to make Q-samples comprehensive and provides the formula for repeating any Q-sample.

Advice on how to construct a balanced design when one is confronted with a chaotic collection of statements for an *XYZ* situation is not easy to give; the possibilities are legion. Usually the situation itself indicates what is required, as was the case for Table 1. Theory of course helps, as for Table 2. But, given merely a collection of Q-statements, one can order them for the logic they themselves suggest. What is certain is that any discourse, in historical, political, psychological, or social science fields, when it is self-referred, can be stated as a balanced factorial design. This is always entailed in such discourse, and it should be a general practice to look squarely this way at its logical connections. I shall provide many examples of this logic later.

In practice I work with Q-samples of size $n = 60$ or so. Except for illustrative purposes, Q-samples of size $n = 20$ are scarcely large enough.

P-SAMPLES

The same logic is used to select subjects. Instead of randomly selecting individuals from a defined population by probability, area, or stratification principles, I seek to represent known interests in the selection, and choose subjects to fit balanced designs.

Thus in the study by Stouffer (150) to which reference has already been made it was deduced from theory that women and rural dwellers would prefer to get their news by radio whereas men and urban dwellers would prefer to get the news from newspapers. Stouffer used a random sample of 5,528 men and women across the northern states from Maine to Oregon to test his hypotheses. I would proceed, instead, with the factorial design in Table 3 to represent the hypotheses. There are 2×2

TABLE 3
P-SAMPLE FOR COMMUNICATIONS RESEARCH

Effects	Levels		No.
A, Region	(*a*) Rural	(*b*) Urban	2
B, Sex	(*b*) Men	(*d*) Women	2

combinations for this design, and a P-sample of size $n = 20$ would be taken by replicating five times for each combination:

$$a a \quad b b$$
$$c d \quad c d$$

One would end with ten men and ten women, five of each group urban and five rural. Whatever one measures the individuals for, whether by questionnaire or Q-sort, the effects can be analyzed by variance analysis; one tests in this way whether (*ad*) prefer radio and (*bc*) newspapers, whether men prefer newspapers irrespective of region, and whether urban people prefer newspapers irrespective of sex. All such hypotheses are asserted in the design, *and in balance*, a matter that Stouffer could not achieve in random sampling.

For my purposes, again, I am not primarily interested in such hypotheses. Many men may have feminine attitudes, and some rural dwellers may be highly sophisticated cosmopolitans. The allotment of individuals to the cells of the design, however, serves as a rough control of such effects, and the design helps us to put together comparable P-samples.

Most hypotheses in social science, such as Stouffer's, can be formally represented P-samples. Thus, for a communications study of Khrushchev's visit to this country in 1959 one could select a P-sample to represent the hypothesis that men and women are likely to have different ideas about the *XYZ* situation; also that political ideology may enter into matters; and, further, that poorly educated people are likely to have harsher super-ego structures than well-educated ones and thus will react differently to the situation presented by Khrushchev's visit. The harsher super-ego introjection to which Wiebe (165) called attention in his study of women's reactions to the Army-McCarthy hearings would be expected more among blue-shirt than among white-collar persons. Such considerations would lead one to compose a P-sample as illustrated in Table 4.

TABLE 4
FACTORIAL DESIGN FOR A P-SAMPLE ON KHRUSHCHEV'S VISIT

Effects	Levels			No.
F, Ideology	(a) Conservative-Republican	(b) Liberal-Democrat	(c) Independent or indifferent	3
G, Sex	(d) Male	(e) Female		2
H, Economic	(f) Blue-shirt	(g) White-collar		2

This is a $3 \times 2 \times 2$ design, providing the following twelve combinations:

$$a a a a \quad b b b b \quad c c c c$$
$$d d e e \quad d d e e \quad d d e e$$
$$f g f g \quad f g f g \quad f g f g$$

The factorial design formalizes the hypotheses and by the methods of variance analysis the effects can be tested for significance, using replication-variance for this purpose.

STOUFFER'S THEORY

The above P-sample for Khrushchev's visit represents a set of hypotheses but no apparent theory. What was novel in the case of Stouffer's (150) study, to which we can now give better attention, was the assertion of a theory from which it was deduced that men would prefer to have their news from newspapers, women from radio, and so on. The theory consisted of a set of "preliminary speculations," consisting of two lists — one of advantages of radio and the other of advantages of newspapers — as follows:

ADVANTAGES OF RADIO

a) Radio delivers news first.
b) It can be heard without cost (once you have a radio set).
c) You can listen to it while doing other things (e.g., during household work).
d) It requires a minimum of mental effort.

ADVANTAGES OF THE NEWSPAPERS

f) It delivers fuller news.
g) It can cater to minority groups (e.g., rural peoples).

h) It does not require attention at a specific time.
i) It permits selection by the reader.
j) The reader can set his own pace of reading.
k) It presents news pictures.

Stouffer deduced that in general rural women have little time to read newspapers, can work while they listen to the news on radio, and so on; therefore they would prefer to have news by radio. A comparable argument in terms of the postulated statements led him to deduce that urban men would prefer to have their news from newspapers. It may not be regarded as a profound theory, but it followed the pattern of the hypothetico-deductive method: postulates were asserted; a coordinating construct was introduced (the assumption that people prefer one medium to another); deductions were drawn; they were stated as testable propositions; and the testing on a 5,528 sample proved these to be true. Men actually did prefer newspapers, and women, radio, and so on.

Why then do I prefer to use factor analysis rather than such well-established methods? The reason is very simple: I do not accept the theories so employed, and I do not agree that they explain what they purport to explain. Thus one can provide a totally different set of "preliminary speculations" and derive the same hypotheses, proving them by the same 5,528 sample. Rural women, for example, are apt to think that newspapers are sinful, promoting sex, waste, violence, and the like; radio, instead, was thought of as a scientific marvel. From such "speculations" one can deduce well enough that rural women will prefer the news by radio rather than by newspaper. In general the hypothetico-deductive method has the failing that it ignores alternative explanations for tested hypotheses. I prefer to keep the door open for different theories, that is, for a different selection of postulates (from among innumerable available) in terms of which to explain data. It is for such reasons that I use factor analysis.

Our Q-sample TRN contains all Stouffer's "preliminary speculations" (really, his postulates for explaining data). But whereas they were all regarded as facts by Stouffer (requiring no proof in themselves) in our case all are synthetic propositions (all have excess meaning and cannot be proved easily except in general [averaging] terms).

It will become apparent that I make more use of information about subjects than is current in social science by large-sample methods. Individuals for us are never merely cyphers or numbers chosen by probability methods; instead, they represent known interests — being young or old, male or female, blue-shirt or white-collar, expert or non-expert, for example — information which is of aid to us, usually, in explaining factors.

FACTOR ANALYSIS

The common practice in Q is to proceed as follows. The individuals of a P-sample each perform one or more Q-sorts, for a given condition or conditions of instruction. The Q-sorts are correlated and factored; the factor loadings are rotated to an acceptable solution; and finally the factors are estimated, that is, a set of factor scores is estimated for each factor. All such calculations are programmed for high-speed computers.

We accept a factor if two or more Q-sorts are loaded significantly on it. The Holzinger-Harman table for standard errors of factor loadings is employed to determine significances (see 44, Appendix, Table B, p. 441).

It is instructive to continue with the Stouffer problem, using Q-method to deal with it. Normally one would conduct interviews with twenty or so adults, men and women, in rural and urban areas, selecting these by P-sample design (Table 3). The individuals would be encouraged to talk about newspapers, radio, and so on, and from the data so reached one would compile a population of self-referent statements relevant to the XYZ situation at issue (X the individuals, Y the media, Z the communication conditions). A Q-sample design would be composed. As an example, however, it is sufficient to accept the Q-sample TRN — which has the advantage that it includes all of Stouffer's original "speculations." I selected twenty-four subjects to fit the design of Table 3. Each performed a Q-sort with TRN to represent his or her preferences as far as radio-television-newspaper "news" was concerned. Table 5 gives the results. (I report only the factor loadings.) There are three factors, designated I, II, III. Several of the loadings are significant at the 5 per cent level, even though the Q-sample size is only $n = 20$. But all loadings greater than 0.50 in the table have some degree of significance and can be used to estimate factors, duly weighting each variable to take account of such degrees.

Thus in Table 5, the three factors are defined by the following variables, allowing a cut-off at 0.50 — anything above has significance, anything below, does not (variables 17 and 20 are on two factors; 12 and 22 are on none):

Factor	Variables
I	1, 2, 3, 4, 13, 14, 16 9 (-ve)*
II	7,* 8,* 10* 19,* 21,* 23*
III	5, 6, 11* 14, 18, 24*

*Rural

TABLE 5
FACTOR LOADINGS FOR A STUDY OF MASS COMMUNICATION ATTITUDE*
($n = 20$ Statements)

Variables (Persons)	Sex	Region	Factors I	II	III
1	M	U	66	41	36
2	M	U	66	−20	47
3	M	U	90	−06	13
4	M	U	72	19	45
5	M	U	35	14	61
6	M	U	23	22	75
7	M	R	36	72	34
8	M	R	−23	58	25
9	M	R	−64	26	17
10	M	R	−11	56	22
11	M	R	30	34	64
12	M	R	15	40	−08
13	F	U	62	34	07
14	F	U	38	15	54
15	F	U	82	07	05
16	F	U	74	−16	12
17	F	U	60	06	66
18	F	U	34	−02	67
19	F	R	−24	74	16
20	F	R	55	56	27
21	F	R	03	50	33
22	F	R	19	−40	40
23	F	R	−11	85	18
24	F	R	−02	22	64

*U = urban; R = rural; decimal points are omitted.

The factors are each well defined by six or eight variables; of the twenty-four variables, twenty are in simple structure (147). This means that clear-cut differences are provided by the analysis.

Anyone who cares to make the calculations can apply variance analysis to the loadings, for the design indicated by Table 3, for each factor in turn. It is enough to observe by inspection, however, that in factor I urban males predominate; in factor II the most significant loadings are for rural persons, male or female; for factor III nothing is significant with respect to male, female, urban, or rural. That is, if we were factorists of R-method, we would probably interpret the first factor as for urban males, the second for rural persons male or female, while the third would be inexplicable.

Q-FACTOR MODELS

The ultimate concern in Q is not with tables of factors and their *load-ings*, but with tables of factor *scores*. These are the scores gained by each statement of the Q-sample, for each factor in turn. I call such tables Q-factor models.

Factor-score estimates are made by adding the scores across statements of the Q-sample for the variables of a factor, weighting each in accord-ance with Spearman's expression (No. 20 in the Appendix to his *Abilities of Man* [135], p. xix). These calculations are also programmed for a computer. Thus, for factor I the scores would be added across each state-ment of the Q-sample for variables 1, 2, 3, 4, 13, 16, and 9 (-ve), each duly Spearman-weighted. For factor II variables 7, 8, 10, 19, 21, and 23 would be used; and for III, variables 5, 6, 11, 14, 18, and 24. Variables having significant loadings in two or more factors are not used in these estimates. The results, for the data under consideration, are given in Table 6. It is usual to report factor scores in standard-score terms (mean 0, standard deviation 1.0), but for some purposes it is more convenient to have the scores in equivalent Q-sort scores; this has been done in Table 6.

Q-factor models are the main focus of interest in Q-method, to which

TABLE 6
Q-FACTOR MODEL FOR STOUFFER'S
COMMUNICATION PROBLEM*

	Factor		
Q-Sample Statement	I	II	III
1	0	3	2
2	+4	1	3
3	0	−1	−1
4	−3	1	2
5	0	0	0
6	1	4	0
7	1	2	2
8	−1	0	0
9	0	−1	−4
10	1	2	4
11	−4	0	1
12	3	3	3
13	−1	0	−1
14	3	−4	1
15	−3	−3	−3
16	−2	−1	−2
17	−2	−2	0
18	−1	1	−3
19	2	−3	−1
20	2	−2	1

*Scores are in equivalent Q-sort scores; differences of 2 are significant across factors.

all else leads. Each statement of a Q-sample is a matter of opinion, that is, a synthetic proposition into which different meanings might be read. Each, in effect, is a tested hypothesis in miniature; each can be compared with every other statement and its scores. Factors are interpreted, and new hypotheses are arrived at in terms of these minutiae. It is worth noting in passing that Q differs from R very remarkably in that in R analysis ends with tables of factor loadings, whereas in Q such tables are merely a beginning of the analysis, which ends with Q-factor models.

INTERPRETATION OF FACTORS

One interprets a factor in terms of the factor scores gained in it by the statements of the Q-sample. By noticing which statements gained the highest scores (positive or negative), which gained zero and so forth, one reaches an explanation. Thus, for factors I, II, III of the above example our interpretations proceed in the following manner.

Examination of Table 6 will show that statements 2, 4, 11, 14, 19 are particularly discriminative for factor I; the factor clearly favors newspapers over radio or television. Absorption in newsreading is characteristic of these readers, who are able to distinguish this from mere entertainment by television (statement 19). Similarly for factor II, statements 1, 2, 6, 14, 18, 19, 20 are highly discriminating, and the factor clearly favors radio and television for news. One should notice the lack of finer sensibility for factor II, at statement 19. The factor is aware of the greater demands put upon the reader of a newspaper, but it recognizes no absorption in newsreading as such.

Factors I and II correspond to Stouffer's hypotheses, tested as factors. But Stouffer had no hypothesis corresponding to factor III; nor indeed had I when I made the factor analysis. It represents a discovery, though perhaps not a very unusual one. Nothing can be said about it from the P-sample or from the table of factor loadings (Table 5); it involves men and women, rural and urban, without distinction. It is not ludenic for newspapers, that is, the individuals do not indicate the characteristic absorption in newspaper reading. The element of "skipping" (statement 10) suggested that perhaps these individuals got their news from news magazines. I could test this by looking back at the interviews conducted with the individuals concerned to see whether they had mentioned the fact that they got their news from *Newsweek, Time,* or the like. I found that indeed this was the case.

The interpretations were therefore as follows:

Factor I. — Rejects TV as a source of news and has formed no habit for TV or radio listening or viewing. The factor has high regard for newspapers as sources of news; if one is an avid newspaper reader, one can find little perhaps to be satisfied about or to form news habits about in television or radio news. Such newsreading requires urban standards of interest and education.

Factor II. — Prefers news from television and radio, without becoming much involved. These media entertain or offer a passing word, but nothing in the way of *interpretation* of news, so that little but bare fact is communicated to these individuals. A lower level of education is indicated, such as would be the case for mainly rural subjects.

Factor III. — Nothing in the Q-sample concerned news magazines, but it seems that some people (men and women, rural or urban) rely more upon these for their news than upon newspapers or TV or radio. They are devoid of deep involvements in newspapers, but might well have wider interests, such as in foreign affairs or art, which are fostered by the major news magazines.

We reach an understanding which in its simplest terms suggests that newsreading for some people is absorbing, whereas television and radio as sources of news are not. Why people relate so differently to these media is not their supposed advantages (such as Stouffer listed) but deeper habits which people bring to the situation. What these habits are can only be a guess at this point. But it is not enough to think that they depend upon the speed of radio news, the "seeing is believing" of television, the small cost of radio, and the like listed in Stouffer's "advantages."

More sophisticated Q-samples are necessary to pursue the matters only hinted at in the above example. The hint is that factor I involves subjective play, whereas II does not. It will be important if it can be shown that newspapers lend themselves to such play about news, whereas the electronic media merely entertain — the former being self-directed, the latter not. The difference is that of deep involvement in play and merely gaping at a spectacular show. These are matters of genuine theoretical interest which Stouffer missed altogether.

In an interpretation one needs to have an estimate of the standard errors of the various factor scores in Table 6. This I have dealt with elsewhere (146).

THEORY OF Q-FACTOR MODELS

In a letter to *Science* entitled "One-tailed Test of Trivia," Ward (160) observes that although a clear statement of a problem in a research is of course essential, its solution is usually not a simple matter of gathering data with explicit hypotheses in mind. Where causal connections are complex, I would add, one proceeds theoretically. This I attempt to do with the Q-sample statements and the scores they receive on the various factors, as these appear in a factor model. That is, I do not stop with an interpretation of the factors, but use the model to examine any hypothesis I care to put to it, irrespective of the factors. Each statement of the Q-sample, in a Q-factor model, has as many scores as there are factors. Each, being a synthetic statement, offers an opportunity for insights and unexpected results from which to arrive at hypotheses that we could never have grasped otherwise. Since there are usually a large number of statements ($n = 60$ or the like), the number of such discoveries can be rather large, each usually involving a combination of statements. The richness of the technique in this respect can only be dealt with by illustration — some attention is given to it later.

Meanwhile it should be said that Q-factor models represent a considerable achievement in technical respects. The one table of factor scores lists the only Q-sorts for an XYZ situation which occur with consistency; it is independent of the size of the P-sample. Theoretically it models major conceptions, images, or viewpoints about a situation for the public at large (if, as is reasonable, one projects data upon the wider public, having regard to any limitations involved).

EXPLANATION IN Q-METHOD

There are some general questions about explanation and interpretation which need to be answered before leaving this introduction to methodological matters.

Toulmin (157) suggests that there are three logically distinct types of explanation — a *stated* reason, a *reported* reason, and a *causal* explanation in a material sense. When a person says he smokes to soothe his nerves, he is giving a stated reason. If his friends say that he is always on edge unless he has a cigarette in his hands, it is a reported reason. If a scientist says that the taste of cigarettes is due to the tar and nicotine content, the concern is with material causes. Philosophers, including Toulmin, are fond of denying any scientific status to stated reasons: if a man says he feels sick, no one need believe him, and what *he* says can never be proved either true or false, that is, by way of any stated reasoning. But this, unfortunately, is apt to be taken too literally — there are some who think of Q-sorts as in some way only *stated*, not reported or causal in any scientific sense. Clearly, no one is suggesting that we have to believe a person's Q-sort self-description, but it is a simple matter to show whether or not what he says is reliable, and easy to show whether other regularities are to be observed for it as well, as when what he says about himself correlates with what others say about him. With such facts as a beginning, it is possible to go further and to give reported and causal reasons °or the facts. Factors are evidence, of course, of systematic conditions.

It is important to distinguish between *ad hoc* and genuine hypotheses. In current jargon a fact is explained if it is the conclusion of a valid deductive inference — only genuine hypotheses explain anything, Thus, when salt is put in water, it dissolves and the salt is said to be soluble in water. Solubility is thus attributed to the salt. But this is an *ad hoc* explanation, not a genuine one; it tells us nothing new and nothing more than is contained in the statement that salt, put in water, dissolves. The explanation becomes a genuine one only if it can be said that in solution the molecules of salt are held in suspension in Brownian movement (or the like), for reasons that can be given deductively, involving other primitive tests.

Factor analysis is associated with R-methodology more than with Q. In R all explanation, however, is of an *ad hoc* nature. Thus, the factorist finds that mental tests involving numbers (arithmetic) are clustered in factor space, that is, they can be operationally classified as alike — and one calls the factor n, or number factor. Similarly v is the factor for verbal tests of intelligence. To so designate factors is clearly only of taxonomic interest — no genuine hypotheses are at issue. It would have been very different if tests of number and tests of color blindness happened to cluster as one factor; in that event the factor could scarcely have been called either number or color, and one's curiosity would have been whetted to find a genuine explanation for such an interesting fact. There is scarcely a single convincing fact of the kind in all R-method and, therefore, scarcely a genuine hypothesis anywhere at issue.[1] Q-method, on the contrary, never concerns itself with *ad hoc* explanations; it is always involved in genuine explanations. Thus, if a woman gives a Q-sort self-description, and then (with the same Q-sample) a Q-sort description of what she thinks her husband is like and these two descriptions are alike, constituting a factor, one seeks a "cause" for

---

[1] This is not true of Spearman's own work, which Thurstone and others quite misunderstood in this respect; Spearman looked for genuine explanations (eduction) for wholly dissimilar tests.

the identity; either the woman has misunderstood the instructions, or she is so identified with her husband that one suspects either idealization or projection. The nature of the factor itself, that is, the order of the statements of the Q-sample for the factor at issue, will allow us to say which it is. The concern in every instance of a factor in Q-method is with such genuine hypotheses, genuine explanations of this kind. Each leads directly to additional primitive tests; each is a conclusion to valid deductive possibilities. The same applies to the hypotheses for each Q-sample statement in turn; each involves a genuine hypothesis, the interpretation as a whole consisting of perhaps several, complexly interrelated. Primitive tests are hinted at or implied in every case; some are undertaken, using perhaps a different Q-sample for the purpose with a different design, and a different P-sample. Interpretation is a matter of successive penetration into data in this way, guided by theory.

Chief among the guidelines for such penetration is a view we have about opinions, attitudes, and beliefs, a matter dealt with later. Q-statements are matters of opinion; Q-factors are attitudinal; and explanation reaches into belief systems which subserve both attitude and opinion. All such, and our knowledge of psychological theory, mainly dynamic psychology, are brought to bear upon the arrays of factor scores in a Q-factor model wherever an explantion is sought for a factor.

SUMMARY

It may be said that I am putting the cart before the horse in defining a methodology without saying what the theory is that it purports to measure. A methodology is not merely a technique, however, but a profound way of approaching nature. The methodology involving the above definitions of Q-populations, Q-samples, and Q-sorting is set in a basic theory placing subjectivity — a person's own reflections on matters — at the hub of all else. This premise extends over all psychological or social science, and thus is not particular to our concern with mass communication theory.

Meanwhile it is important to have the above definitions and principles clearly stated. In summary form they are as follows:

1. Communication via mass communication is grasped by *persons*, not *audiences*.

2. It is in a tripartite context of the person (X), the media or social mechanisms (Y) and an event or message (Z).

3. What communication means, what its effects are, what may or may

not result from it, is never directly a matter of ideas, notions, beliefs, attitudes, opinions, wishes, or the like, but always directly ideas, notions, beliefs, etc., *of a person*.

4. The primary data, therefore, are the person's self-referent statements. These are primary elements of communication theory.

5. A collection of these statements, for a particular XYZ, constitutes a Q-population, samples from which provide Q-samples with which X can perform Q-sort self-descriptions which are homologous with X's ideas, notions, beliefs, attitudes, etc. These are the basic operations of mass communication research.

6. Correlated and factored, these provide an objective basis for classification and comparative study for an XYZ situation, whether for one X or for many.

7. The factors are available for genuine explanation, that is, as matters of scientific theory.

The above, it is believed, lay the foundation for scientific work in mass communication research. From Lasswell's (70) early work to Festinger's (31) most important, all can be looked at afresh in the light of the above fundamental methodology.

3

Principles
Concerning Audiences

I have not completed the methodological framework upon which to launch a theory of mass communication; a position has to be taken about audiences. These, up to now, have been *ad hoc* in nature, as when one speaks of a television audience, a consumer market, or the general public. The concern is with viewers, voters, consumers, and so on, as defined categorically by scientists, pollsters, or market researchers. We have now to look at audiences in a different way, namely, as they are defined by the individual members of such audiences through operations that they themselves perform. It will be difficult for many workers in communication research to make the switch from an objective to a subjective view of audiences. The concern is very like that discussed earlier in connection with the views of the movie critic and essayist Robert Warshow in *The Immediate Experience* (162). Warshow objected to culture being arbitrarily categorized as "high," "low," "middlebrow," or the like; he wanted to study mass communication from the standpoint of the actual immediate experience of the person looking at a movie, reading a newspaper, or sitting in front of a television set. I have the same purpose: audiences are defined by the experiencing person himself and not by what others say about him on categorical grounds.

But some categorical views about audiences deserve mention before I give my own version of what is required. There is a matter of a difference between *mass* and *public* audiences which is important.

MASS VERSUS PUBLIC AUDIENCES

Over the past twenty years a great deal of discussion has centered on the differences between the mass, conceived as a new fact of modern societies, and the public, which has been with us from the days of ancient Greece.

Publics, traditionally, have concerned issues, controversies, faiths, and ideologies. People were supposed to get together to discuss courses of action for their mutual well-being, to share ideas, and to make concessions, so that after due consideration they might act collectively. The object was to reach a consensus, agreed to largely by everyone. We now know, of course, that matters are rarely as simple as this suggests. Voting in a presidential election is not a consequence of rational consideration of the policies of the candidates so much as it is dependent upon early introjected beliefs, social controls, and much that is far from rational or understood by the voter (11).

The mass is differently conceived: people are seen, in the mass, as isolated and separated from one another, millions seated in front of television sets, sitting substantially alone, and therefore directly under the influence of the mass media, whether movie, newspapers, radio, magazines, or television. As such the mass is considered by some to be at the mercy of these media, which can manipulate them at will and arbitrarily. By others, however, the mass is seen as offering at least opportunities for people to free themselves from constraints that limit much of their behavior in social and community life. Man can be free, in a measure, to think as he pleases.

The two concepts, of a public reaching a consensus and of the mass being manipulated, are probably one and the same thing. But the idea of the mass as offering a certain element of freedom to man is something else. I propose to draw a sharp distinction between the *public* (and related concepts of public opinion, social control, and deep belief systems) and the *mass* as relatively free of constraint. Following Blumer (13), I give the term *convergent selectivity* to the latter.

CONVERGENT SELECTIVITY

Political science deals with public opinion, propaganda, and publics; mass communication deals most characteristically with convergent selectivity, advertising, and entertainment. Public opinion and ideologies go hand in hand; and certain aspects of social character and convergent selectivity are related.

Conditions of convergent selectivity in the mass are seen in gold rushes, migrations, land booms, urbanizations, and the like, as well as in the vast audiences of the mass media. At one extreme, for example in a gold rush, it is a case of every man for himself, law, order, and all else being thrown to the winds. Similarly in advertising one characteristically wants to sell *one* old piano to *one* person — classified ads in their tens of thousands every day attest to the convergence of one person on one object for sale. Mass marketing of mass-produced products in free economies has tended to hide the fact that the products become idiosyncratic by the time they reach a buyer; it is difficult to find two cars exactly alike because differences of color, interiors, accessories, engines, and so on make it possible for everyone to have a car for himself, different in some way from almost any other. The diversity and selectivity of this has long been overlooked, and advertising has been criticized for conditions that relate to publics and propaganda and not at all to convergent selectivity.

It is fair to say, also, that in the immediate experience of convergent selection there is a heightened self-awareness, a greater receptivity in the person. One is a free man in front of a television set, or with a newspaper in one's hands, to a degree not achieved before by man in his long history. The same is not true of a man in his concern with public opinion.

AUDIENCES DEFINED

I turn to the operational definition of audiences. When, for an *XYZ* situation a number of persons perform Q-sorts, the factors define audiences, each consisting of all persons on one factor and on no other.

Since I can scarcely hope to pre-empt the term "audience" for my own use, I propose to call operationally defined audiences "Q-audiences."

Certain consequences follow: (1) The *XYZ* situation is likely to be segmented with respect to Q-audiences, because it is usual to find more than one Q-factor for any situation. (2) Q-audiences are always in relation to the particular *XYZ* situation from which they derive.

These definitions are of considerable theoretical and practical importance. They solve, between them, many problems of "audience variables" (154).

Thus, if one is studying the market for tuna fish (to take a simple example), it will be an interactional situation (2), and the market is likely to be segmented (1); some people use tuna fish only for snacks, whereas for others it is a cheap staple food. The two constitute very different approaches to the food; its significance in the family budget, quality considerations, the type of recipe involved,[1] and so forth, differentiate the one segment from the other.

Q-audiences are therefore always dependent variables in our scheme of things; they are at the output end of our studies. Clearly, however, they are of first importance in all marketing studies, in all measurement of public taste (as well as of public opinion), and in all consideration of a "mass society" or "mass audiences" of any kind.

SEGMENTATION OF AUDIENCES

The fact that most audiences are composed of several different Q-audiences presents a difficulty for the principle of convergent selectivity, though not for measurement of public opinion. When we measure public opinion, it is usual to find at least two sides to the question at issue — in an election one group votes for one candidate and another for his opponent. But insofar as the *mass* is segmented into Q-audiences, it suggests that all the people of the same Q-audience are in some sense alike, directed to the same ends or wants and not to idiosyncratic ones.

Thus, advertising practice has learned that markets are segmented. Among buyers of the American automobile the segmentation was quite sharp in 1955 for the big-three popular cars, the Plymouth, Chevrolet, and Ford, each selling in the hundreds of thousands. They were priced at about the same amount and, regarded as value-for-money, there was little to choose between them. But they sold to distinct Q-audiences, not dependent on sociological or demographic circumstances but on differences in *social character* (such as Riesman describes [116]). Plymouths were sold to people of a traditional turn of mind; Chevrolets found their most characteristic buyers among inner-directed persons; and Fords went more to other-directed, youthful customers.

Even so the principle of convergent selectivity applied, supra-ordinate to these more pervasive conditions. The choice available for any of the three was still enormous, and each person could still make his own idiosyncratic purchase.

An example from national advertising is also illuminating, taking the case of two popular soaps, Zest and Camay, sold in every American supermarket. It is true that one is a chemical detergent and the other a fatty soap, but both serve to wash away dirt at the same price and with

---

[1] These statements about budget, quality, recipes, and so on can be expressed by a Q-sample of self-referent statements relative to the *XYZ* situation for tune fish: Q-sorts with such a sample bring the segmentation to light.

much the same efficiency. But a consumer segmentation separates them. Some people prefer the physical stimulation of a shower; others prefer the luxury of a bath. Zest serves the former and Camay the latter. Zest, as the name suggests, is for physical, virile use, for people who want to "get on" with the job of getting clean, and who shower for a "surf-riding healthy glow all over." Camay, with its Parisian perfume, insinuates romance instead, and relaxation in the soothing water of a hot bath. The two segments, each captured by its own soap, are quite distinct. Yet no two persons ever shower or bathe in the same manner. The principle of convergent selectivity would guide the advertiser to foster both the segmentation and the diversity. It would entice women in the one segment to become really feminine, spending an hour in the bath and using bath oils, colognes, powders, and so on, all as adjunct to sophistication and delight. Such image creation, no doubt wasteful in the eyes of economists, is testimony to human expansiveness and versatility. The advertiser does not merely sell a soap; he fosters finer human sensibilities, fashions, manners, new customs, and delights as well.

IMAGES

An important concept in communication research, stemming chiefly from advertising research, is *image* — meaning conceptions of and associations with products or ideas, usually of a dynamic nature (143). Advertising changed the feminine image of the Marlboro cigarette to that of a somewhat psychopathic male. The American image of the Far East has two incompatible elements in it, one of cruelty (of the Fu Manchu), the other of saintly stoicism (Confucian); the two are self-contradictory (105). Thus, it is convenient (in relation to self-justification) to regard Red China as evil now but solidly virtuous a few decades ago "Dumb blonde" is an example of the same incompatibility: she's *blonde* and desirable — but if she is not for me, then she's dumb; or she's *dumb* — but if for me, then she's beautifully blonde. Ambivalence of the kind, or other dynamic factors, characterize images.

A large-scale example of image-changing is described by Matthews (81) for the London *Mirror*, the newspaper with the largest daily circulation in the world. Some years ago it was considered to be a disreputable sort of rag for middle-aged, lower-middle-class readers who wanted sensational rather than straight news. It had such a reputation with the public at large, and it probably was just such a newspaper for just such readers. Its circulation was dropping. The paper was therefore given a face-lifting; its image was made into that of a paper for younger (twenty to twenty-five years old) working-class men and women, for the "common man," with a "warm, colorful, crude but kindly" personality, "often jolly, always downright, with no patience for big words or complex ideas, prone to sudden angers and belligerent questions, irreverent of clerical or mundane authority," but nevertheless a firm believer in its own and its readers' common sense and decency — so writes Matthews (81). The paper became a "vulgar extravert," "definitely not a lady," but one who "knows her way around."

The paper was deliberately designed to be in tune with a segment of the mass in Britain which was new, upward-moving, youthful, yet characteristically British and not American. The conception assumes *one* personality, as though everyone in the segment has much the same strivings, tastes, intelligence, desires; all desire a "little more of what it takes," a little more money, more consumer goods, more fun. The XYZ interaction at issue is very broad: the segment (X) is described theoretically as something of a "vulgar extravert"; the social mechanisms (Y) are the new social conditions, with new cars, new small houses, new possibilities of cheap European travel, new freedom from dire medical expenses, new interests in television, and so forth, all characteristic of the upward-moving working class; the communication (Z) to this segment is the *Mirror*'s daily sugar pill of flattery for its extraverted young Britishers. It does not follow in the least that everyone in the segment wants the same car, however, or the same tea, the same television set; all products, services, or ideas are likely to have their own segmentations, superimposed on the wide base of social character represented by the *Mirror*'s image. No two people are alike, even if they are of the same segment, type, or Q-audience.

The London *Mirror*'s proprietors were clever enough to grasp the social character of the enormous segment of the British mass available to it; the millions of commuters with only ten to fifteen minutes to spend reading a paper as they go to work by train, bus, or tram have a social personality or character of the kind described. The newspaper tunes in on it, cultivating it, no doubt. But discovering it was the initial task — to say it was created would be to suppose that the *Mirror* itself made this upward-moving segment of the British social system. On the contrary, it merely flatters what is already there, doing so, interestingly enough, about nonpolitical, noncontroversial topics, such as being sentimental about animals and babies; it debunks pomposities and laughs at the Establishment; it favors one political party no more than another; it stands no more for one religion than another. Such is the perspicacity of a popular newspaper, as it is of all advertising; ideologies are ignored and personalities and social character are reinforced.

The determination of mass audience segmentation is a major concern of mass communication research. Images of modern corporations, nations, cars, cigarettes, or professions are all communication specifications (of a social character or personality kind) which govern the communication that will be channeled through the mass media to enhance and reinforce the pre-existing segment.

Segmentation and the Popular Arts

There is much discussion of the relation between mass communication and mass culture. The latter implies, where it does not make the point explicitly, an undifferentiated mass of people and an undifferentiated mass of interests. Mass communication becomes undifferentiated too, homogenized (to use Hyman's term [53]), to suit every person and every interest. *Life* and *Look* magazines, for example, appear on the tables of rich and poor alike; and, within the same covers, features appear on such diverse subjects as nuclear theory, Rita Hayworth's love life, starving children in the Congo, brassiered models in New York, an article on philosophy by Bertrand Russell, another on foreign policy by the Secretary of State, pictures of a roller-skating horse, a large spread on Kerima's marathon kiss (a movie sensation), a full page of a housewife sticking her tongue out at an umpire at a baseball game, along with about nine full pages of beautiful colored reproductions of paintings by Renoir and Picasso. The concern is with one vast audience. There is, however, some segmentation in the news magazine domain; *Time* magazine, for example, is in tune with a segment which is differentiated from the mass. In Britain radio broadcasting is provided at three levels: a "light" program of jazz and the like, a "home" program for the public more generally, and the "third" program for culture at a higher level. In this way the needs of different audiences are recognized. The light program can keep soldiers and youthful audiences occupied with the latest hits of the Beatles and the like. The home program, like *Better Homes and Gardens* among magazines in America, can softly please parents occupied with family programs, who want relaxation, dinnertime music, romance, and low-culture entertainment. The Third Program, limited to certain hours of the evening and linked with magazine articles in the *Listener* (which publishes some of the talks heard on this network), is at a high level of culture and sophistication.

We do not know what the real Q-audiences are, in fact, in the above cases. Nor, if these were specified, could there be any guarantee that the media would be put in tune with them. The Q-audiences may require homogenization rather than low, middle, or high cultural programming, but some differentiation in networks would seem in principle to be along the right lines. In the United States the three television networks run parallel homogenized programs, like *Look* or *Life*, but again no one knows what the existing Q-audiences are or whether, knowing what they are, the industry could accommodate them.

A great deal of dissatisfaction is expressed about the mediocrity of the American television networks. British television, though restricted, is said to be much better, being cast at a rather higher intellectual level. In America Gilbert Seldes in his *The Public Arts* (129) expresses concern at the divorce, as he sees it, between Great Art and the Popular Arts. Great Art, he argues, was meant to give meaning to life, to afford deeper understanding of ourselves and others. The Popular Arts, instead, degrade. Seldes admits that there is a place in the mass media for entertainment, for leisure and diversion, but he feels that Great Art can do much in these directions. He points out that the needs of the ordinary man were ignored by American intellectuals during the nineteenth century; today it is the other way around. Few great artists, intellectuals, or authors work creatively for the movies, television, or advertising. The divorce between creative thinkers and the popular media, Seldes concludes, is almost complete. Yet some very fine music has been written for movies by great modern composers, although little of great art has come into advertising, where popular color photography has nevertheless reached true beauty in some instances. There is some feeling among the current practitioners of mass communication that artists and intellectuals cannot do a good job of entertaining people — they are apt to be in the clouds, far above the ready understanding of ordinary men and women. There are others, on the contrary, who maintain that creative people can be *too* effective and that society cannot trust them. Subtly, it is believed, creative people can undermine the masses, leading them astray into communism, antireligion, antiwar, and the like. There are some who argue that in the United States financiers have taken over the popular arts, movies, television, radio, and the rest. Movies are seen as presenting over and over the same reveries, daydreams, and childish fables. It is said that the masses need companionship, but they get these opiates instead and so are kept away from the real problems of life. Even popular cultures, it is felt, should create an awareness of self and of the state of the world and should make the world a better place in which to live.

All of this, however, is armchair criticism. None of it is based on empirical knowledge about existing Q-audiences.

DEFINITIONS

It is now convenient to offer some redefinition of the terms "belief," "opinion," and "attitude" as these apply to publics and public opinion, and "social character," "notion," and "image" as these apply to convergent selectivity.

I have redefined belief, opinion, and attitude elsewhere (144), but a brief statement is in order here:

1. Opinions and notions have the same status as self-referent statements and thus constitute the basic populations from which Q-samples are composed. There is little to distinguish opinions from notions, except that the former relate to deeper *beliefs* (as defined below) and the latter to *social character*.

2. Attitudes are defined as subjective "attitudes of mind." The individual may be supposed to cogitate about matters of opinion concerning an *XYZ* situation. In the process he adopts an attitude of being critical, magnanimous, or the like. Defensiveness, rationalization, displacement of affect, and the like psychodynamic processes ordinarily attend the cogitation. I seek to model this, and do so as a Q-sort. There is plenty of evidence that psychodynamic mechanisms are represented in Q-sorting. The self, as an attitude of mind, is also so represented (143). Thus the Q-sort model and the phenomena modeled are to some extent alike.

3. Images in convergent selectivity correspond to attitudes of mind and are operationally defined in the same way by Q-sorts and their Q-factors.

4. Beliefs and social character, in our framework, are explanations of Q-sorts or Q-factors in the field of public opinion and convergent selectivity, respectively.

5. Q-factors are models of either attitudes or images, as I have said. The same belief system (or social character) may give rise to several factors, that is, to different attitudes in the same or different individuals.

6. The distinctions between wants, needs, and demands are also important. Wants are psychological, or matters of social character; needs are ethical, matters of deeper beliefs; demands are matters of economics

or action. Convergent selectivity is involved in wants; deeper belief systems in needs. Demands can be temporary and are subject to the vagaries of the market. Thus, consumers may want breakfast cereals and can choose from a hundred brands and varieties. The poor, however, need more food, and that is a matter of *our* conscience as well as their physical needs.

Beliefs, needs, and values involve early internalizations and ego structures of people, and all have moral undertones. Wants, images, and social character are related more to the self, and to immediate social conditions, and are without the categorical imperatives of beliefs. A person is rarely aware of his social character and does not rule his conduct by it. He does so in terms of his ethical and other beliefs.

I have a neat empirical system to match these definitions. Opinions and notions are self-referent statements in our system; wants, images, and attitudes of mind are Q-factors; beliefs, values, and the like are explanations of such attitudes. Beliefs are therefore expressed empirically both as attitudes of mind (of which there is a limited number) and as opinions (which are innumerable). The segregationist, and the religious person, expresses unquestionable, profound, God-given truth as his belief. Such beliefs are expressed in innumerable statements of opinion. The segregationist will say, for example, that Negroes really prefer segregation, that they are incapable of the finer sensibilities, and the like.

Rawlins (110) found in a Q-study among women students that belief in segregation was expressed by at least three attitudes, or factors. One was characterized as dour, guilty, petulant, and equivocating. Another was defensive, blaming, and ashamed. Still another was fixed, immovable, unyielding, committed. (The last represented deep faith, well-exemplified by certain southern governors.) The desegregationist belief was shown by at least two factors. One was a highly concerned, a fervent, active, emotional attitude. Another was cautious, conservative, passive, even sanctimonious (110, p. 282). Several different (uncorrelated) attitudes of mind were indicated, but only two belief systems.

Similarly, in studies of the attitudes of lay persons and chronically ill patients about public medicine, Stephenson (141) found eight attitudes but only three basic belief systems, designated *independence, interdependence,* and *dependence.* The former is the fundamental tenet of conservative Republicanism, veering to extremism; the second is the liberalism of a more socially oriented person; the third is the profound dependence of the poor and indigent. Each is a relatively fixed system of belief, corresponding to a firm philosophy of life. "It is God's will," says the indigent Negro. No doubt attitudes may be changed (where they are not direct expressions of the deeper beliefs), but belief systems are apparently unchangeable (63).

As for social character, one need only refer to Riesman's various subtypes, the Do-Gooder, the Moralizer, and the like, to see that the same basic characters may adopt different attitudes. Reference may be made also to my study of public utilities (143): a Q-study showed two factors, one for women who thought of utilities as friendly corporations, reflecting the women's own self-importance, and the other for women who thought of utilities in terms of service, reflecting their housewifely self-sufficiencies. The imagery for the one was pseudo-economic (for the women had really no knowledge of corporate matters), whereas for the other the imagery was service-oriented in relation to home needs.

Notice in the examples, however, that whereas deep matters of faith enter into belief systems, for which people may go to war or die rather than submit to another faith, in the case of imagery few really care much about the issues at hand — the self, rather than the deeper ego structure is involved. The women were not really much concerned, for example, about utilities. Moreover, the social characters represented as factors for the utilities are matters about which the women are unaware; the pseudo-economic imagery stems from *inner-directed* social character, in Riesman's terms, and the service imagery from *other-directed* social character. These, I hold with Heberle (46), are linked to social movements and the like as much as, or more than, to any deeper internalizations of belief.

There is a certain correspondence between our definitions and those to be found in the dictionary. Opinions, according to the dictionary, are judgments which are open to contention or doubt — in logic-of-science they are synthetic propositions and not facts. Attitudes, expressed in terms of such opinions, are neither true nor false; they are modes or instruments of behavior largely involving the self. Beliefs are deeply ego-involving systems, the truth of which are accepted by the person on grounds of authority, trust, faith, evidence, or by exigencies of upbringing. Beliefs, at root, are commitments, largely culturally determined. In Thailand one believes in compassion for others (90). In the United States one believes in independence for oneself. These are not oversimplifications or overabstractions but basic ways individuals have of thinking about themselves and society.

Those who are familiar with the thinking of Pye (109) on the role of personality in politics and nation-building — in which psychoanalytic concepts such as Erikson (27) has espoused are employed — will observe that our term "belief" involves the same cultural determinations; belief is fashioned in early introjections such as Wiebe (165) described in his empirical paper. It should not surprise us, therefore, to find that the same fundamental beliefs enter into political, social, religious, and civic attitudes.

With respect to the terms "social character," "notions," and "imagery," I can only say that it is a new area of concern with which advertising has had most to do up to now. But the related concept of *national character* is a reminder that much has been written about at least one aspect of this area, and that images of different countries are among the most persistent of human frailties. There is, however, something rather trivial, or contradictiory, about these matters of imagery: the image of China as cruel may give place to the image of China as saintly and stoical at almost the wink of an eye. It is hard to think of people going to war to defend their social characters.

CONCLUSION

The above definitions bring about a considerable measure of clarification in our field of inquiry. The difference between social control on the one hand and convergent selectivity on the other is a profound matter. The former is maintained and reinforced by social communication of every kind (familial, educational, religious, economic, poiltical). Convergency is of course dependent on such beliefs up to a point, too, but one would expect mass communication to have most to say about the images of the masses, and therefore about new forms of social character, such as that described by Riesman as other-directed. The concept of imagery, however, is now spilling into the political arena, once the showplace for the exercise of public opinion. One can manipulate political images; one cannot so readily change political faith.

4

Play Theory

Social scientists have been busy, since the beginnings of mass communication research, trying to prove that the mass media have been sinful where they should have been good. The media have been looked at through the eyes of morality when, instead, what was required was a fresh glance at people existing in their own right for the first time. It is my thesis that the daily withdrawal of people into the mass media in their after hours (104) is a step in the *existential* direction, that is, a matter of subjectivity which invites freedom where there had been little or none before.

In this connection we must develop ideas which give the play theory of mass communication a firm theoretical basis. Among these the idea of *communication-pleasure* is of first importance.

PLAY

Modern thinking about play for our purposes begins with Huizinga's *Homo Ludens* (52). I began my own applications of Huizinga's theory in 1958 and others had clearly been busy at the same time, including Szasz (152), Caillois (15), and Plath (104). Most people distinguish play and leisure from work; leisure time is our free time, time for recreation, hobbies, or self-cultivation. Work deals with reality, with earning a living, with production. Play, on the contrary, is largely unproductive except for the self-satisfaction it provides.

There are, of course, thousands of games, toys, and ways of playing in leisure time in every culture and era of man and many explanations have been offered for man's tendencies to express himself in play. Huizinga's viewpoint, and the one I follow, sees play in terms of culture; the study of play, in short, has become the concern of cultural anthropology, as Plath's work on the "after hours" of the modern Japanese testifies. Culture, according to Huizinga, depends on play; rather, the spirit of play is essential to the development of culture. Many of our games, toys, and customs are residues of earlier phases of our culture and lie outside the evolving cultural process, but much of what characterizes current culture is rooted still in play — in law, stagecraft, military "science," debate, politics, liturgy, academic learning, prosody, business conduct, marriage rules, and much else — all forming the civilization in which we live. Scholars before Huizinga considered play a degradation of real living, a waste of time, a meaningless mask. To Huizinga, on the contrary, playing is a source of culture, giving rise to useful conventions that permit culture to evolve and stabilize — it teaches loyalty, competitiveness, and patience (the Chinese *wan*): "To the degree that he is influenced by play, man can check the monotony, determinism, and brutality of nature. He learns to construct order, conceive economy, and establish equity" (15, p. 58).

Clearly very tricky matters are at issue as to what is play and what work. Our own distinction between them turns on what is fantasy and in some sense unreal, which is play, and what is real in the world, which is work.

Playing is *pretending*, a stepping outside the world of duty and responsibility. Play is an *interlude* in the day. It is not ordinary or real. It is *voluntary* and not a task or moral duty. It is in some sense *disinterested*, providing a temporary satisfaction. Though attended to with seriousness, it is not really important. The British, for example, would never cry when their team loses a match; Americans do. Games in Britain, though played seriously, are never confused with the serious things of life. Play is enjoyed, no matter who wins. It is astonishing to observe how often winning a fortune in a lottery or football pool (in England) makes no difference to the lucky person's way of life — he just goes about his daily work as a plumber or porter as before. Play is *secluded*, taking place in a particular place set off for the purpose in time or space: it has a beginning and an end. The child goes into a corner to play house. And play is a free activity; yet it absorbs the player completely. The player is unself-conscious if he plays with proper enjoyment.

Play has been explained by psychologists as abreactive, wish-fulfillment, instinctive, and much else. All that seems certain is that it is "fun," as Huizinga (52) remarked.

Caillois (15) differs from Huizinga somewhat in his account of play and games; he agrees that play is free, is subject to rules, is an interlude, is often uncertain about its ends, is unreal (as against real life), and is unproductive — except in lotteries and betting, which can be either highly lucrative or ruinous. A man may win a fortune at roulette or lose his proverbial shirt at cards. But even here the play is still the thing; as I observed above, a man may win a fortune in a football pool and then go about his daily work as though nothing had happened — this is most telling for play, which is always detached from "real life." Caillois distinguishes between four classes of play: *agon* (the agonistic principle of games involving two sides, as in football), *alea* (games of dice, roulette, lotteries, etc.), *mimicry* (acting, pretending), and *ilinx* (producing dizziness, as by swings, roundabouts, etc.). Much in play is a combination of two or more of these basic forms. There are also, Caillois indicates, at least three main ways of playing. *Paideia* is primitive, pure play of carefree gaiety, uncontrolled fantasy, and the like. *Ludus* is formal play, as in games with rules and conventions, requiring patience or the development of skill. *Wan* is the quietly sensual Chinese way of playing, as when jade is caressed to polish it, or with every subtle sniff or touch at issue, as in the sacred Hindu book of *Kama-Sutra*. Thousands of customs, devices, and occasions are employed to gratify playing in every culture of the world, in all its history.

Although there are hundreds of words for this or that aspect of playing, the general concept itself is little represented in any language. There is no common Indo-European word for play; the Greeks had a specific name for each child's game and different words for childish games, contests, and ritual plays. The Chinese languages have separate words for fun in the sense of romping, jesting, trifling, fingering things, sniffing pleasurably, and the like activities; for gambling, playing with dice, dancing, and so on; and for formal games. The Japanese have a definite general word for play function, covering recreation, relaxing, pastimes, amusements, jaunts, gambling, idling, playing the fool, imitating, jugglery, aesthetic tea-partying, and the like. And whereas Greek has numerous words for play functions, Latin has only *ludus, ludere*, meaning illusion or semblance, and this applies to children's games, recreation, contests, theatrical and liturgical presentations, and games of chance. I call my theory of mass communication the *ludic* theory, but for the sake of euphony I take a liberty with Latin and coin the word *ludenic* for play theory. It is so used in my paper dealing with newsreading (142).

RELEVANCE TO MASS COMMUNICATION

It is of course obvious that mass communication serves to inform as well as to entertain, but for theoretical purposes it is wise to distinguish that part of mass communication dealing with work (and therefore with reality, such as concerns the weather, farm information, shipping news, educational projects, and the like) from that concerned with leisure-time pursuits. Schramm (126) does not make this separation in his proposals for developing mass communications in the new countries of the world — with serious harm, in my opinion, to all concerned. Schramm sees a direct causal relation between mass communication and national development. It informs nations of their five-year plans; it "raises the goals, spreads the news, widens their acceptance," and thus raises the level of development in every nation. It fosters "nation-ness," Schramm reports, and the growth of loyalties. It helps to teach skills, literacy, and technology. It extends markets. It prepares people to play their roles in a country and among nations. All of this looks like hard work. It would seem better to maintain the distinction between this work and the pleasure-time pursuits of rising (or any other) nations.

Mass communication in its play aspects may be the way a society develops its culture — the way it dreams, has its myths, and develops its loyalties; what it does in the way of inculcating work may be quite a different matter. What kind of a culture is it, for example, that thinks only of learning, production, and work? The American, who knows all about work and technology, may be the least able to see what is required for the entertainment and play of a country, and therefore for its culture.

THE DAILY "FILL"

Hyman (53) observes that social and political communication in all countries, especially the newly developing ones, is apt to be brief; it is set in a daytime "fill" of entertainment material which is nonpolitical and might be quite unreal in social respects (as when Congolese enjoy an American Western movie). Soviet radio programs transmit the basic Communist values, but the propaganda is an interlude in a daytime program of music and similar entertainment; 50 per cent of radio broadcasting is serious music (56). Mystical Arab music is broadcast for hours on end in the Middle East, in the intervals of which there is news and propaganda. Hyman suggests that apart from the obvious fact that people could scarcely be expected to listen all day to pretentious monologs on reforms, the "fill" serves a positive function: it keeps an audience available for the coming short messages of reform. The hint is taken from modern marketing, "Pleasant packaging pays!" The "fill" of mass communication is therefore not seen as flight from reality, escapism, or the like; nor is it debasing or seducing the masses as critics suppose. Hyman sees it as a "buffer" against conditions which would otherwise be anxiety-inducing. Without question a constant barrage of political propaganda would find few listeners or viewers or, if it found many, would arouse deep anxieties in an unsettled world.

Hyman does not propose that the "fill" can teach people to accept pleasure and to make free choices about minor matters of taste. He proposes, instead, that the principle of preselection should be looked at essentially as a defensive mechanism. People in the United States, for example, are confronted with massive offerings of subject matter — there is the voluminous *New York Times* Sunday edition; and TV, radio, magazines, movies, and journals are constantly harassing everyone. There is, Hyman suggests, a "blend" of such mass content, of a relatively constant kind under given circumstances: one copy of the *New York Times* is very like any other. The story "mix" of a murder or two, a civic scandal, a dope or other addict, is much the same in every edition of the New York *Daily News.* This "blend" or "mix," Hyman notes, might account for two sets of facts: ". . . the Western public doesn't suddenly change many of its topical opinions as a result of a particular exposure but, at the same time, the media do mold the rather odd ways some see the political world and relate to it" (53, p. 147).

The individual, Hyman concludes, has to maintain his own viewpoint (his own values) in terms of this daily bombardment of news. According to Hyman the individual cannot possibly respond to all of this fare and therefore becomes preselective about it out of self-defense. This is a rather negative way of looking at things, but it is true that people react in the world in terms of their own interests and that they perceive (or, strictly, *apperceive*) most of the world around them in relation to these interests and values.

These ideas have direct connections with play theory. The daily "mix" is repetitious, like a child's game played over and over with variations on a familiar theme. In its content the individual can muse, at random if he is of a childlike mind, but skillfully with measured steps if he is well developed in ludenic respects. The "mix" is the way a person has to think of the wider world around him, so that he will be able to talk to himself and others about it; and in the process he does, of course, "learn" something to argue about for a day, he acquires a taste for this or that, and he is generally able to hold his head a little higher because of the daily incursion into the "mix" that suits him. On the other hand, what is molded by the mass media should not be confused too readily with what is poured first into the mold by introjected beliefs, which are subject to social and not to mass communication controls.

Thus, without denying what can be described as an informational function to the mass media I agree with Hyman that this (however important it may be) is only an interlude in the almost full-time function of the mass media in general, and of the press in particular, to entertain mass audiences. But whereas this is soporific for Hyman, a way to keep the masses quiet or more receptive to the sudden shots of propaganda given to them as "news" or the like, I take a more generous view of the actual function of such mass entertainment. To begin with, I do not think of it as merely entertainment in a non-ego-involving sense, but at its best as a highly developed form of subjective play. I go a little further: though it is true that a person's selfhood is formed largely in relation to social controls (68), I want to look at the possibility that new aspects of self arise out of subjective play, such as that fostered by mass communication.

SCHRAMM'S THEORY OF PLEASURE

We can take it for granted that people find mass communication, on the whole, enjoyable. Schramm (127) has speculated about the source of this enjoyment and proposes in his well-known theory of newsreading that the pleasure stems from two principles. When people read the news, certain of their impulses, needs, wishes, or wants are gratified, and the enjoyment is the feeling of pleasure so engendered. Sometimes the pleasure is immediate and sometimes it is delayed. The two are discussed as immediate and delayed reward. News about crime, corruption, accidents, disasters, sports, recreation, and social events provides immediate pleasure; news about public affairs, economics, social problems, science, education, public health, and so on gives delayed pleasure. Kingsbury and Hart (62) had suggested a similar division, many years earlier, into the "feebly socialized" newsreader and the "socialized" — the former no doubt having immediate enjoyment and the latter delayed. Schramm associated his two principles with Freud's pleasure and reality principles, respectively.

This, however, was scarcely fair to psychoanalysis because Freud's pleasure principle had reference to deeply unconscious mechanisms, whereas at least much of the immediate pleasure in newsreading is quite open and aboveboard. Schramm considered, even so, that from sensational news, crime, disasters, and news about entertainment and social events, newsreaders received immediate rewards: they could enjoy the pleasures of crime or sex, for example, vicariously ("shivering with the axe-murder" as Schramm put it, and gloating at the voluptuous blow-up of the queen of the call girls). This suggests, of course, that people prone to such vicarious pleasures are "feebly socialized"; their preoccupations are with accidents, crime, sex, and so on, because of their own unassuaged hostilities, aggressions, and sex-starved lives.

Reading about public affairs, however, and all the more intellectual or aesthetic subjects such as economics, literature, religion, art, and politics was considered by Schramm to be governed more by delayed reward. Indeed, the immediate reading about such matters, Schramm suggested, is apt to be unpleasant, annoying, or even alarming. To read of any world crisis is scarcely a delight for educated peace-loving men; news about the national debt and taxes is unlikely to please the hardheaded economic man; and news on the incidence of cancer in old age is scarcely likely to warm the hearts of elderly newsreaders. All such reading, Schramm supposed, requires the intelligent or socialized reader to endure immediate pain; but the end result would be pleasure because the "threat" provided by such news items prepares the reader the better to meet the future. So one dies of cancer the better pleased for hearing about it long before! Clearly this is nonsense. What is in error is the assumption that people are necessarily self-involved in such news items at the time of reading. If they are, the result will be unpleasure. If they are not, then the black news is just news like any other, no less or no more interesting.

What indeed are we to mean by being self-involved? I find it necessary to distinguish two meanings for our purpose. To see one's photograph unexpectedly in the newspaper is definitely self-involving in the sense that it matters to us, as self, to our sense of pride, conceit, or the like. But when one is absorbed in doing something, like reading a newspaper intently, all sense of self is absent; afterwards you may say how much you enjoyed it, but at the time there was no self-reference, no pride, no vanity, no sense of oneself, no wish, no being-with-anything, no intrusion of the self upon the news. How, then, is the self at issue in such absorption? Note that what is at issue is not deep concentration, such as one needs to read a book; it is merely quiet absorption in the news. Indeed it can now be no secret that in such absorption one is being highly subjective, and that the report afterwards about it is that one has enjoyed it! It is more like being in a trance than being in touch with reality.

For Schramm, however, the feebly socialized were out of touch with reality, whereas the socialized — those subject to delayed rewards — were regarded as serious-minded, reading the news with their thoughts on "the world of surrounding reality to which he can adapt only by hard work." The truth could be quite the other way around.

Schramm provides evidence to show that the more education a person has had, the more he is inclined to read "reality" news. The more un-educated, the more he is likely to prefer vicarious pleasures. Similarly, New Englanders and people from the eastern states are more "reality" oriented, and Deep Southerners, more "vicarious." But this merely indi-cates that as people become better educated, they may take more stock of public and international affairs.

The Pleasure Principle Reconsidered

Freud's principle is worth attention, however, for reasons not associ-ated with Schramm's use of it but with our own theory of mass communi-cation.

Freud wrote about the pleasure and reality principles in a brief paper called "Formulations Regarding the Two Principles in Mental Func-tioning" (33). Mankind's mental life began, Freud argued, in fantasy; the oldest primary mental process was the pleasure-pain principle, that is, a "waking tendency to shut out painful experiences." We strive, funda-mentally, for pleasure and to avoid pain. This was the hedonic process at work before any consciousness of the person and before any aware-ness of self. It is little use arguing, in terms of this principle, that the "feebly socialized" are shutting out thought of the "real" world of inter-national tensions, taxes, and so on, preferring instead to bask in the vicarious pleasure of comics, crime, and sex. Freud's primary principle does not apply directly to such conscious matters at all. The truth is likely to be rather different: the "feebly socialized" person is probably un-aware of the trials ahead in international crises and similar "painful" matters, which the socialized person knows about and yet still prefers to read about.

Freud's second principle, concerning a later stage in development of the individual, maintains that fantasy cannot produce real gratifications, so that the individual is forced to strive not only for what is pleasant but for what is real, even if unpleasant. This is the *reality principle.*

The principles were conceived by Freud as primary processes, operating at almost a physiological level (*id* processes), before the individual has any awareness of self. The process of repression is similarly lowly placed. But as the person develops consciousness, the processes of attention, memory, judgment, and thinking arise, replacing the primary mechanisms. The latter, however, are very tenacious — the organism finds it difficult to give up pleasure and to face realities, and the individual represses when he could better face the facts. For this reason two new psychological functions were postulated by Freud. One was *reality-testing,* in which consciousness and self take part; and the other was *fantasy-making,* in which, though consciousness and self are involved, there is a closer relation to the primary processes, to repression and to instinctual life, as in daydreaming and in the play of children. Repression is quite effective in fantasy-making, which is again free of reality-testing. One can understand how important these considerations are for any theory which relates the entertainment of the masses to childlike play.

Such are the principles on which Schramm based his theory of newsreading. Fantasy-making, and the primary processes of pleasure-pain, corresponds to immediate reward; in newsreading of this kind, wishes and fantasies are used to avoid unhappiness and unpleasant ideas. The reality principle corresponds to more conscious control and to delayed reward; the concern is with what is *useful* in life. But here too the pleasure principle is not altogether abandoned; it is merely deferred — a momentary pleasure, wish, or fantasy is given up in order to gain an assured pleasure later on. Thus, the religious person forgoes the pleasures of this world for greater joys in heaven. The growth of one's ego and self is characterized by reality-testing; the person grows into selfhood by conquering his primitive pleasure processes.

Thus, analysis of Schramm's self-evident fact suggests that, theoretically, we must expect signs of repression among the feebly socialized, since wishes and fantasies are at issue. With socialized readers we must expect, instead, much stronger ego-development, better judgment, greater thinking powers, a more elaborate memory.

Now it may well be true that the feebly socialized are more prone to fantasy, wishes, and repressions, to judge by their somewhat morbid interest in the sensational — crime, sex, accidents, divorces, and so on. But this cannot be taken for granted. Their more socialized fellow citizens could be even more repressed, differing from the others in the *kind* of fantasy they have rather than in its amount. Freud, of course, thought that really normal people, living by reality-testing, would be fantasy-free; the more fantasies one has, he assumed, the more neurotic one is. But can we regard the masses of the feebly socialized as neurotic in any way? Clearly not by ordinary standards. There is little doubt, however, about the richer intellects and greater knowledge of more socialized individuals — it is indeed likely that people who have been to college are more ego-developed (or something of the kind) than people who failed to graduate from a high school.

Paralleling the two meanings I have distinguished for self-involvement above, there are two for the word "pleasure." The one concerns our moods of elation, joy, sorrow, and the like; the other is retrospective, as when we say that we were so absorbed in an activity, so engrossed in it, that we "enjoyed" it. In the latter case the person may not have been experiencing any particular feelings — on the contrary he may have been so absorbed that he lost all sense of himself in the process. Thus, as I have said earlier, when people say they enjoy reading a newspaper, sheer absorption may be involved and not feelings at all.

These thoughts should lead us to be cautious about any too facile regard of a term like "pleasure." The pleasure-pain principle has indeed been considerably tempered, in recent years, by considerations like the above. Fenichel (30), a well-known psychoanalyst, has replaced the pleasure-pain principle (as a primary process), by one of *functional pleasure*. This is the exercise of a function, not for gratification of instinct or other primitive impulses but in some ego-developed sense. The child enjoys reading the same story over and over, not out of some deeper fantasies, but out of a sense of mastery over the external world by repeated exercise of the function. Similarly the person who reads a newspaper "with enjoyment" may be involved not in gratification of pleasurable fantasies or wishes, of sex or crime, but in a sense of mastery and achievement over them. *Others* are shot, robbed or raped — but not the newsreader — and one's enjoyment lies in the constant affirmation of one's mastery over these everyday threats. I have no evidence pointing in this direction, but no doubt there are times when readers gloat over the downfall of others.

Still another viewpoint from the most far-reaching school of thought in psychoanalysis rejects Freud's primary principles altogether. Fairbairn (29), and Klein before him (64), supposed that the individual is primarily object-seeking, not pleasure-seeking. This looks at the individual from the standpoint of how he is influenced by what he takes into him-self (primary introjection), rather than from what is instinctual in him to start with (the id). What matters is what the child eats, so to speak, what it smells and touches, not what is libidinal in it to start with. Ac-cording to this view, pleasure-seeking is merely a safety valve, doing little for the individual other than to stop him from exploding altogether. But there is a long chain of connections from early object introjections to the pleasure-seeking behavior of the feebly socialized. Indeed, in all the discussions so far, whether about the primary processes, Fenichel's *mastery* conception, or Fairbairn's just mentioned, complicated develop-mental matters in which the self is everywhere involved are at issue, rather than ultimate *processes* only. We need Langer's (67) reminder about the fallacy of reductionism: "There is a wide-spread and familiar fallacy, known as the 'genetic fallacy,' which arises from the historical method in philosophy and criticism: the error of confusing the *origin* of a thing with its *import*, of tracing the thing to its most primitive form and then calling it merely this archaic phenomenon" (67, pp. 201–2). Schramm saved himself from this fallacy in his theory of reward in newsreading because he clearly recognized ego-identifications in it, and it is to this point that attention has now to be turned.

Szasz's Theory

We need a better theory of pleasure than Schramm had to work with; for this a beginning has been made by the psychiatrist Szasz (153), who presents what he calls some conceptual "models" for it. He begins with the reminder that pleasure is a *concept*, and not a feeling or mood ex-perience. The whole wide range of phenomena to which the concept of pleasure applies requires four very different definitions for the word.

There is, first, pleasure at a physiological, id, or economic level; the term is used in connection with the reduction of physiological need, as when hunger is appeased and satisfaction results. Psychoanalysts have used the word at this level in the past — the id alone is involved, without the mediation of the self. Freud's initial understanding of anxiety, too, was at this level; it was conceived as a discharge of affect which had been repressed, involving no conscious mind, no ego-involvement. It was a process of energy-like displacements. (He later modified this view, but it is doubtful whether it was ever fully abandoned.) The modern psychia-trist, like Szasz, wants to use the word "pleasure" at other than this proc-ess level — to lift it into conscious levels of mentation. Szasz remarks that this has already been done for the concepts of guilt and shame: "Up to now only the latter (shame, guilt, etc.) have been approached in terms of ego-functions, signals and communications, and our understanding of pleasure has remained rooted in physiological and Id-oriented concepts" (153, p. 207).

A second use of the term "pleasure" is in connection with its associations with objects. The child is gratified with an empty bottle — when it is satisfied with food, and up to a point even when it is hungry. In the latter case the pangs of hunger, a painful matter, are replaced by the associated pleasure of an empty bottle to suck. Already, it seems, the child is playing; the point arises again whether the child has an awareness of what it is doing, that is, that it is conscious of the deception, or whether purely mechanical matters, or processes, are at issue. If it is aware, this is a very different state of affairs from that which supposes that the child is motivated by a search for pleasure and avoidance of pain *as processes*. If aware, the child is controlling objects for its own purposes. This involves its self. The facts are not reducible to those of process only. Similarly for much else discussed in process terms: what is more likely to be at issue is not *persuasion, anxiety, reward*, or the like, as processes, but relationships between the self and things, as actions or behavior. When it is said that what the world is suffering from is a lack of love ("there is not enough love in the world"), this does not mean not enough affect or feeling of love, conscious or otherwise (of love ladled out by the gallon so to speak) but not enough actions of a certain kind — for example, of tolerance for others, concern for the poor, interest in suffering, joy in the pleasures of living, and the like, in all of which the self is everywhere involved. We have constant need of a reminder that this is so. It is all too easy to slip into the mistake of talking about a process when in fact what is at issue is an attitude of self in relation to things around it.

A third use of the term "pleasure" is the familiar one attributing it to objects: food itself is said to be pleasant, as though it has pleasure in it like vitamins and proteins. Wealth, adornments, possessions, are satisfying in themselves — so we think. But, again, it is only when the person adopts a certain attitude toward them that they are pleasant. No art gives pleasure per se, nor is a jewel, or a lover's body, a pleasure per se. In all cases the person behaves toward the objects in some way — which may indeed be far removed from anything that could be called pleasure as a mood, or as something which on later reflection we attribute to the objects, saying how pleasing they are, what pleasures they hold, what a treasure, what a delight. At the time the actions were being experienced they may have been quite astonishing, erotic, sensual, "off the beam," unbounded, sadistic, grasping, and much else indeed. But afterwards we say we enjoyed it.

A fourth use for the word "pleasure" introduced by Szasz he called *communication-pleasure*. When two people meet and converse, they may say afterwards how much they enjoyed it. They have been talking in a complex way, now serious, now in fun, now at cross-purposes, now with gusto, in intricate interaction. The talk serves no apparent purpose as far as one can see; one person is not necessarily trying to convince the other, to subdue the other, to get anything out of the other. They are not trying to please one another — nor is the one in some remote degree having fantasy about the other, or seeking to seduce, influence, or in any way become involved in the other's purposes. Afterwards, they both say how pleasant it was. This is communication-pleasure: its characteristic is that the two so talking are not expecting anything. Quite different from it is communication which is meant to bring about a change in one or both persons talking — such as a command for action, a cry for help, a demand. Such we might call "communication-pain."

Thus, communication-pleasure, parodied by smugness and self-satisfaction, is contrasted with communication-unpleasure or -pain — which alone is apt to bring about action and change in the status quo. It is well known that unfavorable affects can bring about social change, and the wily advertiser knows that his job is half done if he can make the consumer dissatisfied with what he has. Communication-pleasure calls for no action: communication-unpleasure is a command for action.

Thus, the self is involved in all but the first of the four uses of the concept of pleasure. But there is a profound difference in the way the self enters into pleasure compared with its involvement in pain. In the latter there is a *loss* of self, in the former a *gain* in self. One would like to "hide one's head" in shame. The guilty person becomes suspicious, furtive, or confined — "secret guilt by silence is betrayed." But communication-pleasure is attended by a gain of self, a feeling that somehow it "did one good," that one's stature is increased; something is added to the self. This is *after* the event. Our two happy talkers, for example, male and female, both young, talk without expectancy of anything. There is not an implication of a wish or desire — and yet, afterwards, both go their ways with higher heads and a gain of self. Some people achieve in this way a profound contentment, a prolonged well-being and serenity. It is not in the least necessary to suppose that this is reached only by way of complex sublimations. Eskimos with little but seal to eat were said to be the most contented and serene of peoples. So, too, the homely farmer and his wife may be sublimely happy in the communication-pleasure they jointly experience.

SCHRAMM'S THEORY RECONSIDERED

Clearly, anticipation of eventualities is characteristic of any developing self and planning for the future is the stock example of the reality principle at work. But where is the immediate pleasure in Schramm's theory? What is its character? And what, really, is involved in delayed gratification of the so-called reality principle? Since he mentions the pleasure principle and the reality principle, these must be developed or his view is subject to the "genetic fallacy." He leaves open an important consideration, that self-identification somehow relates reward on the one hand with what is selected in newsreading on the other. If this is taken to mean that self factors enter into the scheme of things, what he means by the basic principles (pleasure-reality) is not the primary or economic matters discussed by Freud. Rather, the differences between Schramm's concepts of immediate and delayed reward is a difference in the organizational complexities of the individuals. If one person elects to read crime and sex stories, the fundamental process is not reward of immediate pleasure, or reduction of tensions, like a child given a candy — rather, it is a certain kind of self which is gaining something. Similarly the person who elects to read about public matters and keeps in touch with international affairs need not be suffering now for gain later, but could be a certain kind of person, probably more highly developed in the self-integrative sense (along with which he is likely to be better educated), who is gaining something, too. The gains are always gains in the self.

But what of the actual newsreading? It is quite possible here, too, that besides becoming absorbed in it the reader is interacting with the newspaper as communication-pleasure. This could apply to both the feebly socialized and the more socialized readers. Their reactions in relation to their own self-involvements could well be communication-pleasure — that is, the reading is undertaken without any expectation of anything, of any reward of any kind, other than being able to say later, if asked, that it was enjoyable; and if studied, one might indeed find the newsreader's self is all the better for it. Thus we come a long way from

Schramm's early formulation to this: *newsreading is a communication-pleasure, sans reward.*

Our theory more generally therefore is to the effect that mass communication, where it concerns entertainment, is characteristically a matter of communication-pleasure. It brings no material gain and serves no "work" functions, but it does induce certain elements of self-enchantment.

PRIMITIVE COMMUNICATION

Before leaving the theoretical consideration of communication-pleasure, we should mention two special examples of it. News of the assassination of President Kennedy in 1963 flashed around the world with powerful impact in every country — Communist, Western, and neutral alike. Pope John XXIII's death engendered something of the same universality: his humility spread into every corner of the world, transmitted instantly by vast communication networks. Here was a tragedy, and a goodness, each on an Olympian scale, gripping the world — transcending creed, color, or ideology. Each was universal. The one touched youth and the other age, and both pulled at the deepest primitive feelings. One may doubt the reality of these men; one can be sure that myth more than truth surrounded Kennedy's impact. But that both touched the world massively and deeply cannot be doubted.

What, then, had happened? The cynic will say the mass reactions to the deaths were mere emotional binges, weekends of sobbing and pathos signifying nothing. I would rather think of each, instead, as an example of primitive communication, of primitive comradeship, of primitive communication-pleasure. Each was enjoyed, as a wake is. Surely, too, the events seemed to make little difference, everyone going on his way afterwards, as before. But was the self of anyone quite the same afterwards? From French-Canada to the Vatican and into India, the emotional comradeship engendered by Pope John seems to have had lasting effects. This is more apparent for the church than for the political changes brought about by the Kennedy image, but that Kennedy symbolized something of far-reaching significance is certain. We need to study therefore the conditions of primitive comradeship, such as Bartlett (6) has described for small-group situations, to seek answers to the problem posed by these universal effects. The question will then arise whether the effects can be produced, as good theater.

For the moment, however, I merely draw attention to the communication-pleasure aspects of such events. They are absorbing; we enjoy the tears; we feel better for it; we are indeed not a little self-improved. Primitive communication is well illustrated by the inroads made by music, often called an international language. Music from modern jazz to classical symphonies and musicians from Benny Goodman to Van Cliburn have found a warm welcome from all conditions and classes of people on both sides of the Iron Curtain. Even as London was being bombed by German airplanes, Mozart's music was being played by Myra Hess in the National Gallery in Trafalgar Square — with not a thought about its German origins.

WORK AND PLAY

For theoretical reasons it is important to distinguish sharply between the concepts of work and play. I shall consider all work to be communication-pain (work gets something done), and all play to be communication-pleasure (play is just fun). Moreover, I shall consider all social control to veer toward communication-pain, and all convergent selectivity to veer toward communication-pleasure.

This is the essential simplification of our theory. I am well aware of many contradictions in relation to it. Some people work for the fun of it; others work hard at having a good time. Social controls are put upon us in our cultures by customs, institutions, and creeds, which are all couched in play and are therefore enjoyed. But it is precisely the purpose of such play to give communication-pleasure and thus to soften the hard realities of control and work by a leavening of enjoyment.

We shall see politics from the public viewpoint, for example, as *play*. The diplomats and politicians do the work; the public merely has something given to it to talk about, to give them communication-pleasure. Much of religion is play, too; people dress up in their Sunday clothes and go to church, there to sing and praise. During weekdays they go to work, not entirely unmindful of the precepts and hymns of Sunday but not exactly indifferent either to the hard realities of making a living.

The separation of these two areas, play versus work, is of course schematic and theoretical. The ordinary man does not find it difficult to distinguish between his work and his play. But his distractors confound matters. He is told that he should work for the joy and glory of it; that his work should be his play; that some play at work, and others work at play. For my part reality and work alike concern actions, attended more by pain than pleasure. So the "ploughman homeward plods his weary way," and the seamstress "with fingers weary and worn, with eyelids heavy and red" epitomizes labor. It is the taskmaster who asks us to work for joy, and the devout who say that work is worship — *laborare est orare*. Most of us, left alone, prefer the enjoyment of play.

The methodology which we recommend for either work or play from the subjective viewpoint, Q, is common property, applying to both equally. The definitions of *XYZ* situations, of self-referent statements, of P-samples, Q-samples, Q-factors, Q-models, Q-audiences, and the like, introduce systematic procedures where before there were none of the same comprehensiveness.

These ramifications of our theory into culture take us outside our immediate interest, except insofar as the concept of *social character* (and therefore also of national character) has to be developed as a matter of communication-pleasure. It will be suggested that social character is how we discourse in common in after-work, or in outside-of-work situations. That is, social character is merely what we have conversations about. As such it is communication-pleasure, a sort of unending bull-session. It involves self-psychology rather than ego-psychology.

PRAGMATICS

The principal use to which I put the theory is in the study of key symbols and creative themes for mass-media consumption. I propose that these should be studied objectively and decided upon scientifically, and my theory and methodology make this posssible. The great themes of freedom, social justice, communism, and the like in the domain of public opinion and propaganda are nowise different from the catchy slogans of advertising in the domain of convergent selectivity. My studies are therefore all directed to this end: that key symbols can be recommended for mass communication on a basis of research rather than by guesswork or hunches. It is perhaps anticlimactic to see how much research one has to undertake in order to come to grips with what seems to be a simple theme. The key themes, however, are not slogans to learn by heart; rather, they are prescriptions for *all* communication for an *XYZ* situation. Thus, when Chrysler Corporation chose the theme "Compare All Three," this was a prescription for the full purpose of the then struggling automobile manufacturer to bring its Plymouth into line with Ford and Chevrolet, against all other competition. And today, decades later, the key to Chrysler Corporation is still embodied in this simple slogan. It is for this reason — that key themes are meant to proliferate into every aspect and facet of communication — that all the preparatory research is necessary.

We arrive at key themes by the following procedures. First, for a given *XYZ* situation, its basic segmentation into Q-audiences is determined. This provides a "think piece" about the situation, so that one has a grasp of the audiences at issue. One can then consider what statements in the Q-sample appeal particularly to the segments, as well as which have equal appeal to all segments alike. From such consideration one arrives at the first hints about themes of importance for specific Q-audiences, or for all alike. We end with specifications for promotion of the selected theme in "imagery" respects.

In this connection we study communication in a two-way context. The public is studied to determine its wants and needs and then we seek to fit the communication to the existing conditions.

It is well to have in mind what can now be done for practical communication from this standpoint. For example, the documentary is a valuable mass communication medium. It was developed by John Grierson (see 43), who was responsible for many notable documentary films in the 1930's and 1940's. Grierson, like all the early mass communicators, was imbued with the desire to make people better — not, in his case, to reform anyone but to make them better citizens and more informed about the world. Grierson felt that only by keeping people up to date in information, especially of a sociological nature, could we hope to keep democracies alive. His famous documentaries, *The Drifters* (about fishermen), the *Song of Ceylon, Night Mail* (about the London Post Office), *Coal Face* (mining), and a hundred others, were all meant to be informative and entertaining at the same time. People, he argued, do not have to be taught what to enjoy at a movie; might they not learn as effortlessly, with enjoyment, some of the fascinating facts of modern sociology? But after producing hundreds of documentaries, he had to admit to failure in his objectives. After all, what a lot of sociological facts there are for people to digest and is it certain that they want such a diet?

The basic themes of movies, by comparison, are very few in number and about simple matters of the eternal triangle, the moral superiority of sons (in American films) and of fathers (in British); the good-bad girl (of American movies) and the prostitute redeemed (in French). The symbolization is no less simple, vigorous, and constantly used — the "bowed blonde head" of the heroine in Britain (where men seem bent on destroying the women they love) is an example; or, in pre-Nazi movies, the image of the hero with his head bowed on a woman's bosom (symbolizing the return of the son, beaten and chastened) is another symbol used repeatedly (167). What Grierson overlooked was the necessity of simple themes and sharply defined symbols for constant use. Sociological facts do not provide them.

Consider, therefore, what would have to be done to make a success of documentaries such as Grierson produced. An example is provided by a public service presentation on the N.B.C. network, sponsored by Westinghouse in March, 1962. It was a documentary on the farming problem in the United States, narrated by Chet Huntley. The sociological facts were clear. Thousands of farmers were leaving farming every year, hundreds of small rural towns were falling into desuetude and decay, and millions of acres of land were lying fallow, while at the same time a relatively small proportion of farmers were growing vast quantities of food, with costly surpluses, in the flood tide of the revolution that is still taking place in farm technology. Farms had disappeared at the rate of 150,000 each year, as they had over the past ten years. The documentary was alive with beautiful photography, and Chet Huntley's commentary was, as usual, urbane, believable, and warm; he could not, of course, involve the documentary in political matters, yet he managed to say, very gently, that politicians were doing little to help the situation — some pulling in one direction and others the opposite way.

Of course human motives were portrayed — the sorrow of the farmer leaving his farm, and the sadness of decaying rural townships. The documentary, however, was merely a sequence of shots of farms, wheat fields, farm machinery, cattle feeding, public auctions of farms, and the like, illustrating the theme that small farms were disappearing, large ones waxing prosperous in the wake of an agricultural revolution made possible by chemical fertilizers and mechanization. All were facts. What was missing was a theme of more universal appeal, which is more than the sum of sociological and economic facts. It should have been a theme applicable to all communication on the farming problems, to every documentary, all feature stories and novels, records, pamphlets, or anything else dealing with the problem.

Can any such theme be found? The director of a documentary might take as his theme the love of farmers for farming or the love of the countryside, common to us all. My own approach, instead, is to undertake motivation research on both farmers and the public for whom the propaganda is intended. Among farmers I discovered that some merely want to be left alone, independent of everybody — all they want is to farm and to make a living. They have little conception of their dependence on the rest of the nation and the world, but are vociferous whenever their "rugged independence" is threatened. There are others who recognize the wider world around them; they wonder why the bounties of their mechanized harvests cannot be used to feed the hungry everywhere in the world. Their humanity is not mere pity or compassion so much as it is largess and generosity. The two dimensions of rugged independence and competent largess are also in the public's mind, as subsequent research indicated. Here therefore is the beginning of thematic material; the drama is that of the failure of ruggedness and the success of generosity. These are not sociological facts but explanations and suggestions of myths and symbols. In every documentary and every poster or feature article there could be both the rugged individualist and the prince of bounteous harvests — the former with his broken scythe and the latter knighting the poor with a lusty stalk of corn. My research explanations are never far away from such themes and symbols. Not that I can do more than pretend when I try to create any. I merely offer a research foundation for the creative artist, writer, dramatist, or director to work upon, recommending less guesswork and more science in the derivation of effective symbols and themes. These and other pragmatics are to be considered in the chapters to follow.

SYNOPSIS OF THE THEORY

Play theory applies to all customary institutions, whether of state, church, court, school, college, factory, or home. I see the role of the mass media, compared with these playful culture-forming institutions, as serving two purposes. One is to give people something to talk to each other about, to foster their mutual socialization. Q-factors, approximating as they do to inner talk — as a sort of conversation with oneself and thus also to one's conversation with others — are scientific models of sociability. Here the term is used technically to mean attitudes adopted to maximize sociable interaction *for its own sake*, a "play form" such as Simmel (132) discussed, or such as Huizinga (52) described more widely. For my part I accept the viewpoint that mass communication may influence customs, as play. Its purpose can be to "normalize manners" (as Toeplitz [155] puts the matter), to suggest to the masses certain standards of conduct, to provide for the leisure of such peoples, to make life easier for them. I see nothing oppressive or nefarious in this. On the contrary, it is beneficial. The classical study by Warner and Henry

(161) of the audience for daytime radio "soap operas" showed how clearly supportive these programs were for the hard-pressed housewives who listened to them every day.

The other purpose of mass communication is to "rock the boat," to be in the forefront of change in status quo conditions. The press, traditionally, has served revolution and revolt. It is important to notice that it is difficult to change basic beliefs, though in a revolution that is perhaps exactly what happens willy-nilly. It takes a cataclysmic event, however, to bring this about. The achievement of mass communication lies in the way it short-circuits older beliefs, substituting new values for them.

In the latter respect I keep in mind the role of *social control* on the one side, upon which all our institutions are based, and of *convergent selectivity* on the other, with which mass communication is more particularly concerned. Social controls are subserved by deeply internalized beliefs which are difficult, if not impossible, to change. Convergent selective conditions concern trivial matters in comparison with the above. One's religious faith is a matter of social control and belief; one's wish for a Coke is more likely to involve convergency. Social controls involve ethical needs and moral injunctions — the problems are in the realm of the public good. There is little but communication-pleasure in attendance upon convergent wants; communication-pleasure is in many respects what our theory is about.

5

Reduction of International Tensions

This is an era of revolutions, of threatening thermonuclear holocausts, and of anarchy in scores of newly developing nations. It presents communication with its most pressing problems, solutions for which have been sought by many of the leaders in communication research, starting with Lasswell (70). Recently Lerner (74), Osgood (99), Pye (109), Schramm (126), and others have given much thought to the matters. We shall look at some of this work to abstract from it what I believe to be essential for a theoretical position in the area. It is a very limited position, but the theoretical implications are interesting. For the shattering revolutions and threats of war, ways can be found to represent them for theoretical regard. Their ludenic character can then be examined.

THE THEORY OF ELITES

In 1935 Lasswell published his *World Politics and Personal Insecurity* (70), which marks the beginning of communication theory. From it stemmed his theory of elites. Lasswell saw society as pyramidal with a few, the elites, at the peaks and the many rank and file down below. According to the theory, the elite of any pyramid preserves its hold over the rest not by reason or good will but by manipulating mass symbols, by using force, by controlling the means of production, consumption, education, and so on. We witness it at work in Russia and China. Lasswell sought to study such elite-pyramids, comparing them in terms of origins, the traits they engendered, the attitudes involved, their modes of control, their values and symbols. He called his method *configurative analysis*; but it was merely his own speculation, his own contemplative thinking about elites and the masses they subdue.

Revolutions, of course, are rapid turnabouts in the pyramids, and Lasswell wondered how far a study of an existing elite-pyramid would enable him to predict what would happen to it in a revolution; what would happen in South Africa, for instance, in the face of a Negro revolution. The bottom of the pyramids is seen as filled with restless, embittered, insecure people — the whole world, indeed, rooted in insecurity. Almost anything that relates to the position of the rank and file — unemployment, threats of depression, the growth of wealth elsewhere — will raise the level of insecurity. This presses upward and is held down by the elite, using "significant symbols" to do so; the rulers who used to dispense bread or who put on circuses or who went on the Crusades to protect themselves from revolution at home are now superseded by others "adept at diverting, distracting, confusing and dissipating the insecurities of the mass by the circulation of efficacious symbols." For this reason the Chinese peasants are provided with "Freedom for Formosa" as a distraction and the new masses of Western culture with the bounteous entertainment of the mass media to keep them quiet. Such is Lasswell's theory.

Lasswell saw himself as a political psychiatrist, bent on alleviation of insecurity by studying its sources and the devices of its control by elites. He felt that the hope of the world lay perhaps in an elite of men like himself, political scientists, using the methods of "vocabulary, footnotes, questionnaires and conditioned responses," to control society more humanely than by elites based on "vocabulary, poison gas, property and family prestige." A brave new world indeed![1] Lasswell never said, however, what the restless masses would be like in such an antiseptic world of questionnaire controls. Perhaps he had in mind their subjugation by mass entertainment methods, such as television is held to do!

What Lasswell overlooked was some reference to selfhood. One of the most obvious characteristics of modernization and rejection of colonization and the Western influence is the *desire to do it oneself* (as Lerner [73] has indicated) and a belief that somehow one *can* do it onself. It was vividly evident in Cuba and Egypt, but seems to be characteristic of all revolutions drastic or mild — a bolstering of self-pride, of

---

[1] Yet we may note that polls on a world-wide basis were reported to be so strongly opposed to any resumption of atomic bomb explosions that a meeting of President Eisenhower and Prime Minister Macmillan in Washington to discuss disarmament proposals (March, 1960) had to take account of the fact.

one's own distinctiveness, was apparent as Girard (40) indicated for Chile and Uruguay.

Mass communication is very much involved in these dramatic events. President Nasser, for example, relied heavily upon radio as the significant means of mass communication for indoctrination and propaganda. Our Voice of America speaks for itself. The mass media are everywhere at the service of the state in Russia and China. But they were no less significant in the liberal tradition where the press was regarded as an indispensable condition of government by the people for the people. "Freedom of the Press" is a creed of democracy. The study of "significant symbols," therefore, is of obvious concern in communication research.

There are classical examples to examine. In the Spanish-American War, the Hearst and Pulitzer presses in this country made hay, increasing their circulations enormously by dramatizing what were rather mundane matters about the sugar market in Cuba. Who wants to hear about sugar? To have the events dramatized, however, as "epic campaigns" (with "Butcher Weyler" as the Commander of Cuba, and with Cuba offering at that time some of the "worst insults to America in its history") made dramatic news out of mundane incidents. Give it the drama of the prize fight and create for it villains, heroes, and crises — such is mass communication at its liveliest.

Yet, as Helen Hughes (51) suggested, jingo patriotism and the conversion of news into dramatic personal events opened the way for the American public to become interested in foreign affairs. This process, of dramatization into human interest stories, success stories, and so on, became the *modus operandi* of the popular press; but it led to "talking points" about homosexuality (the Leopold-Loeb trial), about moral values (the Chessman death sentence), about scientific issues (Sputnik and Explorer I), and the like. Thus, Helen Hughes conceives of "human interest" as crucial in a free society; it puts the reader, the viewer, the listener in the position of a confidant, revealing (some will say encroaching upon) inner feelings and experiences; it induces reverie and self-reflection; it expands the personality of citizens. In the Soviet Union, on the contrary, where mass media are not free to be interesting but are notice boards for the state, human interest is apparently contracted.

MATHEMATICAL THEORY OF CONFLICT

It is worth looking at Lasswell's theory in a systematic manner. Smith (133) in a comprehensive review of literature and research on problems of communication between nations concluded that there was then no better theory than Lasswell's. Nothing quite so comprehensively meaningful, it seemed to Smith, had appeared over the twenty-five years or more since Lasswell wrote his book about the insecurity of the masses. Note that what is at issue is *insecurity of masses* — not anything about a man for himself. As Warshow observed (162), the concern was with *social facts* rather than with the individual psychology of the person, and this in spite of the use of psychoanalytic doctrine by Lasswell to add color to his theory.

If, then, one intends to develop Lasswell's theory, it would have to be in mass terms, not individual psychological ones. The concern would be with social insecurity, power, force, grievances, and the like *in the mass*. There is an excellent development of the kind in the mathematical theory of politics by Richardson (112), whose studies were published posthumously (111 and 113). Richardson represents the matters algebraically. He uses only a few concepts, such as national "revenge," "fear," "rivalry," "expense," and "grievances," and develops for these a set of differential equations to represent the conditions of foreign politics. The same expressions hold for Lasswell's theory of elites.

The mathematical-theoretical argument for Lasswell's theory is as follows. The elite and the rank and file are in a sense preparing for revolution. The elite builds up its army of "significant symbols" — the total communication effect of which may be designated as x. Opposed to it is the insecurity of the masses, designated y. "Conditions of balance" may be reached, in which the propaganda (significant symbols) is moderate and the insecurity low; but if the insecurity is high and the propaganda extreme, a crisis is likely. This is to say that if, in the 1964 circumstances in South America, Castro's Cuba were to be blatantly destroyed by the United States, the insecurity in the South and the heightened propaganda value of Castro's presumed martyrdom would set off revolutionary movements in South America far exceeding the boundaries of Castro's Cuba. In short, x and y vary together. We assume that any increase in one increases the other; that is,

$$\frac{dx}{dt} = ky,$$

where t is time and k is a constant, which we shall call the communication coefficient. Similarly,

$$\frac{dy}{dt} = kx.$$

But the cost of the circuses, symbols and propaganda, and so on, has not been considered: this has a restraining effect:

$$\frac{dx}{dt} = \mathbf{k}y - \mathbf{a}x,$$

where **a** is a coefficient of "cost" or "fatigue" for the elite. Also, the rank and file are subject to "fatigue" as well:

$$\frac{dy}{dt} = \mathbf{l}x - \mathbf{b}y,$$

where **b** is the coefficient of "fatigue," and **l** a coefficient of insecurity or communication, now probably different from **k**.

There are also more permanent conditions to consider of the grievance kind; the elite thinks of the rank and file as racially inferior, as heathen, Communist, and so on, and the rank and file thinks of the elite as colonializers, exploiters, aristocrats, or the like. Such we must regard as of a constant, pernicious nature, so that the two equations become:

$$\frac{dx}{dt} = \mathbf{k}y - \mathbf{a}x + \mathbf{g} \quad \text{and} \quad \frac{dy}{dt} = \mathbf{l}x - \mathbf{b}y + \mathbf{h},$$

where the constants of grievance are **g** and **h** for the elite and rank and file, respectively.

The solution of these equations is well-known:

$$x = Ae^{\mathbf{k}t} + Be^{-\mathbf{k}t}$$
$$y = Ae^{\mathbf{k}t} - Be^{-\mathbf{k}t},$$

where A and B are arbitrary constants. If **k** is positive (as we suppose) $e^{\mathbf{k}t} \to \infty$ *as* $t \to \infty$, meaning that the situation is one of instability.

These equations for Richardson's theory clearly fit Lasswell's elite-pyramid theory. By a series of brilliant assumptions Richardson derived constants for the solution to these equations of motion (as they are called) for foreign affairs, but these need not concern us. Other consequences of the mathematical formulation are of direct interest, however. Thus, if x, y, **g**, **h** are made zero simultaneously,

$$\frac{dx}{dt} = \frac{dy}{dt} = 0,$$

which means that there are no grievances, and no symbolization or insecurity. This corresponds to the situation of "permanent peace" between
two countries, such as between England and Scotland since 1603, the
United States and Canada since 1817, and Norway and Sweden since 1905.
The situation corresponds to the conclusion reached by Buchanan and
Cantril (14) to the effect that we must give everyone security and remove
the grievances ("bring his world into perspective") in order to make everyone happy as citizens of the world. But this might be achieved at the expense of communication — the elite and the rank and file could live at
peace, like Norway and Sweden, incommunicado. Buchanan and Cantril
said, as well, that UNESCO should "improve facilities for communication"
between nations. What is wanted is not improvement of facilities such as
telegraphic communication, common language, and the like — they may
be perfect; the real problem is what *kind of communication* has to be
broadcast — what order of things in the communication sense of significant symbols or the like.

The condition for a revolution, corresponding to a race in armaments,
occurs when the communication-insecurity terms predominate, namely:

$$\frac{dx}{dt} = \mathbf{k}y \quad \text{and} \quad \frac{dy}{dt} = \mathbf{l}x.$$

x, y tend to the same ∞, which if positive is to be interpreted as revolution, with a complete *volte-face*.

And what of unilateral conditions? If an elite decided to take off pressure, corresponding to putting $x = 0$, we have:

$$\frac{dx}{dt} = \mathbf{k}y + \mathbf{g} \quad \text{and} \quad \frac{dy}{dt} = \mathbf{b}y + \mathbf{h}.$$

This means that if **h** is positive, *y* can never remain at zero; insecurity will
constantly grow, and no doubt the elite pressure would have to be put on
again.

Richardson's theory has many consequent theorems, concerning conditions of stability and instability and the like. Balance of power can be
reached, for example, as between the communication of management and
labor unions. Stability occurs when the coefficients of fatigue are greater
than those of communication ($\mathbf{ab} > \mathbf{lk}$). The actions of a nominally quite
independent and sovereign nation are really controlled by its neighbors —
and, *pari passu*, the actions of an elite are controlled by the pressures of
the rank and file.

There is complete correspondence between Richardson's theory and the above representation of Lasswell's theory. In Richardson's case, however, one could also consider conditions in which the signs of the equations are reversed, corresponding to "love and co-operation" as distinct from "hatred and war." The chief stimulus to falling in love, as is well known, is a sign of love from the other person. It follows that the antithesis of war (and revolution) is not peace as a mere tranquil state of inattention and noncommunication with others, but cooperation, as a positive effort to please the opposite member, not to suppress it. So, we must suppose, assistance will provoke reciprocal assistance (as imports and exports tend to equality). Is this not the logical substitute for what Lasswell had in mind as the rule by an elite of political scientists?

The situation is comparable to that of international trade regarded as the opposite to war (see 80), and Richardson deduces the consequences. Most important, perhaps, is his conclusion that in the case of Germany, the constants k and l are the same in magnitude for trade as for war preparation. In the elite-pyramid, then, we can expect that whatever it costs to maintain an elite supreme by way of war-provoking pressures, no less will be at issue for the condition of active benevolence. The concern would not be with insecure masses (as Lasswell thought) forever held down by symbols but with something quite different, namely, self-expressive people who need "love" to maintain them.

We reach the conclusion that the opposite of "significant symbolization" is the replacement of it neither by rationality nor by inattention, but by "positive benevolence" of some kind — an exuding of cooperation and an enhancement of the selfhood of all concerned. This may seem like fantastic sentiment, but the consequences could be remarkable for international communication no less than for the theory of elite-pyramids.

The above rapid view of a mathematical formulation of Lasswell's theory surely asks for more careful study. The concern is with one elite-pyramid, but it can be generalized to cover many elite-pyramids. In ancient times the elite-pyramids existed without intercommunication; the ancient Britons had no communication with Spartan Greeks, although each separate system was an elite-pyramid (in Lasswellian terms). Today the situation is one in which there is the possibility of instant and complete mass communication around the world.

In the political case Richardson's equations indicate that the condition of least stability is one in which there are n equal states, all making war preparations against each other; the condition of greatest stability is when all but one nation has been reduced to zero size, so that there remains only one power. This might have been grasped, for example, if the discovery of the atom bomb could have been in the hands of one nation only. But now there are three, then four, then five . . . nations with the same powerful secret, and unstable conditions are inevitable. In communication-theoretical terms, following Lasswell's theory, the outcome has to be *one* elite, with *one* set of significant symbols to maintain the rank and file of separate nations in subjugation (we are assuming that insecurity will remain, and grievances, fatigue, and expenditures). But what symbols?

The choice in communication is not limited, however, to Lasswell's theory of an insecure and suppressed rank and file and an elite: there is also the opposite of this, that of in some way *giving*, with reciprocal acceptance. Thus, in considering the battle for the minds of the nonindustrial nations (the modernizing ones, as they are now called) the whole area of significant symbolization could call for serious revision, away from conceptions based on Lasswellian and Freudian notions of insecurity, to those of existence by benevolence. The cost would be much the same in time, money, and human effort.

PSYCHOLOGICAL CONSIDERATIONS

So rapid are the changes in the world that Richardson's theory of a decade ago is no longer sufficient. The situation has changed; it must be assumed that no power is prepared now to push the button that will set a thermonuclear war on its path of world destruction. Psychological factors, and not power politics, are therefore more profoundly significant.

This does not mean that matters are any less threatening. Large military interests exist in the United States as elsewhere. Without attributing any sinister plotting to them, whereby they foster wars in order to exercise their sinews and to prosper, the fact remains that they cherish weapons as a child does the most costly toys; they call for vast expenditures of public funds; they introduce military considerations into all international and national affairs, perhaps without relevance to matters at issue. From the very nature of the military profession, it runs counter to much that might be peaceful and presents a constant threat of secret military advice at the highest levels of government, out of all reach of the public, that could spell disaster because of public indifference rather than because of military villainy. The press has a special responsibility to be vigilant in this matter, more so now than ever before in history.

It is reasonable to suppose, however, that the knowledge of thermonuclear destructiveness has Communist leaders particularly on the horns of a dilemma, one which was apparently separating Soviet and Chinese leaders in 1964. The current impasse has put an end to the historical justification for Marxism as a scientific prescription for socialism; wars between capitalists, it was held, served to make way for communism over the dead bodies of exhausted capitalist nations. The argument no longer holds water. We must suppose, therefore, that the Communist elites are taking a second look at basic principles; great wars can no longer be instruments of Communist, or any other, growth.

What, then, can mass communication do in such a state of affairs, assuming that the above ABC of foreign politics is not too inaccurate?

In my view, very little. Psychologists, almost every one of them, will attest to the aggressiveness of man under conditions of frustration. Wars occur in spite of wide opposition to them; a referendum in Europe at any time in the past sixty years probably would have outvoted any resort to arms. Nor is it enough to suppose that antidemocratic personalities (*The Authoritarian Personality* [1]) are the source of wars. There is a great gap between the psychology of individuals and the happenings that lead to war. One has only to read Tuchmann's *Guns of August* to catch a glimpse of the autonomous character of war; or to read Rowse's *Appeasement* (121) to learn of the stupidities of prime ministers — Churchill described Neville Chamberlain as an old Birmingham businessman "looking at world-affairs through the wrong end of the municipal drain-pipe." One sees how wars come from ignorance and miscalculation, from mismanagement and conceit, and scarcely at all from any displacement of aggression or the like simple human mechanisms. It is better to say that wars happen out of stupidity rather than out of anything else — out of political-historical factors rather than out of psychological factors.

Psychologists, however, still try to explain these terrible mistakes in their own terms. Osgood, a case in point, is a communication theorist and psychologist whose book *An Alternative to War or Surrender* (99) offers a scheme based on psychological principles for his premise that either we shall have a thermonuclear war soon, or else within decades we will have to surrender to the superior might of Russia and China combined by then into an invincible single power. His proposal is not to seek disarmament, but to pursue a policy of unilateral actions designed to reduce world tensions. Osgood calls his program GRIT, meaning Graduated Reciprocation in Tension-reduction. It consists of taking the initiative in helping modernizing countries to grow in the image of the great powers. Thus, the United States might help Latin American countries (as the Alliance for Progress proposes); it was hoped that the Soviet Union in turn might help, say, Pakistan. We know, of course, that such help has never been selflessly given, "with no strings attached." Russia helps Egypt to build the Aswan Dam, but there are political, economic, and military implications; we foster the Alliance for Progress with the expectancy that the Latin countries taking our help will see the cold war our way. We are always prepared, President Kennedy said, to help those who are going to be our friends. Osgood's GRIT seems to be oblivious of these political matters; the initiatives he proposes are outpourings merely from goodness of heart. Thus, he talks of exchanging scientists, of fostering tourism, of encouraging uncensored front-page coverage of views by Latin American journalists in United States newspapers, and the like. In this way, he suggests, by kindness, tensions can gradually be reduced (leaving armaments untouched). At best the initiatives would be transferred from national to international authority (99, p. 126); they would be designed to reduce the imbalance between "have" and "have-not" countries; they would strengthen "democratic as against totalitarian ways of life" (99, p. 132). GRIT is a glorified cultural outpouring from the United States to "have-not" nations, or from the Soviets to other "have-not" nations. It fits fairly into preparations for "love" or "un-war" in Richardson's terms.

What, then, can one say against it? First, with Bauer (7) I would suggest that communication has to be conceived as "two-way," that is, as a transaction between two equal parts, and Osgood's proposals are "one-way" in conception. The great nations are to *do* something, but it is not clear what the smaller ones have to do, not so much in return but reciprocally, as the basic theory requires. In Osgood's GRIT the "initiatives" are unilateral. We would no doubt seek to make Latin America in our image, and the Soviet Union would do no less for its own image wherever it gave of its bounty. This ignores the principle that the growth of a nation is a growth in selfhood, involving a wish to "do it oneself." Under "one-way" circumstances the more the well-wisher gives, the more it is resented. The United States has poured tens of billions of dollars into newly developing countries with, it seems, little thanks and less reciprocity as the result.

Second, to be effective, the cost of Osgood's proposals would have to match the cost of current military preparations, requiring whole armies of personnel and services, a revolution in itself. That the world is ripe for such a revolution is perhaps true. But, with Max Lerner (New York *Post*, January, 1965), I wonder how far the key concepts at issue about even the much lesser revolution proposed by President Johnson, leading to the Great American Society, have really been grasped by anyone. Revolutions are generated in a climate of excitement and triumph, the status quo tumbling down like a thousand avalanches, and there was little of this in the American situation in 1966.

Third, our principle of Q-audiences is damaging to Osgood's argument. Osgood describes, as in some sense characteristic of the United States, a primitive mentality, which maintains that what is good for the United States is good for the world; that foreign aid should be used to keep people in line; that "we are powerful enough to do it alone, and that goes for the United Nations as well." The mentality is backwardlooking and would repeal twentieth-century social advances. It is terribly alarmed at the Communist conspiracy here. Few have ever seen a Communist, but if none can be found they are said to exist as subversives. It is a mentality that cannot think, out of anxiety; the only way out for it is to assume toughness, to deny any danger of war, to sneer at pacificists, to destroy humility and social welfare everywhere around. Such, Osgood admitted, is a caricature; for us, however, it is true of only one segment of the American public and happily not of others, as my study of public opinion about Cuba (139) indicated, and as I indicate in chapter 12 in connection with the study of Khrushchev's visit to the United States.

Is there anything that mass communication can perform which will cross national boundaries and ideologies, which can bypass the current schisms and antagonisms that plague the world? I look at this, finally, in the light of a problem peculiar to the United States and its Latin neighbors.

THE ALLIANCE FOR PROGRESS

This American alliance went into effect in 1961, having as its objectives the pumping of United States money into South America for programs of direct benefit to the Latin American masses. It was expected that as these nations achieved greater economic stability and higher living standards, and a measure of social justice and democracy, they would be more willing to cooperate with the United States and its policies. By 1963, as reported by Obaid and Maritano (95), it was clear that the millions of dollars given under the program to Latin governments had done little to achieve Alliance objectives — politicians, wealthy landowners, and businessmen had put much of the money into their own pockets, shipping it back to European and United States banks.

The difficulties are no doubt enormous. Obaid and Maritano observe, particularly, that the American press does a very poor job of reporting on its southern neighbors, distorting the news; these neighbors, for their part, have a black image of the United States. It is obvious that American policy has "yet to identify itself with any genuine democratic movements" in South America. "We are woefully ignorant of each other," these authors conclude. We are pictured in Latin America as grossly materialistic and crude, with no cultural or humanistic preoccupations; and Latins are seen by us as lazy, uninterested in the cold war, the space age, and the like. The idea of the Alliance for Progress has not sifted down at all to the Latin masses.

We are told that the spirit of enterprise is missing in Latin America; that its Spanish background has produced "an incurable hatred" against all law and order; that there is little sense of civic responsibility, little spirit of cooperation. And to cap it all off, the peculiar Latin social character is said to be incompatible with the creation of modern forms of society. The picture is the usual one, common to all modernizing countries, such as Lerner (76), McClelland (86), and others have described. The obstacles are certainly enormous in every direction of culture, history, politics, social institutions, geography, economics, racial prejudices, and psychological quixotism. In England what is accepted as simple social justice is viewed by the conservative Latin press everywhere as communism.

What, then, is to be done? Our two authors, Obaid and Maritano, suggest what common sense recommends: that the flow of dollars should cease, to be replaced by surplus from this country to help build housing, hospitals, schools, and so on; our colleges and universities should be linked with counterparts in Latin America to develop extension work, to teach the masses simple skills, as in agriculture. All of which sounds very much like an Osgood prescription, "one-way" in direction — big brother helping poor little brother.

My own suggestions would center, instead, upon "two-way" action. I would learn first what motivates Latin America and what motivates the United States, and then see what might be done to gratify both. Q-audiences indicate what motivations to look for, after which one can set about finding themes to tie in with them.

Obaid and Maritano (95, p. 83) observe that Rodó's *Ariel* (117), a classic south of the Rio Grande since 1900, has had deep impact upon Latin Americans. Rodó wanted a new ethic for Latin America which would be rooted in aesthetics. His concept of democracy was a beneficent utilitarianism which retained the "aristocratic spirit" — a scholarly, gracious trade-unionism. Rodó wrote disparagingly of the United States at that time as imperialistic, materialistic, dollar-minded, and devoid of any idealism or truly creative thinking. The country was described as unaesthetic, hating "noble superiority," belittling intellect and genius, and rewarding mass mediocrity. Rodó wanted to steer Latin America away from such Calibanism and, instead, to have instilled the symbolization and lofty idealism of an Ariel:

> Ariel represents in the Shakespearian symbolism that noble and winged part of the spirit. Ariel is the rule of reason and sentiment over the base impulses of irrationality. He is the generous zeal, the lofty and unselfish motive in action, the spirituality of civilization, the vivacity and grace of intelligence, the ideal goal to which human selection aspires [Rodó, 1957, pp. 202–3, translated by Obaid and Maritano (95)].

Ariel was widely used in the education of Latin American youths (of the elite) and it may have contributed to the image that these Latins have of Americans as plebeian, vulgar, and intelligent but uncreative. Even today a great section of the Latin elite apparently thinks of Americans in this way — "they still look at us with Rodó's eyes, and are not aware of the changes that have taken place in our society in the past twenty years" (95, p. 85). A few, throughout Latin America, think of their culture as having already achieved just such a lofty Ariel's ideal, as perhaps it has — for the wealthy elite.

But who shall say that something of the kind, a loftiness of spirit, is not precisely what motivates far more of Latin America than we are prepared to admit? In any case it is some such socially oriented, self-directed motivation for which we should look. I am foolish enough to believe that with a few-score depth-type interviews, followed by a Q-sample to represent them, a beginning could be made in the direction of determining what would flatter Latins, and with good enough reason. It might not be an Ariel; nor need it be a scholarly, gentlemanly "Montesqieu" with the full romantic treatment of castles, guilds, craftsmen, and, no doubt, trade-unions thrown in. But it would be something for a new Latin America. Insofar as assistance from the United States would be involved, it would have to be tied in with North American motivation. The solution would be a mood, and a climate for it, which fashions the conduct and lifts the hopes of all concerned.

Again this sounds like preaching for goodness. But it is obvious that the mass communication put out in Communist countries provides some such mood, and the climate which fashions the culture of their vast masses. The American continent has all the facilities required for communication, or could make them available — the radio, television, newspaper, news magazine, movies, documentaries, paperbacks, and all other forms of modern communication. What it does not have is a central source of ideas or inspiration to feed into them.

Of course, very difficult matters are involved for the democracies. One can only raise the bare possibility of a nonpartisan group of directors, playwrights, producers, editors, and social thinkers who with the support of "backroom boys" working along the lines I am here developing could tell the Americas what sort of mass communication they are getting and what they could have instead. Jean-Luc Godard, the French film director, remarks that he can learn more about France through the advertisements in the magazines and newspapers than he can from the news they contain. The advertising campaigns of oil companies, banks, and brassiere manufacturers tell you more than is learned from reading how de Gaulle shook a thousand hands in Marseilles or Caracas. If we could feed into the directors, producers, and editors objectively determined motivations, in relation to specific Q-audiences ready for them, then something might be achieved of lasting effect for everyone. At present there is mere anarchy instead. I can do little more than illustrate what is involved in such a backroom. In each case an *XYZ* situation has to be defined, to grasp its Q-audiences; these have to be examined for their deeper motives; and finally these have to be translated into key communications. In each instance the theoretical stand is taken that one has to grasp primitive moods and feelings within a framework of communication-pleasure. There are problems enough in this direction, but none is insuperable. The greater difficulty lies in having the weight and authority of a central body of directors and producers to begin the process of a new acculturation.

6

Theory of
Social Character

In the present and each succeeding chapter the data come from factor analysis, involving many tables of correlations, factor matrices, rotations, and Q-factor models. Computers do the calculations, fortunately, and I propose to take them very largely for granted. The reader without statistical knowledge will not find it difficult, therefore, to follow the discussion. Since I believe that the most important problems are in international communication, we began their study in the preceding chapter and now continue their consideration in the present and subsequent three chapters.

We are to examine in the present chapter how far social character, especially other-direction, depends upon the principle of convergent selectivity. Inner-direction, as it is described by Riesman (116), is dependent upon inner beliefs, upon early internalizations which fix the person's character. The concern is with social controls such as LaPiere (68) describes. Other-direction, instead, is much more in relation to mass communication — to what is "popular," to new experiences, to fads, and so on. It is important to understand what might be done to influence social character in any consideration of communication, national or international.

RIESMAN'S THEORY

Riesman (116) defined directedness as different from personality. It was conceived as a growth of character, dependent upon "movements" across the centuries, spanning Western civilization from feudal times to the Industrial Revolution and so down to today's age of affluence and plenty. American social character today, therefore, was supposed to have in it vestiges of the directedness of all previous historical movements.

Everyone was considered by Riesman to be traditional, inner-, and other-directed in some degree.

Tradition-direction is a dependency on conformity to tradition, by both institutions and individuals of a society. This conformity, Riesman suggests, is assured by a type of social character to which the term "tradition-direction" is given (114, p. 4). It is characteristic of preliterate and peasant cultures. When individuals are taught instead to conform to internalized values, characteristic of Western civilization, the type of social character which assures this is called inner-directed. The individual in this culture is directed by very general goals, for wealth, achievement, fame, goodness, and the like, values which are modeled upon one's parents or other influential father figures in one's early childhood.

Other-direction is a type of social character which apparently supports the "new middle class" in the United States. Its quality is a certain sensitivity to one's peers; its characteristic is the impermanence and fluctuating nature of the new American's goals rather than his internalized values. Short-run objectives, and the "world of interpersonal relations," are primary factors in this form of social character. Thus, whereas European values are set in firmness, stubbornness, doggedness, a concern for hard work, and indifference to the opinions of peers — all in the pursuit of fixed and often very distant goals — the new American is characterized by "variability, sensitivity to others, the taking of goals from peers and mass media, and concern for consumption" (114, p. 13).

In tradition-direction there is fun, in myth, legend, and song. God is responsible for everything. The person is nowhere sufficiently self-aware, sufficiently separated psychologically from himself (or sufficiently close to himself), his family, or group, to think in other than day-to-day terms. Shame is the great controller of behavior; one behaves in an approved way out of fear of being shamed, and since there is an approved way for almost everything one has to do, it is easy to see why shame is all-pervasive.

In his description of inner-direction Riesman puts emphasis upon the strength of character needed by Western men to break away from feudal and traditional ties. It is indeed easy to forget how strong were the terrors of hellfire that scourged feudal times with centuries of dogma, inquisitions, and witch-hunts, and how difficult it was for a modest burgher to cut loose a little, to travel, to begin to think differently, and for himself. The reverberations are still with us. To break away required a special kind of inner strength, a self-sufficiency and mastery of oneself. But the new character could only be built upon the older models of harsh authority, ruthless, without compassion. Thus, while Protestantism and the Reformation gave each man his own soul, it was at the expense of pity. The age of rugged individualism was the age of child labor, of sordid slums and slavery. Business was impersonal — one could ruin one's brother with impunity. Sexuality was a frigid posturing. Money, it was well known, "talked." Social classes were cut off from one another — and nations, of course, too. The laws of the jungle, in the name of Darwin, were proclaimed as verities by industrialists and scientists alike and were sanctified and sanctioned for human conduct. Such is the age of free enterprise and rugged individualism. It was also the age of the internalization of guilt, of the harsh superego structures described by Freud.

Homo Americanus of the future, if we are all to become other-directed, will be a very different creature. The breakup occurred in the "fabulous twenties" (well reported in Frederick Lewis Allen's *Only Yesterday* [2]), a decade of scandals, ballyhoo, alcohol, the Florida boom, the Big Bull Market, and the sickening crash of the Great Depression. The aftermath has been one of sober problem-solving. The problems of production are solved; technology, automation, and nuclear energy have revolutionized industrial prospects. It is now widely proclaimed that in 1970 the standard of living in America will be 50 per cent in real values above what it was in 1960. The problem is how to consume what can be so abundantly automated. What is required is a new kind of social character to consume the wealth and bounty — not out of ostentation and vulgar display but out of genuine, sensible pleasure in supermarkets, parks, rivers, seashores, highways, and foreign travel. All of it, in our theoretical framework, is a matter of communication-pleasure. Nothing much is gained, except enhancement of millions of selfhoods.

Again Riesman gives a fascinating account of such an other-directed social character. The *popular* is important in it, not the good, the best, or the great. The interests are in people, not things — as in our study of a state library system where it was found that the modern librarian prefers people to books. Teachers, professors, children, are all of equal status, none more significant than another. Adjustment matters more than ability. Taste counts, not morality — so that the young have babies, and are "cute," "darlings," "good guys," "swells," or the like in the process — if not, they would have been "square" or "lousy." Success now depends upon what others think of you, not what you do; one understands everyone's motives cleverly. Parents can no longer feel superior to their children; the children's models are no longer great men but their own idealized peers, jazz crooners of television or radio. Children have become more realistic, however, — they *know* more than their parents. Whereas the tradition-directed child propitiates his parents, and the inner-directed fights or succumbs to his, the other-directed manipulates his or is manipulated by them.

Without having to deny that inner-direction has its roots in history, the facts for other-direction suggest more immediate causal agencies. Heberle (45) holds that directedness may be more immediately interactional than is contemplated by a slow historical and cultural process. He suggests that with increased economic freedom people can move about more freely; the mass migration into Florida, Texas, and California from northern states may have immediate effects on the social character of the movers. New Yorkers moving to California or Texas want to behave like everyone around them; they do so in terms of the trivia of modern consumer goods — cars, homes, dress, barbecue pits, swimming pools, and the rest — not out of any sense of shame but out of dissonance, followed by self-expansion, self-respect, and self-expression. They change their ways, and their social character follows suit. Whether their deeper value-systems fall in line as well is another matter; our own view is that it would be well to recognize that early internalizations remain untouched. So conceived, other-direction is a person's free conduct, an adjustment to conditions in which peer groups and mass communication play crucial parts. It is to that extent nearer to conditions of convergent selectivity than was the case for inner-direction, which was dominated by institutionalized social controls.

Riesman thought that there could be no neat "litmus-paper test" for his typology; the concern, he considered, was with tendencies only, with matters of balance, emphasis, and interrelationship, and not anything clear-cut. It was clear, also, that individuals adjust to their culture with different degrees of success — some are well attuned to it (adjustment), others are sociopathic (anomie), and some transcend it and are free to act autonomously (autonomy). In relation to special areas of concern individuals were further typed by Riesman as Moralizers, Indignants, Oldstyle Indifferents, Inside Dopesters, and the like.

FORMAL REPRESENTATION OF RIESMAN'S TYPOLOGY

It is a simple matter to put certain aspects of Riesman's theories to test, using Q-method.

Riesman placed his emphasis on the subjective individual, as his *Individualism Reconsidered* (115) so brilliantly indicates. When Riesman wanted to provide empirical data, he resorted to interviews with individuals; he read and reread these through many times to provide for each an explanation in terms of his theory (with dynamic psychology thrown in most perceptively). The interviews covered the complete milieu in which the individual may be supposed to have come under the influence of the culture in which he lived. In the course of the interview each individual expressed his views about the culture, his attitudes toward his society (of course without any direct awareness of the purpose in hand). Riesman had then to interpret the material with his theory in mind.

This is along the right lines. The problem is to bring a little system and science into it, so that research might continue by anyone, especially by those who cannot hope to match Riesman's interpretative gifts. This can be done by taking Riesman's heuristic method a step further, by asking the persons who are interviewed to offer a more direct account of how they see themselves in the context of their cultural milieu, using Q-method for the purpose.

It is a simple matter to represent Riesman's theory formally, as in the following Q-sample design:

effects	levels			No.
Direction	(a) Traditional	(b) Inner	(c) Other	3
Adjustment	(d) Adjusted	(e) Anomie	(f) Autonomous	3

I have covered the design with several different Q-samples for statements typically as follows:

1. I feel bothered when I'm in a new environment; but I meet people or forget about the ones I can't meet.
2. My tastes in music cater to the semiclassical, in particular to the works of Jerome Kern and George Gershwin.
3. I respect money and fame — it takes something to get either.
4. I think the man should be the boss, especially in the home and with the children. The hand is meant for spanking.
5. I seldom regret what I do — I'm self-sufficient in myself. Some people can't do anything on their own, but I'm hard to get to know because of it all. I make up my own mind.
6. I just don't like people who shut themselves off from others — the weirdies.
7. I guess I never did have any ideas of being great. I want to do a good job of course. I think I'm very normal in these respects.
8. Mario Lanza — I like to hear him sing the Student Prince. I also like Perry Como and Pat Boone. I like musical movies.
9. I like an interesting person — one I can learn from, a broad con-

versationalist, one I can appreciate — I like to find out their goals and values, and why they have succeeded.

10. Happiness is the most wonderful thing on earth, when it is contentment and peace in religious respects.

The statements are in the language of the individuals interviewed. They touch upon how one lives, one's taste, self-sufficiency, ideas about others, values, habits, personality, opinions on success, achievement, sex relations, military views, and, one might say, almost everything that jostles about in the mind of every one of us in some way or other, or at some time or other in relation to one's social behavior.

With Q-samples for the above design it is a simple matter to ask individuals to represent themselves in Q-sorts — one invites them to give a self-description. One can proceed further by asking a person to offer as a Q-sort what he believes others (whose opinion he respects) think of him, and the like. From self-descriptions alone, however, the various types described by Riesman are readily made apparent.

It will be remembered that in the domain of social control Q-factors correspond to attitudes of mind, and their explanation to belief systems. Several attitudes of mind may require the same explanation in terms of beliefs. Similarly for social character: Q-factors correspond to types described by Riesman as Do-Gooders, Inside Dopesters, Good Providers, and the like. Their explanation reaches into directedness — that is, traditional, inner, or other — and adjustment. Thus, several different Q-factors may require explanation as inner-direction.

Riesman thought of his types as tendencies only, as matters of emphasis, for which there could be no neat "litmus-paper test." Q provides precisely such a test. Nor is it arbitrary. The Q-sample is as comprehensive as one can make it, governed as it is by the Q-sample factorial design for Riesman's theory (as the above table indicates). Each person's self-description involves every statement of the Q-sample. Quite distinct types appear, each as a Q-factor, yet each may be inner-directed, or other-directed, as the matter of tendency or emphasis.

Consider a study for adult (white) Americans for the following P-sample:

Age	(a) 20–40	(b) 40–60	
Sex	(c) Male	(d) Female	
Educational level	(e) Grade	(f) High school	(g) College

For a Q-sample of size $n = 48$ one found in the Midwest three factors,

A, B, C. Factor A was other-directed; B and C were both inner-directed.

Factor A favors white-collar individuals, and a glance at the statements scoring +5, +4, +3 in the factor array indicated very clearly that other-direction was at issue. The following statements of the Q-sample illustrate this:

Statement	Score on Factor		
	A	B	C
I have never sought out responsibility for its own sake.	+5	−3	−5
I am attracted to a "warm" personality.	+5	+4	−5
I appreciate jazz music because I understand it.	+3	0	+1

Factor B is focused more on blue-shirt individuals, of either sex, and any age. The factor is patently inner-directed, showing a need to respect others and to be respected by them, all matched by firm ambition and an eye to success. There are many facets in the Q-sort pointing in the same direction, that what is represented is a stable, materialistic, somewhat grim creature of the Puritan ethic. Probing quickly shows that the factor thinks religiously and not affectionately about warmheartedness. Discipline and sobriety are at issue, rather than the softer qualities of factor A.

Factor C is inner-directed, too, but with anger and evidence of dynamic factors at issue. One individual of the factor, a woman aged thirty-nine, works all day, six days a week — she is married, with a daughter and one grandchild. Another is a physician in his late thirties, educated in the Middle West, who "takes an active part in church and altruistic pursuits." The factor is pointed and personal. These individuals say they enjoy a "binge," and they display themselves as ambitious, intolerant, argumentative, indignant (at political events — but no doubt more generally, too). They are the hard workers, the moralizers, the intolerants, the conspicuous spenders, the people who say they know what they want.

The model points to one form of other-direction and to two of inner-direction, and some individuals are mixtures of these. That other factors exist, for this Q-sample, is no doubt certain. Thus, the many types described by Riesman as Moralizers, Inside Dopesters, World-Improvers, and the like, can all be supported empirically.

RIESMAN FACTORS AND "SOCIABILITY"

The above must serve to show how it is possible, very easily, to provide an objective basis for Riesman typology. Much more could have been reported, had space permitted, concerning the outstanding questions of autonomy (Riesman) and of related problems — such as those concerning loss of self-identity, which Wheelis discusses (164). Here, however, we must turn to theoretical matters at issue. What, really, is Riesman's theory about?

Riesman calls his theory a typology of societies; he thought of the types as "ideal" only. They point to social conformity, and a suitable theory to fit the conditions is probably that of George Simmel (132). In the broadest sense the concern of Riesman's types is with *sociability*, which Simmel regarded as a "play form" — something done for itself, rather than for any gain or other purpose. So people in a society have shared values, shared interaction, shared identifications in relation to their society; and in societies as in smaller groupings all the participants tend to have these values equally — in this way participation by everyone alike is facilitated. It is much easier in a society if everyone thinks alike about the necessity for hard work, diligence, owning property, and the like, characterizing, as we see, inner-direction; this is especially the case when production of goods and capital is essential for the growth of the society's wealth, as during the Industrial Revolution. Thus, in small groups as in larger societies social character is adjusted to suit the conditions, not the reverse; the social conditions essential to the Industrial Revolution, as to the Reformation, demanded something very like inner-direction. Moreover, it had to express itself, in spite of some exceptions to the rule, as much the same sort of thing — the same values and identifications — for everyone.

It is apparently agreed, however, that we are now a society of abundance, such as man has dreamed about for centuries. The sociability corresponding to abundance is consequently bringing about other-directedness, that is, forms of interaction to suit these new conditions. To be able to spend leisure time on fun, sport, travel, picnics, movies, television, stereo records, paperbacks, and all else calls for a different social character — a willingness to spend, to be in debt, to enjoy oneself without a conscience to mar the pleasures. The epitome of other-direction is beauty, leisure, sun-tanning, and the like, married to peer-group sociability.

The firm hand of inner-direction, however, still lies heavily on the

possibilities of such a happier sociability: the *Moralizers* say we are decadent; the *Pessimists* see corruption, idleness, loss of identity, and weakness of character everywhere around. The truth may be that inner-direction is now largely inertial, standing in the way of the American's
enjoyment of the fruits of his cleverness.

SOCIABILITY AND CONVERSATION

The Q-factors we find for social character are what a person is prepared to talk about with others. They are indeed his social conversation with others, summarized in a characteristic form.

Conversation, as interpersonal communication, is of course at the heart
of communication theory. Conversation serves a social function, as when
one talks about the weather, dogs, babies, and the like to one's neighbors. One is not exchanging ideas — because everyone knows what the
weather is like, and what babies and dogs are like, too. One is just being
sociable, that is, attitudinizing, *playing* for no gain, as Simmel said —
and one is not aware of this "play." Conversation between lovers or in
the intimacy of the family is quite different from one's sociable talk,
with which social character is concerned — and different again from
one's professional talk or from what one talks about at work.

Research in mass communication however has emphasized the ideational contexts, that is, the exchange of ideas as a means of influencing
people and to bring about changes in their attitudes. One seeks to per-
suade people (49) by giving all the facts. This is putting the cart before
the horse — or, rather, it is to put no horse to the cart at all. One should
be studying the interchange of attitudes, that is, the art of being conversational for reasons of "sociability."

The great trouble in the world is that we now find it difficult to have
a conversation with others; sociability fast became a lost art in the rational centuries of inner-direction. The English psychologists Bartlett
(6), Pear (101), and Oldfield (96) have long pointed to the disparity
in this matter between the current view of conversation as ideational and
its more basic form as attitudinal. When the house is on fire or in any
common danger, people return to more primitive conversational forms
("primitive comradeship"). We are quite sure, for example, that if
Americans and Russians could speak the same language, they could not
hold a sociable conversation — except in a situation of common danger
or, as we believe, except in situations mediated by what is "popular,"
such as might appear at a carnival, a fair, a picnic, or wherever Pepsi-

Cola, cigarettes, bubble-gum, or the like are freely dispensed. It is therefore a striking characteristic of other-direction in the United States that its peer-group sociability is spreading its open arms into the family, into lovers' talk, into professional talk, and into work talk. In short, other-direction is restoring conversation to its original role — that of increasing sociability, of making it easier for everyone, of any estate, age, intelligence, class, or color, to converse with everyone else inside and outside the home or the factory. It still has a long way to go. But if mass communication methods cannot achieve something in this same direction, it is hard to believe it can be effective in any way whatever.

The vision of such "primitive comradeship," of primitive communication-pleasure, has already been mentioned in connection with the universal impact of Pope John's humility and President Kennedy's youthful image. I see other-direction as pointed in the same playlike, youthful, childlike directions. Riesman concludes that there are some weaknesses in the other-directed social character; but that is to confuse cause and effect. Other-direction depends on an achieved affluence, rooted not in retirement from work but in skills and cleverness that make work less and less essential, since automation does what is required. The real problem will be to maintain this utopian character. The less fortunate peoples of the world, out of need, may misunderstand these movements of the affluent American.

CONCLUSION

I see other-direction as a play form such as Simmel described, done for itself and not for gain. Whereas inner-direction brought about sharp segregations into the "haves" and the "have-nots," other-direction bids fair to restore conversation to its original role of common communication that can be shared by almost everyone. Its connections with "primitive" communication have been indicated. The other-directed social character fits the needs of an affluent society as a glove fits a hand.

The connections with convergent selectivity may seem remote. Much in social character calls for everyone to think alike, to have the same identifications, and thus to be conforming. The rules for other-direction are not laid down, however, by churches, parental figures, or any existing social institutions — whether political, educational, legal, or any others ordinarily associated with social control. Rather, they are generated within peer groups, stimulated by the mass media, by movies, records, and any popular personalities. The concern is with relatively trivial commodities and limited wants — all are pleasures, without deep commitments; all are fashions, like the wearing of a new hat at Easter, at best for the fun of it.

In the development of other-directedness it is hard to believe that the mass media have failed to be, if not the major, then one of the major influences in its formation. We can accept Heberle's view that social mobility, due to increasing affluence, produces the characteristics of other-direction in certain material respects (of a willingness to spend for leisure pursuits and the like); but the conversation still has to be accounted for, and this, in other-directedness, seems to depend little on church and more on movies, little on the home and more on the peer-group allegiances, little on the heavy reading of classical novels and more on implicit understanding of Beatle recordings. Fads, fashions, and styles for clothes, chewing gum and drinks (Pepsi or Coke), music (records), automobiles, and homes — all are heavily supported by mass communication. And these epitomize other-direction.

7

National Character and Charismatic Leadership

The above treatment of Riesman's typology affords an idea of what I believe is at issue in any consideration of national character, which should be conceived of as in relation to the needs of the culture and as something about which every citizen can make conversation. The process of developing national character is no doubt basically rooted in social controls (as LaPiere described them [68]), in which church, home, school, work, and all else mediate. But national character is also what a nation *thinks* of itself, as something to talk about, to sustain ongoing social or national conditions. It is best regarded as communication-pleasure, which has little effect on anything but gives self-satisfaction all around.

There are now over a hundred new nations in the world, all proudly flying their own flags, all seeking or expressing their individual identities. Some, like India, with dozens of subgroups, speaking hundreds of dialects in a dozen major languages, have to create almost *de novo* a common national sentiment. It was easy in the early days of the Industrial Revolution in England for James Mill to point the way to such common allegiances; one need not worry about the votes of the working classes, he wrote, if they can have before them the idea of a hard-working, respectable middle class to which to aspire. The same English character, of stability, dutifulness, reliability, and diligence, would serve the rest of the world very well if it could be transplanted everywhere into its teeming masses and new nations. The problem is, is it possible? National character has not been considered seriously in this way. Much of course has been written about it.

THEORY OF NATIONAL CHARACTER

There is much interest in general discussion of national character, as Northrop's *Ideological Differences and World Order* (94), or Hsu's *Americans and Chinese* (50), and many others attest. Riesman's *The Lonely Crowd* (116), and *Faces in the Crowd* (114) have led, in papers edited by Lipset and Lowenthal (78), to important commentaries on American (United States) social and national character. But we would agree with McClelland (87) that such work leaves much to be desired, although he adds that the study of national character is basic to communication theory. Lerner (75) proposes that people make social change self-sustaining by way of "empathy," but he puts national character in place as the *modus vivendi* for an ongoing social state — it does not cause conditions but merely sustains them — which is perhaps not far from my own viewpoint.

McClelland (87), writing of national character and economic growth, remarked that national character is not taken very seriously because it is difficult to define. This is no longer the case, as I said, indeed, much earlier (147). All the more, therefore, is there need for theoretical positions in this field, whether about national character and economic development or national character and militarism or, as here, about national character and communication.

The trouble begins in analogies. Simon Raven, writing in the *Spectator* about modern Turkey, describes its landscape as alternately savage and boring, its mountains as all sheer, its lakes all deep, salt-filled, and treacherous, its deserts pitiless, its plains unending. Therefore, to live in such a country men must be brave and resourceful; parents for the same reason have to be harsh and cruel; in this context a virtue has to be made of inefficiency; and courage is extolled. All of which makes interpretation sound so easy — the country made the character, and the character makes the economic, the military, or the political picture what it is. In point of fact, Kemal Atatürk's Turkey was a small elite, educated entirely on Western lines (35), surrounded by the savage and inefficient peasants and the petty, greedy shopkeepers of the plains and mountains. If the character of the elite had been measured, it would have been more French than Turkish. That of the peasants and petty middle class might have had reflections in it of the kind described by Raven, for certainly Atatürk never reached down out of the elite into the masses. But modern communications are doing so not merely by transportation, so that people are now physically mobile across the length and breadth of the country, but also by radio. It is in such a context of a dissolving elite and evolving lower classes that we must have a viewpoint about national character to see what it might offer for mass communication. In this respect our answer is quite clear: national character is what a nation is prepared to talk to itself and others about — it is essentially communication-pleasure, a conversation piece. It is what citizens are going to talk about in clubs, meeting places, and factories. It is what gives a nation a sense of its own identity. As such it is important enough, in all conscience, and offers basic directions to media writers, to propagandists, and to national leaders.

One should observe here the suggestions by Shils (130), concerning the development of elite cadres for newly developing nations. The prerequisite for a stable nation is not demagogy, he remarks, but stable institutions of public opinion, education, and work. There can be no question that there is a most important need for engineers, doctors, university teachers, higher civil servants, businessmen, and editors, journalists, and broadcasters; these, constituting an elite, are the hub about which all else can turn, the center of gravity of a nation. But in the circumstances such persons have an obviously superior position and prestige, and unless care is taken they will separate themselves from the public at large — as is happening in Turkey. The result is a separatist culture within a country, and this bodes no one any good.

How, then, to remedy matters? Even Shils, it seems (almost as an afterthought to judge by its position in a note appended to his paper [130]), has to remark that it is to the communication networks that these elite groups should turn for an answer. They should consider what newspapers, periodicals, clubs, colleges, and radio stations can do to help them bridge the gap to the mass. One would have to study "images and responses of the less educated to the educated," and the "images of the political elite to the highly educated who are not engaged professionally in politics" — so writes Shils. Shils knows full well, however, that the availability of mass communication favors the demagogue, especially where the public is illiterate. It is easy to say that what is required is a "redefinition of the image of the self" of a growing nation, as Shils does, recommending that administrators have to be punctual, dutiful, and devoted servants. But there is no James Mill to indicate the truth that there is no respectable middle class in these countries to which the poor can aspire through hard work and diligence. We have seen how quickly black demagogy can take over; yet the solution probably lies in something of the kind, except that we would call it charismatic leadership, and it need not be demagogy at all.

Shils proposed that cadres of educated men should be formed for new nations, but, as these nations can scarcely wait for such slow growths, the tendency is to fall back upon mass communication to see what it can do.

For this we should study the mass media in relation to the whole public in its segmented parts with no a priori conceptions other than this: to let people *play* more, even if they have also to *work* more. Communist China apparently succeeds in this (170) by heavy use of entertainment as a "fill" against the obduracies of hard work and reiterated dogma and doctrine. One probes the public, in politics as in advertising, to determine needs and wants in relation to existing possibilities, and in this matter no two nations are ever likely to be alike anymore than Q-audiences are alike for every consumer product. Demagogy may turn out to be what is really required in some cases. What is most required, however, is something for everyone to talk about. The daily "fill" is far more important than the education of professionals. This is how social character and culture is formed, in songs, gossip, sports, dances, competition, or whatever is required to give people communication-pleasure. What is required, as well, is charismatic leadership and deeply involving themes and symbols.

Our prescription for studying new nations, therefore, is to examine the existing social controls and ethical needs, and to represent these thematically. To this we add a "fill" of convergent selective pleasure.

PLAY THEORY OF NATIONAL LEADERSHIP

When it is concluded that the leadership of a Winston Churchill or a President John F. Kennedy is in good part charismatic, eyebrows may indeed be raised. The events of November, 1963, of Kennedy's assassination, have been described earlier as primitive communication. It is obvious that President Kennedy is rapidly becoming a legend — more myth, as Muggeridge has said (91), than man. He is widely extolled as great — a dedicated public servant, orator, writer, Christian, a devoted husband and father, a genius among statesmen. That he had some such attributes need not be denied, but their exaggeration is patent. The legendary image bears little relation to his real abilities, capacities, and true self.

It is also true that to a considerable extent the legend was synthetically produced. President Kennedy's father demonstrated how a great deal of money, machination, and a keen Bostonian type of political gerrymandering was able to fashion the image of his son; the egghead, the Harvard man, the do-gooder, the New Frontiersman were all synthetic productions. Muggeridge adds, indeed, that the senior Joe "almost invented, besides begetting, the late President." That the method was eminently successful cannot be denied either.

The adoration of President Kennedy has been scathingly described as turgid, hypocritical, grisly, sickening, and the like, and compared with the "degraded monarchy-worship" in Britain (91). His public appearances have been called mechanical, robot-like, pervasively sad, as though he belonged more to a comic strip than to real life. But there can be no doubt whatever of a certain sense of high tragedy now enveloping the Kennedy family, a sense of doom that has struck it, giving it a Shakespearian rather than political or historical significance.

Accept all of this as one may; for my part I draw attention to its obvious charismatic attributes. However, unlike Muggeridge, I like the legend, the myth, and the model of all the virtues. The sycophancy and sickening deception seen by the Muggeridges is legitimate theater for millions who want something of the do-gooding and the charm of a young prince among men. What millions saw about Kennedy need bear no relation to reality; in his case, however, what they saw in pity, and continue to see in compassion, was a Holy Grail, symbolizing much that can never be articulated except in dreams or by poets. People will continue to talk about it, and President Kennedy's memory could well be with us for a long time. The conversations will be enjoyed, as all communication-pleasure is.

COMMUNICATION THEORY OF MODERNIZATION

We can now compare such charismatic leadership with what communication theorists have had to say about the growth of nationality. Much is heard of it now in relation to the modernization of underdeveloped nations.

Lerner (75) is perhaps the best-known theorist in the area of communication and modernization; how does it come about, he asks, that the mass media function effectively only in modern and rapidly modernizing nations?

Lerner supposes that communication media are major instruments of social change. It can scarcely be doubted that urbanization, industrialization, higher standards of education, greater political awareness, and increasing use of mass media are all interwoven; everyone will agree that communication networks are the nerve centers of modern societies. Studies of diffusion in modernizing nations (24) indicate that social status, the media, and "mobility" are interactional, each influencing the other. But how to get such systems moving in the first place and what is important in them is still anybody's guess. That all is not well in nations under the aegis of Western communication principles is certain. We see this in the most modern of nations themselves, where the media are subject to constant criticism for their shortcomings and puerilisms. But the most damaging criticism comes from those who, like Lerner, believe that Western mass communication has done little but induce dissatisfaction and frustration in the new nations receiving it. Western movies and ideas raise the expectancies of the poor nations far beyond any possibility of immediate realization. We face, according to Lerner, a revolution of rising frustrations in the modernizing nations.

My conclusion to be considered later is that the function of "news" is little understood. Most of the newspapers across the world were started by Englishmen with the general idea that they were to serve public enlightenment, for social and political reform, and it is true that the early newspapers in Asia were involved in reform movements. The news was incidental, however; the cause was the main thing (so writes Passin [100]). This is clearly the case today in Communist countries, where mass communication gives only such news as fits the party line. In doing so, however, it gives the public a sense of unity. Yu (170) gives us an account of the process in China, where there is monopoly over all channels of communication. The Communist theory of communication begins with the doctrine that thought determines action — therefore one sets out to make people think "correctly." One shapes the mind of the entire nation. Class consciousness has to be awakened. In principle, one determines what the masses want and this is fed back to them. Mao Tse-tung writes, for example, as follows:

> Whether or not the party leadership is correct depends upon the party's ability to analyze, systematize, summarize, and consolidate the opinions and experiences of the masses, to transform them as the policy of the party and then to return them through propaganda, agitation, and or-

ganization, to the masses as their own guide to thinking and action [quoted by Yu, 170, p. 264].

How thoroughly the opinions and experiences of the masses are indeed probed may be debated, but there can be little doubt about the thoroughness with which the communication system can be put to work. The commune is full of blackboard newspapers, handwritten posters, street-corner plays, and face-to-face talks by agitators, all fed from a central source. Some of the communication is communistic; some is traditionally Chinese — so Tao and Marx are cheek by jowl. It has resulted, Yu informs us, "in new images, new symbols, a new language, a new audience, new communication channels, new communication methods and behavior of the masses." Yu's account of the communication in a commune before and after this onslaught is more instructive. A region with 20,000 population was originally largely illiterate, without contact with the national government. It had few primary schools, and only a few reading rooms which were poorly equipped and infrequently used. A few families received prestige newspapers; there was no radio station; movies were a novelty. In 1959 the region had become a commune with a similar population. There were now 267 newspaper-reading groups; 267 art and literary groups; 390 blackboard newspapers; 17 libraries; and various exhibition, current affairs, and recreation centers. There were 200 schools, including high schools. Since the Great Leap Forward, we are told, 13,000 in the commune had written poetry, folk songs, plays, novels; and even the number of wall drawings had been counted at 190,000! If only partly true, it represents a wonderful change. To read a newspaper in China is now an obligation. Radio is all over the country, in buses, trains, even in the trees in parks. What is important, of course, is the very fact of so much *play*, carrying along the hard work of a growing society.

Lerner (76) proposes that what has to be induced in the modernizing process is "psychic mobility," as well as physical and social mobilities. Everyone can now travel by bus in Turkey and such physical mobility is of course significant. Social mobility is also important — it is said to be maximized in the U.S.S.R. But psychic mobility has top place in Lerner's regard:

> The acquisition and diffusion of psychic mobility may well be the greatest characterological transformation in modern history, indeed since the spread of the great world religions. It is in any case the most fundamental human factor that must be comprehended by all who plan rapid

economic growth by means of rapid social change. For psychic mobility — what we have elsewhere called empathy — is the mechanism by which individual men transform themselves in sufficient breadth and depth to make social change self-sustaining [76, p. 332].

All of this is no doubt true, but it does not help. The fact of the matter, according to Lerner's own observations on the disruptive effect of Western-style communication, is that there is a rising tide of frustration everywhere. Lerner's theory could suggest nothing that might be done to stem the tide, except to propose that people everywhere must learn the virtues of hard work, the rewards of effort, and the necessities of achieving moderate stages of development step by step. He said nothing about how to plant these seeds in the poor and illiterate nations.

My own theory is more practical. It picks up from *homo ludens*. I assume that there cannot be stability in a new nation without an element of play. Play sets a limit upon aspiration; the child plays and never confuses this with what he might indeed like to have in reality. In the new nations there are on the one hand the higher goals of modern life, of education, political justice, increased education, better health, increased leisure, and all other hopes; on the other hand there is what is realizable in the immediate future. The latter is inevitably much less than what everyone yearns for. To teach hard work is no doubt commendable; but mass communication serves to keep people busy *pro tem*, to let them play, and therefore to enjoy themselves en route to the promised goal. The play should be such that no one will confuse it with what is immediately realizable; that is, the mass communication must serve as a substitute for the ultimate goal. It is not to be conceived as escapist, or with Hyman (53) as a way to relieve mass anxieties. Rather, one's culture grows out of such play if it is properly constituted.

We may note, here, that in China the communication system led to the writing of poems, plays, and novels, and to drawings on the walls. This, in a country leaping forward into modern industrial life, is testimony to the strength of play where it might have been little expected. The hard-working Victorians missed all such playfulness: there was little time for play in the Industrial Revolution. Emphasis was on educational aspiration, on scientific judgment, on social consciousness, all free from folly, all taken seriously — to which the dead black suits of Victorian dress bore sardonic witness. How much wiser it might have been to induce poetry-writing, novel-writing, play-writing, and the making of 190,000 drawings on the factory walls! Not by alienated writers or artists, of course, but by everyone.

Nor is this farfetched. In every small town in the United States men and women are painting pictures, heaven knows with what unaesthetic feeling, with little thought of gain. All of it is genuine play. We should remind ourselves of the eighteenth century with its teeming clubs, secret societies, literary salons, brotherhoods, and innumerable associations, all bearing witness to wholehearted abandonment of an elite in play; and we should wonder how to bring genuine play into the lives of all nations today, modernizing or modern. The form must be appropriate to the possibilities. One seeks to blend old ways and traditions with new customs, styles, and manners; and perhaps one would be wise to steer clear of the puerilism that characterizes some American broadcasting.

Such communication maintains the status quo, and that should be its primary function. But it does so with pleasure in attendance. The communication is communication-pleasure, doing no one much material good and no one much harm, but giving time for the fruits of work to make the essential economic gains upon which a modern society rests. So Nasser learned to give his Arabs Arabian music on radio, and the U.S.S.R. wisely filled its radio networks with serious music; aspirations for all that the world can offer are symbolized in Mozart, Beethoven, Berlioz, Bach, and Tchaikovsky. The Chinese Communists wisely purvey Taoism blended into Marxism. All of this is play, to serve *pro tem*, but always with the distant goals in mind. It is not without importance that American women paint pictures, or that the ordinary man in China writes his poems or makes his drawings on his walls; but it is supremely important that what they play in this manner is somehow in the image of what people want out of life, ultimately, for themselves or their children. It should never be a matter of entertainment to assuage anxieties, or to lessen frustrations, but a matter of allowing people to be self-enhanced in play.

This is why we do not deride but praise the Kennedy legend. It would be well for the United States to play it, as *Hamlet* is played on the stage, for all it is worth — and what it is worth is human decencies, and the reduction of poverty, disease, and ignorance the world over. There were enough of these virtues, and enough of charm, youthfulness, and honesty-of-purpose in John Fitzgerald Kennedy to merit the image. More important, there is perhaps enough of a demand now for the same virtues, all over the world, to make the image live.

8

The Democratic Myth

When a list of errors is drawn up for the conduct of the world's political affairs, the cold war of ideologies will rank high for its astonishing follies. It was, and still is, Western democracy's policy to defend democracy and to encourage it everywhere. Yet most of the new countries of the world have found democracy unsuitable, if not unthinkable. American dollars, poured into scores of new nations, failed to help any of them clutch the tender nettle of democratic freedom; all fell to authoritarian forms of rule of one sort or another from Formosa to Korea with Turkey, Egypt, Pakistan, Iraq, Ghana, Cuba in between — to mention the more obvious of the early 1960's. Yet democracy is the most pervasive of all ideological concepts. National Socialists, Communists, Anarchists, Liberals, Socialists, Conservatives, Republicans, Democrats, on this or the other side of the Iron Curtain, are all votaries at the shrine of democracy. But there is little agreement about what in fact is being worshipped.

Democracies such as Britain and America are a slow growth of Anglo-Saxon political traditions, supported by Protestantism and a steady growth of economic wealth, and kept free from authoritarianism by legal forms and by the absence of military castes. Britain and America had no need of large armies until recent times, and therefore no Napoleons, Hitlers, or Francos could usurp for themselves the seats of authority. There can be no guarantee that a system so slowly nurtured, under such special conditions, would be applicable to totally different circumstances — of poverty, different religions, agrarian economies, instead of industrial economies and the like.

How did it come about, then, that slogans seem to have governed the conduct of nations, when in fact complex matters of social control have operated?

In the present chapter we look at two studies, one comparing the democratic attitudes of five nations (Britain, Germany, Italy, Mexico, and the United States) and the other looking at the concept of democracy from a philosophical standpoint. In both cases the search is for key communication concepts.

STUDY OF FIVE CULTURES

The intensive study by Almond and Verba (4) of democracy in the United States, Britain, Germany, Italy, and Mexico indicates how complex are the differences in democratic process in these ostensibly democratic countries. The study took several years to complete, under the aegis of the Center of International Studies at Princeton. A thousand interviews were taken from each of the five countries under careful sampling conditions, two questionnaires being used in each interview — one of 94 questions (with many subquestions) and the other of 131 questions (again with several subquestions). It was assumed that people adopt attitudes about their culture, government, and political institutions. The object was to determine what relationships exist between these attitudes and each ongoing nation. A wealth of data and inferences are the outcome.

One will observe at once that the attitudes are inferences by Almond and Verba and not direct expressions of such by the individuals (as they are in Q). The authors express regret, indeed, that they could only present their data "dimension by dimension," in one chapter after another, and that this "tends to obscure the wholeness of individual countries and the reality of the individuals who constitute them" (4, p. 402). For this reason they resorted (at the conclusion of their report) to the clinical method of reporting, presenting a number of intensive interviews with two individuals from each of the five countries, as "summary country profiles and illustrative case histories." Almond and Verba considered that these were merely illustrations of the various patterns of attitudes analyzed in the main body of the report; the case histories were held to be "unique" and not open to easy generalization. For our own part we would *model* the attitudes at issue, and seek to relate these directly to ongoing governmental action. We would in fact begin with case histories, such as Almond and Verba describe, though we might be more precise in our definition of the XYZ situations.

The authors of course come to many interesting factual conclusions. The theoretical framework in which they interpret their data involves the assumptions that for true democracy to develop there must be a sense of national identity, competency in discussion, and acceptance of a stable government, civic cooperativeness, and social trust within a country. Education tends to increase each of these, as do urbanization and industrialization. Education is thus the prescription for growth of democratic attitudes.

Broadly, the United States was shown to be active in its political culture, but with no strong allegiance to a central federal government. (We may add, in passing, that education did not produce democratic attitudes in the extreme rightists of recent political history in the United States.) Britain was found to believe more in the independent authority of government, but was considered to be deferential and relatively inactive in political matters (nothing corresponding to the New Deal has come out of Britain in the past thirty years). Germany has a purely pragmatic view of democracy; Germans are passive about planning and democratic discussion and accept any government if it satisfies their pragmatic needs (in Hitler's day and today alike). The situation was the same for Italy, except that it was alienated at both ends of the democratic machine — nothing is put in, and there is little trust of anything the government puts out. Mexico discussed democracy vociferously, but under the banner of the Mexican Revolution, so that all is myth; and all political and governmental actions were derided and rejected. Mexico's aspirations for democracy were high; its actions were negligible. Almond and Verba concluded that the situation vis-à-vis democratic functioning was highly unstable in Italy and Mexico — Italy lacked the passive acceptance of authority of Germany and the aspirations of Mexico. The authors added that the new nations of the world are trying to do in years what took centuries for Britain and the United States to achieve, and it is highly doubtful whether the attempts can be successful.

The exceptions to the theory of national identity, stability of government, civic cooperativeness, and social trust (all assumed to grow with increase of education) are of course dramatic. Germans are well educated by acceptable standards; yet they are shown to have little sense of citizenship or cooperation with their fellows (yet socialized medicine and housing, pensions and cooperatives, are everywhere in vogue). Mexico lacks the educational skill, but stands high in democratic cooperation. The theory, in short, merely lets one see what one wants to see a priori, and leaks heavily at every seam. The two authors are aware of this and therefore add that what seems to be essential, though puzzling, is leadership of a charismatic kind: ". . . there must be a symbolic event . . . or [a] charismatic leader . . . to create commitment and unity at the symbolic level" (4, p. 504).

Application of Q to the Study

I agree that cultures require charismatic conditions to symbolize their commitments. So Nasser of Egypt, Castro of Cuba, Stalin of Russia, and many another has focused the commitment of a nation and set the pattern for new cultures. Hitler's Nazi regime had similar magical roots. Each, however, had foundations in a literature, a pseudo-science, or the like, that gave it verisimilitude. Hitler could depend upon the dogma of German race psychology, believed in by many German psychologists before and after World War I. Castro had his Marti, and Stalin his Marx and Lenin. Pan-Arabia had a wide vogue, to which Nasser added his own writings. One would have thought that these charismata should have been the objects of study by Almond and Verba rather than academic categorical matters of civic cooperativeness, social trust, and the like. For of course nothing but categorical facts come out of studies based on such assumptions.

We can show first, however, that Q-sorts performed by relatively few persons from each of the five nations studied by Almond and Verba, say fifty from each, are enough in principle to reach theoretical positions which these authors reach with five thousand.

We may begin with the ten case histories reported by the authors (4, chap. 14), two from each country. From these, self-referent statements pertinent to the XYZ situation are readily collected (where X are persons, Z the acquired information, and Y the cultural, governmental, and political mechanisms or institutions involved), which in turn suggests the following factorial design for a Q-sample:

Effects	Levels			No.
I, Opinions	(a) Political	(b) Governmental	(c) Others	3
II, Valency	(d) Positive	(e) Negative		2

(Combinations: $3 \times 2 = 6$)

For eight replications a Q-sample of size $n = 48$ is composed, maintaining a broad basis so that it is applicable to any nation. Examples of statements for a Q-sample with this structure are given below; they are taken from the interview material provided by Almond and Verba.

1. I have always been concerned about the outcome of all the socialist principles — social security, etc. — what will the end result be?
2. The government favors the industrialists and the rich — the poor get little out of it.
3. Politicians make a lot "on the side" — there is a lot of waste.
4. I would like to see better conditions for everyone.
5. War is always terrible.
6. I don't think that politics affect my life very much.
7. Without a government people would kill, and kill without fear.
8. I consider myself an agnostic, though religion undoubtedly plays an important part in the country.
9. Social security, safer mines, more health benefits, and unemployment benefits — these have made things better for the country as a whole.
10. I have been interested in politics for as long as I can remember.

I found in a study of adult male subjects (ages 25–35, all college graduates) that their Q-sort self-descriptions gave rise to four factors, A, B, C, D. Cutting across all were statements for which there was agreement; all expressed confidence in their country, government, and social developments. They expressed the well-known American distrust of politicians and disquiet about moral problems. These are salient opinions, suggesting an attitude of considerable hopefulness and confidence in civic and social respects. There were high aspirations for betterment and progress. But there was little integration of politics into these high social expectancies; political feelings have not developed in step with the attainment of pride and confidence in one's own culture.

The factors, except for B, proceed differently. Factor A has the common deficiency in developed political attitude, but is deficient also, basically, in firm civic and cultural feelings.

Factor C puts on a strong political front; all the statements involving politics are upgraded (or downgraded as the case may be). Love of country and politics have the highest saliencies. But the translation of politics into governmental action is conspicuous by its absence for this factor. Politics is the putting-on of a shirt without awareness of the responsibilities in wearing it; there is no well-integrated growth from social aspirations into governmental action. War, for example, is not regarded as terrible. Statements given neutral scores all attest indifference to government action and change.

Factor D is alienated, rebellious, and pessimistic in attitude. Interest is only grudgingly given to politics, and lack of home influence is seen. The statements given neutral score show indifference to country, politics, segregation, religion, and so on. The factor "wants it good," but has no faith in much happening. There is resistance to the culture, to government, and to politics; it is the protest of angry young men.

Looking back, therefore, I came to the same conclusions as Almond and Verba, but in direct focus: the citizen of the United States, to judge by our model, has high aspirations for betterment and progress with confidence in the culture; but he is negative about politics — much as Almond and Verba concluded. Similarly, none is an ideal citizen, if by that one means a person with firm roots in the culture and a stable faith in government and in politics, the latter integrated into the culture and government. Factor C is little better than the Mexican condition described by Almond and Verba; it waves the flag of nationality, but scarcely knows why.

In the above manner the over-all viewpoint of each person is retained on the basis of analysis, and there is never any need for thousands of persons to be compared — twenty or thirty at a time are enough. A Q-model for Englishmen, another for Germans, and so on, would give at least a first look at the facts, and usually at those of immediate importance.

Our interest is not in merely arriving at Q-audiences or types with respect to the matters in hand, but with the ultimate problems of communication in relation to them. First, however, a somewhat paradoxical conclusion must be drawn: it seems true that the American culture is achieving, in education, technology, social mobility, affluence, and everything else, a degree of success far in excess of anything to be found elsewhere in the world or in its whole history, and our Q-model reflects this, precisely, but the achievement would seem to be in spite of politics, or at least political attitudes are less well adjusted than are the cultural and governmental attitudes.

This would ask us to be cautious about any assumption that the attitudes of a nation's citizens have any one-to-one relationship with the functioning of the state. This is for two reasons. I would echo the following thought in the *Economist* of October 17, 1964, in its comments upon the defeat of the Conservative party in the 1964 parliamentary elections in Great Britain:

> It may be a comfort to fearful Conservatives to remember how small a margin of the acts of any government are significantly influenced by its party colour. Of what is done in a government's name much the largest proportion is always determined by the pressure of events, the momentum of past policies, or the prevailing habits of mind of the civil service. A government ought to be turned out either when its small margin of entirely political acts has become generally inept and malign or when it allows the proportion of its actions which are determined by passive acceptance of events, the mere momentum of past policies and prevailing civil service attitudes to become altogether too large [pp. 225–26].

Second, it is doubtful, as I shall shortly indicate, how far a large proportion of the United States is genuinely democratic; conservative Republicanism seems to be democratic only in a rudimentary sense. The United States is still in many respects a frontier nation in which the principle of convergent selectivity applies; the virtues of rugged independence are still uppermost, and socialism is a very dirty word indeed. Yet again, the attitudes in these respects bear little relation to ongoing affairs — veterans have free medical treatment; students have almost free university education; industry is hemmed in everywhere by pension schemes; and "social security" is rather well established in the land of individual opportunity.

Almond and Verba, in looking at what might be done to produce attitudes congruent with democratic ideals, observe that all political cultures differ from the "rationality-actionist" model of classical political science. People do not debate issues rationally, reach a consensus, and take action accordingly. This is an ideal, it is suggested, which is difficult to achieve because of the complexities of matters, but to which democracies are directed: ". . . given the complexity of political affairs, given the other demands made upon the individual's time, and given the difficulty of obtaining information necessary for making rational political decision, it is no wonder that the ordinary citizen is not the ideal citizen" (4, p. 475).

The real problem is whether anyone would welcome rationality in politics. Berelson, Lazarsfeld, and McPhee (11) concluded that people in the United States range on a scale from "social" on one extreme (characterized as indifferent to public affairs) to "ideological" on the other (absorbed in affairs, but rigidly, in a highly partisan manner). In the center is "political man," with only a moderate interest in politics. Our Q-model for the Almond-Verba case does not quite parallel such a scale, though factor C is the most ideological and factor B corresponds to a moderate "political man." It is clear that political theory will have to come to grips with our factors. Here, however, it may be the case that the United States is all the healthier for having a skeptical attitude about its politicians; inconsistency between political attitudes on the one hand and actions on the other may well be the key to much that is really healthy in the ongoing affairs of the United States. This, again, is a conclusion close to that reached by Almond and Verba.

Let me repeat, however, my concern is with mass communication in relation to the above. My tendency is to approach communication through the consensus items of a Q-model. In my study there was only one cogent, highly salient statement common to all the factors. It is as follows:

	Score on Factor			
I would like to see better conditions for everyone.	A	B	C	D
	+5	+5	+4	+5

It may be said that no one could possibly disagree with this — yet, as we see, factor C can find statements with higher saliency and the statement is not highest in saliency in other countries, unexceptionable though its aspirations may seem to be. The main point about it, however, is its prescription for cultural, governmental, and political communication in the United States, insofar as our Q-model represents the general public. Content analysis of advertising in the United States will show, without doubt, an insinuation toward such betterment. Mass magazines, such as *Successful Farming* and *Better Homes and Gardens*, are right in line with the sentiment at issue. Better conditions for the indigent and chronically poor in the country seems to have wide support in politics. The themes of better schools, better public libraries, better homes, better automobiles — indeed the proverbial better mousetrap — are so familiar that they almost breed contempt. But there are fewer of the kind in the less-developed nations — even in Great Britain.[1] Such, for us, is the prescription for the mass communication of any achieving nation. It has to be proved how far such communication can induce an achieving culture. There are indeed suggestions (76) that poor nations which are promised

---

[1] A Q-factor study, made in England in 1964–65, shows this to be a striking difference between the attitudes in Britain and the United States in this respect, supporting McClelland's position on achieving societies (86).

too much too soon become bitter and frustrated. But infusion of a little of the methods and outlook of the man in the gray flannel suit, selling improved services and goods, might be a better stimulus to modernization than much else that has been tried with little or no success.

PHILOSOPHICAL DISCUSSION OF DEMOCRACY

A set of papers put together for UNESCO, entitled *Democracy in a World of Tensions*, and edited by Richard McKeon (88) (in which over one hundred experts examined the "philosophic grounds" of the current conflict of ideologies in world politics), showed very clearly that everyone had his own ideas about what democracy means. The experts were leading philosophers, men of letters, historians, legal authorities, and social thinkers from all the major nations of the world (excluding Russia and China, but with the Eastern views well represented by professors from Hungary, Poland, and Czechoslovakia). They were invited to give their views of democracy, and the result is a remarkable set of scholarly papers laying bare the thoughts of experts who presumably take a broad view of their endeavors and of the problems facing the world. Thirty-four of the respondent experts have papers in McKeon's book. In addition an "analytical survey" of the views of all one hundred men was undertaken by two professors, Arne Naess and Stein Rokkan, whose report is included in the book. The conclusions were disappointing. So complicated are the arguments, references, assumptions, and contextual involvements that Naess and Rokkan had to conclude, hopelessly, that "it is beyond the powers of present-day research to determine in any exact way the lines of agreement and disagreement between [the] ideological doctrines" (88, p. 510). The two professors concluded nevertheless that all men are created equal, but that the difficulties occur when one sets out to define who are men, what creation is, and in what equality consists.

Even so, the discussion by a hundred experts cannot but be illuminating and scholarly. Their views provide us with a ready supply of Q-statements, and from Q-studies we can hope to determine what goes with what in the philosophical mind. Two problems are of particular interest: first, how far are one's views about democracy based on one's political faith, or, conversely, does one's political faith determine one's views about democracy; and, second, are there any key concepts that the McKeon Committee missed that should have been handed over to UNESCO to help in its work?

LUDENIC THEORY OF DEMOCRACIES

Among the various papers in McKeon's report (88) there is one (chap. 25) by J. P. Plamenatz, Fellow of All Souls, Oxford, which seems to me to be more down to earth than any of the others. Plamenatz notes that the primary meaning of "democracy" is the same in Russia, Poland, Yugoslavia, France, Britain, and the Americas; it means government by persons freely chosen by and responsible to the governed. The difficulties occur when steps are taken to implement this in practice; it gives rise to many secondary meanings now attached to the word, such as that democracy is characterized by freedom to form associations, to discuss what one pleases, to criticize the government, to emancipate women, to have independent political parties, to abolish state involvement in religion, and the like. All these, variously held to be preconditions for democracy, are essentially not so, Plamenatz asserts.

The real question is to ask on what grounds a person "freely chooses" his government. Government today is a vastly complex matter about which only a few persons have expert knowledge — only civil servants and professional politicians really know about affairs of state, the economy, and administration. The ordinary voter is largely ignorant of the matters; ignorance and prejudice, rather than knowledge and altruism, are indeed the common characteristics in politics whether local, national, or international.

In politics, few really know what they are doing; yet all speak knowingly. They have learned to use a vocabulary of politics, a language of charades and clichés to use in disputation. One can recognize it very easily, for example, in Reiger's essay in the McKeon book (chap. 27), where the talk is of "victory for bourgeoise capitalism over feudalism," "the total removal of economic bases of class antagonisms," and so on. But there is comparable language for Republicans in this country, as there is for Democrats or Socialists. The working classes had to acquire a political *patois* suitable to their needs — they had nothing of the kind, for example, when they first got the vote. Now they are highly articulate, as any speech by a Reuther or a Hoffa will attest. In every instance the "argotese" is without real meaning, involving little adequate understanding of anything. But in its terms one can dispute and argue as well as the next person. Politics is carried on, as far as voters are concerned, in a context of relative ignorance and prejudice as on a stage, outside reality — it is a play, so as to make political conversation possible.

The experts in politics, the professional politicians, do have some expertise; it is not necessary to suppose that they are deliberately keeping the voters ignorant to serve their own professional ends or for the benefit of propertied classes or munitions manufacturers. On the contrary, circumstances are controlling factors to a great degree. Politicians have no sure answers to outstanding problems, and it is easy to appreciate how party and pressure groups influence them to take courses of action often far removed from the will or intentions of voters.

Plamenatz concludes that when there are several political parties each will try to please the voters in order to win power, and that this alone preserves an element of individual freedom for the people at large. Since the issues upon which voting takes place are chosen by the professional politicians rather than by the voters, individual freedom is circumscribed correspondingly.

In my theoretical framework, political language is indeed very largely *play*; it keeps people talking with little reference to reality as a scientist would understand it. Yet things get done this way. Every now and then the talk gets down to realities, as in the "war" against poverty, medical care for all as a human dignity, public education for all, and work (or a substitute) for all who want it. But apart from such needs, still being fought for, everyone enjoys the rough-and-tumble of an election; and everyone expects name-calling, innuendoes, and mudslinging — as a famous President said, "No one should be in politics unless he is prepared to stay in the kitchen when things get hot!" There is, in innumerable details, little that distinguishes political mongering in the United States from the Eskimo drumming contest described by Huizinga (52, p. 85) in which no distinctions are made between well-founded accusations, slander, and anything funny that is calculated to humor an audience.

EMPIRICAL STUDY

The views of the various experts could have been studied systematically along our lines. Following my usual procedure, a collection of self-referent opinion statements can be taken from the McKeon report by going through it, page by page, abstracting from it all opinions bearing on matters of democratic belief, institutions, and values. For my purpose a sample was taken by selecting at least one statement from each of the contributors to the symposium. The result was a Q-sample of size $n = 54$. In this case there was no design for the Q-sample.

I feel that one example of Q-method should be available in more detail to the reader, and I have chosen a study using this Q-sample for the purpose. The topic, besides, is of considerable general interest and importance. The complete Q-sample is given in the Appendix to this chapter.

The Q-sample has in it several statements which apply more particularly to the ludenic theory, notably statements Nos. 18, 23, 35, 38; but there are statements to the contrary, for example, Nos. 13, 36, 39, 47. Indeed, every slant and viewpoint is built into the Q-sample in the haphazard manner of a chance selection.

The Q-sample implies innumerable hypotheses, and still more are involved in the choice of respondents. I could not have Q-sorts performed by the symposium experts, but this scarcely matters because the principles can be dealt with without their help. Nor was I able to include in my initial studies any Communists to represent the Eastern philosophies. It was desirable, however, to cover the following "interests," following a Thompson design (see 158) rather than a balanced P-sample:

A. "Special": three hypothetical variables were performed by the present author to represent (1) an expert opinion, (2) the East-West dialectic, (3) Dr. Plamenatz's viewpoint. (They are discussed later.)

B. "Experts": three professors of history and two of law, all with distinct scholarly interests in constitutional matters.

C. "Authorities": these are people who presume to speak "with authority" about matters, in the present case individuals holding political party office, five Republicans and five Democrats.

D. "Class" interests: since the Q-sample is a difficult one to comprehend no attempt was made to ask uneducated blue-shirt workers to perform Q-sorts. Instead military and religious interests were included, two Army officers and two ministers of Baptist and Catholic churches, with the idea that their views may be reflections of their professions.

E. "Anybody": a category including the ordinary man-in-the-street, in the present case represented by four housewives, four white-collar workers, two bright thirteen-year-old children, and four university graduate students.

There were thirty-three individuals in categories B to E, thirteen of them female. Each performed a Q-sort to represent his or her philosophy vis-à-vis democracy, using the following forced frequency distribution, for scores ranging from +5 to —5, respectively:

$$3 \quad 4 \quad 5 \quad 5 \quad 6 \quad 8 \quad 6 \quad 5 \quad 5 \quad 4 \quad 3 \quad (n = 54)$$

The "special" category consisted of three Q-sorts performed on different days by the present author to represent the following positions theoretically:

1. A Q-sort of an *ideal* viewpoint (i.e., from an expert standpoint and having all information available, such as is contained in the UNESCO Report and other sources) is performed to represent what, under present conditions, would be a sensible view to hold in this domain. It represents what we might expect informed, unbiased, reasonable judges to hold if, for example, they were members of a commission asked to report on what people *should* believe about democracy.
2. A Q-sort of the West-East dialectic with respect to democracy; that is, a Q-sort which shows the Western view as diametrically opposed to the Eastern. Statements highly valued by the West are highly rejected by the East and vice versa; the Q-sort is thus bipolar.
3. A Q-sort to represent Dr. Plamenatz's views; it would have been admirable to have Plamenatz himself perform the Q-sort, but, failing that, it is easy to provide a Q-sort which obviously represents his viewpoint.

These three Q-sorts are theoretical or reference values, of interest in the subsequent validation of empirical data.

A table of thirty-six variables for the above Thompson design provides us with a table of factors (Table 1), and the table of factor scores (the Q-model, Table 2).

THE FACTORS

Any factor loading of size 0.50 or more in Table 2 can be considered significant. Factor F_1 is well defined by variables 8, 9, 10, 11, 12 and 13, all Republicans, largely those who presume to speak authoritatively about their political faith. F_2 is as clearly defined by variables 7, 14, 16, 17, all Democrats. F_3 is little in evidence, except for the hypothetical viewpoint of Dr. Plamenatz (variable 3). Neither of the children is on a factor; nor do the graduate students show up clearly.

Because variable 2 (the dialectical Q-sort) is loaded on F_2, this factor must represent the West-East opposition in democracy; Communists would presumably be loaded negatively on this factor. The Republican

TABLE 1
Rotated Factors for Q-Sample $n = 54$ (Democratic Principles)
(Decimal Points Omitted)

Variable Number	"Interest" Class	Sex	Loading in Factor		
			F_1	F_2	F_3
1	A. Expert	—	—15	58	56
2	B. Dialectical	—	08	67	—09
3	C. Plamenatz	—	—04	07	56
4	Historian (R)	F	53	39	—13
5	Historian (D)	F	05	54	—03
6	Historian (R)	M	75	03	14
7	Lawyer (D)	M	18	76	02
8	Lawyer (R)	M	43	28	03
9	Republican	M	65	29	19
10	Republican	M	37	05	02
11	Republican	M	69	37	25
12	Republican	F	66	15	08
13	Republican	F	60	45	—02
14	Democrat	M	24	57	09
15	Democrat	M	25	23	—17
16	Democrat	M	13	59	10
17	Democrat	F	30	50	16
18	Democrat	F	46	20	46
19	Military	M	26	24	45
20	Military	M	27	54	12
21	Minister (Baptist)	M	—02	38	21
22	Minister (Catholic)	M	42	13	02
23	Child	M	33	07	14
24	Child	F	33	36	25
25	Housewife	F	25	54	—02
26	Housewife	F	45	10	05
27	Housewife	F	60	37	—17
28	Housewife	F	38	29	03
29	White-collar worker	M	22	37	00
30	White-collar worker	M	54	52	—13
31	White-collar worker	M	60	29	30
32	White-collar worker	M	40	42	—16
33	University student	M	52	05	25
34	University student	M	29	00	47
35	University student	F	28	36	44
36	University student	F	24	05	33

factor F_1 is not on this democratic axis, a most significant result, as we shall see. There is no sex difference. Nor are the "experts" of one mind: on the contrary, they are what their political faiths happen to be, i.e., the Democrats among them are on F_2 and the Republicans on F_1. It is apparent that a person's political faith determines his views about democratic principles. This explains why the experts of the UNESCO symposium were so much at loggerheads; however scholarly, however legalistic, philosophical, or social scientist, none can look at democracy with detachment or sound judgment because of the intrusion of his own political bias.

F_3 is defined purely only by variable 3 (the Dr. Plamenatz viewpoint) with a significant loading on 1 also.

Table 2 presents the Q-factor model, i.e., the factor-scores for F_1, F_2, and F_3, respectively.

These are significant data; substantially the same factors are reached whenever American citizens are tested, as I have shown by taking probes here and there. Interpretation can be quickly undertaken by looking at

TABLE 2
Q-MODEL FOR SAMPLE $n = 54$ (DEMOCRATIC PRINCIPLES)*

Statement Number	Factor Score			Statement Number	Factor Score		
	F_1	F_2	F_3		F_1	F_2	F_3
1	1	3	4	28	5	0	1
2	6	2	8	29	5	9	5
3	7	3	4	30	7	5	7
4	3	4	2	31	8	8	4
5	5	7	7	32	1	2	6
6	9	9	5	33	10	4	7
7	6	7	7	34	2	6	1
8	6	5	8	35	4	5	5
9	8	6	6	36	7	8	3
10	2	4	3	37	0	0	0
11	6	2	8	38	4	4	10
12	5	1	3	39	9	9	9
13	3	7	6	40	6	8	2
14	4	6	6	41	3	2	7
15	10	8	8	42	8	4	1
16	5	6	2	43	4	5	6
17	5	5	5	44	1	7	3
18	3	5	6	45	5	3	9
19	1	6	3	46	2	8	2
20	4	5	5	47	6	6	4
21	8	3	10	48	9	9	5
22	0	3	0	49	4	5	0
23	10	10	10	50	2	4	4
24	7	1	2	51	9	10	9
25	7	7	5	52	0	2	5
26	3	1	8	53	5	1	4
27	2	0	1	54	8	10	6

*See Appendix to this chapter for a copy of the Q-Sample. In the table +5 has been added to each sum to remove signs.

the statements which discriminate most between the factors, beginning with F_1 and F_2. A glance at Table 2 shows that statements 33, 21, 42, 24, 3, 2, 11, 28, 12, 53, in that order, score significantly and saliently higher on F_1 than on F_2. There is a comparable set for which F_2 is higher than F_1, namely, statements 29, 13, 19, 34, and 3, 24, 21, 2, 12, 28.

My interpretation is as follows: F_1 is a factor provided by men and women who are conservative (Republicans) or southern Democrats in political faith. It differs from F_2 in being more concerned about the individualism of man. This is how one must interpret the high saliency given to statements 33, 21, 42, and 7 — which are the most characterizing of all the statements for F_1. The desire to be somebody (statement 21), the favorable view taken of competitiveness (42), and self-realization of the individual (24), all support the high point of the factor, that individuality is paramount (33).

Conversely, it is clear that F_2 gives little credence to this sort of individualism, out of which the rugged individualism of the industrialist was forged. F_2 is not prepared to think of man as self-assertive by nature (21); he obviously holds that there can be agreement about ideas concerning social welfare and affairs of state (33) — whereas these are red flags to the Republican bull. F_2 also does not believe that man is by nature competitive (42), or that restrictiveness and defensiveness will be necessary, so to speak, in a well-run democracy (2, 3). If we interpret statement 24 correctly, F_2 thinks of self-realization in the political context as selfishness. Note that the low position given to statement 53 by F_2 is due less to a lack of understanding of democratic matters than to defensiveness toward any threat to *voting*. Type F_1, apparently, cares neither one way nor the other about it, since he places it in the neutral position in the Q-sort.

The highly discriminative statements for F_2 are fascinating for the broad principles they unfold. The Lincoln formula (29), the idea of democracy as critical discussion (46), the ideals of freedom of speech and press (44), of the pragmatic nature of things in democracy (13) — these are very profound faiths which F_2 holds, and which F_1 simply does not. Does it not seem very astonishing that statement 29, the eloquent words which the McKeon report accepted as self-evident, finds no salient place in the minds of the Republicans whose great leader it was who spoke them?

Similarly, whereas mention of a science of society (19) is not rejected out-of-hand by F_2, it is wholly disbelieved by F_1. The poverty, ignorance, and so on of the world (34), with which Communists make so much play, is rejected by F_1 but not by F_2. The type F_1 of course rejects completely any mention of co-operatives, collective farms, and the like (22) — and the liberal Democrats are of the same mind, only less so.

There surely cannot be any doubt about the import of these factors, that F_1, held by men and women predominantly of conservative political faith, place great value on individuality and little on democracy as Western democrats ordinarily understand it — the type does not even value their own great leader's words (29). On the other hand type F_2 greatly values the social-democrat principles. I submit that so profound a difference, which one can repeat anywhere across the country, is evidence of a serious cleavage in the United States, between individualism of the frontier ("rugged individualism") and the liberalism of the northern Democrat, as among liberals now the world over.

Factor F_3 penetrates behind what people are conscious of in political matters and sees them as engaged, unwittingly, in play. The discriminating statements for F_3, contrasted with statements which for F_1 and F_2 are on common ground, are given in Table 3. Statement 38 is the ludenic viewpoint in a nutshell, and although F_1 and F_2 do not reject it out-of-hand (each giving it score — 1 as though they are not sure about it), on the whole they think it is not really true. F_3 gives it a maximum value. Statement 45 is also a precise play-theory formulation; it is surely fascinating to see so obvious a truth rejected by the liberal Democrat F_2 (of course

TABLE 3

Statement Number	Score			Statement
	F_1	F_2	F_3	
38	—1	—1	5	Democracy is talked about, as is politics, by a *vocabulary;* people are articulate, can *talk* about democracy and politics without really knowing what is going on. It is a "game," with its own rules and vocabulary, but the people do not really know what is happening.
45	0	—2	4	Democracy does not mean government in the interest of the people; it means government by persons chosen by and responsible to the governed.
26	—2	—4	4	Communism, liberalism, and Western democracy are all based on a common arsenal of values, with a common heritage — although it is exploited for different ends.
41	—2	—3	2	Every democracy tolerates only those opinions that uphold the social order on which that democracy is based.
32	—4	—3	1	The great factor making for optimism about the sanity of the world is technology — it encompasses all nations, all strata of populations, and all conditions of life.

*The scores are on the Q-sort scale from +5 to —5.

because he wants to believe that democracy is government in the interest of people), and placed in the neutral position by F_1 (as though he would hide his head, ostrich-like, against any responsibility to the governed). Statement 26 is historically indisputable; but only the play-theorist apparently can accept it — even the historians of our study rejected it, so strong is their political faith. Similarly for 41, liberals will tolerate culture and political divergences only up to a point. Finally, 32, which is almost a prescription for the world's sanity, is completely rejected by F_1 and F_2, but accepted by F_3.

Thus, neither F_1 nor F_2 is aware of the patois character of much democratic language (38), or of the literal meaning of democracy (45); they reject any thought of Marx sitting in the British Museum conjuring up communism in typical Western terms (26); nor can they think of democracy as in some way a delusion (41); nor have they any faith in an understanding of the place of technology in the world (32). In all these respects F_1 and F_2 are woefully uninformed. It would be better for both, perhaps, at least to recognize the common heritage of capitalism and communism that statement 26 implies; and certainly some faith in technology as a positive force in world affairs might be healthier than much else in this area of dispute.

THE AMELIORATIVE THEMES

What I found, as I suspected, is a difference between political faiths in this country as profound as any that separates Eastern and Western philosophies more generally. The evidence is that a large section of the United States has one conception of democracy and the other a different conception.

The problem is to influence both sides in the direction of amelioration of political conflict (so that what is a game in our play theory does not become something vicious, a fight, such as would happen if Nazi or Birchite sympathies got the upper hand in the extreme Republicanism of this country). Our theory, like that of Plamenatz, is represented by factor F_3; at present this is not common conversation, but is merely a more objective position than either F_1 or F_2 affords in view of the obvious political partisanship of these two viewpoints. Setting this alongside F_1 and F_2, the Republican and liberal Democrat views, respectively, it is a simple matter to determine where these differ most from F_3. This is at or below the psychological zero point for F_1 and F_2 but where there is positive saliency for F_3. With this rule in mind, we reach three statements of great interest, each of which is a prescription for vast thematic development. These are statements 26, 38, and 32 of the Q-sample, concerning the common heritage of Western and Soviet democratic ideas (26), the ludenic nature of democratic practices (38), and the real force that is changing the world, that of technological advance (32). Their scores are given in Table 3 above.

These are of course hints at specifications for communication, rather than much else. Number 26 will be considered highly controversial or un-American, even high treason, by many Americans. The *New York Times* reader was being told in 1962 (in a series of articles by the dean of correspondents, Harrison E. Salisbury) that neo-Stalinists and "liberals" in the U.S.S.R. were currently engaged in a bitter struggle for the dominant role in the Soviet future and that, if Khrushchev succeeded, the results would be a momentous linking of Russia to the West again. This is where the United States and the U.S.S.R. belong by history, culture, technology, and ultimate aspirations, and we are sure that what statement 26 means, however put into operational specifications, is highly significant in that direction.

Statement 38 will also be hotly contested by those who can see little to laugh about in the current cold war of nerves and thermonuclear bombast. All that it recommends, however, is to restore to international relations a sense of interest or awareness of it as a "game." By this we would mean the interjection into it of such playful things as royal visits — whether by a Queen Elizabeth or a Mrs. Khrushchev or a Mrs. Jacqueline Kennedy. A few such perambulations would be worth a hundred meetings of foreign ministers. There is need of a light touch in the world that need not descend to mere entertainment, but one that elevates instead and softens the game of politics — as of life. One operational specification alone, such as the interjection of more women into the political scene, might do more good than anyone guesses. At the least it might make for fun, so that people might begin to laugh again in national and international affairs, as Benitez (8) so wisely recommended.

And, as for statement 32, I would echo the thought that one discovery of a wheelbarrow or a printing press may have more effect on man than a score of ideologies. It should not fail to impress us, and in a positive direction, that American chewing gums and Westerns and supermarket methods, as well as Cokes and hot dogs, all spread easily around the world, whereas our ideologies have heavy going. Technological advances can sail before calm and peaceful winds.

The three statements are all that the Q-study brings to light. In themselves they are as small as mice. Yet the Q-sample covers a wide sweep of philosophical thought — the best available at the time the McKeon report appeared — and the significance of the three mice should not pass unnoticed. They are what would have been proposed to UNESCO had I been asked to advise it on what an objective study of the philosophy of democracies has to offer those who are struggling with a divided world.

Nor are the formulations farfetched. Any good advertising agency could make a fine job of telling the country about the common origins of Western and Eastern forms of democracy — who would sponsor it, of course, might present a problem. It could be done without alienating either Democrat or Republican, and giving more salience to it by promotion would at least enrich the respective beliefs at issue. Technological developments have often been regarded as the primary source of cultural change (164); wheelbarrows, printing presses, machinery, electronics, nuclear energy — these, in the final analysis, make change inevitable. Such instrumental factors have had their advocates, facetious though it may be, in *The New Yorker* (August 19, 1961), where the editor asks, "Why not turn the thoughts of the world from the space race and the missile hustle to the power for peace of notions and novelties?" Do the Russians have pinking, pruning, and poultry shears, or cuticle nippers? Combination bookrest and three-umbrella receptacles? Green and red wool coasters? Ruffle-edged makeup capes? Expandable hangers for growing children? Home sewers? Giant Yo-yos made of heavy walnut? Few people are aware in any real way that technological advances are changing the world. Again, any good advertising agency could work wonders with the formulation that it is high time technology was made to tick in people's minds. And as for the ludenic matter, I can scarcely do better than mention Chancellor Benitez' (8) observation that much of American (United States) reporting of Latin America betrays a puritanical sense of guilt. The achieving giant of the United States has a dead-set urgency to *do* something; but, Benitez adds, this "lacks its own breathing space, its sense, if one may use such a word today, of poetry, enjoyment of life rather than merely of activity" (8, p. 9). Certainly there is no joy anymore in international politics.

A method exists, therefore, for finding not merely the hidden assumptions of political and ideological beliefs but for determining what their shortcomings are on theoretical grounds. We see that ideology plays second fiddle, in our example, to political beliefs. As I pointed out the evidence is very clear that large sections of the United States have different conceptions of democracy; this of course is likely to be so all over the world. But by comparing these beliefs it is always possible to see what in them might be enriched or developed from a theoretical standpoint. In the present case the theory is that of Plamenatz, or mine of ludenic behavior: it is by comparing the existing ideological viewpoints with a theoretical one that new directions can be given to communication at the mass level.

ADDITIONAL CONSIDERATIONS

Mass communication research at the hands of Pye (109), Lerner (76), and others is imbued with the belief that its efforts should be directed toward learning about the best ways to foster modern, free, democratic institutions. There are indeed intimate relationships between political and communication processes. After all, very few of us can observe politicians at work in legislative halls, and we depend upon mass communication to keep us in touch with governmental matters. Mass communication provides a basis for discussing politics en masse in such a way that there is at any one time a common fund of ideas for political discussion. Politics calls for an understanding of the motives of others, in other political parties and in other nations; political discussion resolves issues and sets goals for legislative action. Or so it would seem. There is a sense, certainly, in which the Western concepts of democracy are concerned with immediate problems and not with the more utopian schemes of Communist countries.

Grierson (see 43) wrote feelingly of democracy, arguing that mass communication must create a flow of ideas to inspire people. There had been too much emphasis in the past in Western democracies on a narrow view of individualism, "geared to the person in private rather than to the person in public" (43, p. 193). We have taught democracy (in schools), he felt, in the manner of a gentleman in a library; the ideal has been one of rational citizenship, where the individual makes cold judgments on the basis of facts. "The burden of the books," he concludes, "is still upon us." What is required is a complete change of outlook in which the newspaper story, the poster, the movie, television, and radio all concern themselves with the vital problems of a democracy. But matters (in a free society) are not at all as simple as this suggests — much of what Grierson stood for is regarded as socialism, communism, or worse, the work of the devil, in quite large segments of the United States.

Lerner's earlier work (74) is nearer to mine in its methods than are his more recent excursions into modernizing nations (73, 75). His 1952 study (74), entitled "International Conditions and Communications Content: The Case of Neutralism," deals with the problem of the spread of neutralism. At that time Lerner argued that the neutral peoples really belong in the American fold; looked at dispassionately, their purposes and those of America seemed exactly the same. Therefore, not to identify with America could only be regarded as political irresponsibility, resulting from a retreat into self-indulgence or a flight from reality or sheer cowardliness. Thus, unless the neutral peoples could make up their minds to be either for us or against us, Lerner believed they would inevitably become more and more anti-American and a total loss to United States influence. They must be brought back, therefore, where they belong, in the American sphere of influence. Such was Lerner's "theoretical" position in 1952.

Neutralism has of course grown since then, though it is complicated by the excursion of Communist China into world affairs. The problem remains, however, except that it is now of much larger and more complicated proportions.

Lerner proposed that appropriate symbolization of democracy could change this. Research would be necessary to isolate key symbols with which to do the job. The research has apparently never been done. Lerner (74) suggested the use of *content analysis* for the purpose and indicated at some length what could be expected from it by referring to a study of a related kind that had already been completed at the Hoover Institute at Stanford University in California. The study had examined the fate of the concept of democracy over the period 1890–1950 with content analysis as the research tool. From 1890 to 1910, the analysis indicated, the mass media and elite in France, Britain, Germany, and the United States gave much the same meaning to democracy; it meant, very generally, a "stirring of individual liberty" and "involvement in representative government." These two were the key themes of the press, speeches, books, and magazine articles of those twenty years. The analysis for 1918–30 showed a very different state of affairs. Democracy now had the meaning of "mass rule" and "social welfare." In the Soviets these key symbols took over completely, as was true to a considerable extent in France as well. The Nazis of course derided these, providing instead the symbols of national socialism. But Britain and the United States dropped the symbolization altogether, as though, when confronted with these new key themes for democracy, they had to be silent, having nothing to say. Thus democracy lost its stature as the key symbol of humanity under American sponsorship, and accordingly there has been a decline in "ideological effectiveness" in the West ever since. It plagued the Allies in World War II and clearly still does so today.

The Hoover Institute study indicated, in the same research, that post-war (1948) Europe was highly receptive to ideas of *peace, security, safety,* and *relaxation* — a not unlikely set of key motivations after suffering two world wars. The symbols given to Europe instead, by the Voice of America and the policies behind it, were those of *struggle, conflict,* and *effort.* The reminder has to be made that these are not theoretical conclusions, but the outcome of elaborate content analysis of the mass media and elite communications in Europe. Political science, based on the deepest wishes of the peoples, would have developed the security symbols; international politics led, instead, to those of struggle and conflict.

Lerner was fully aware that the propagation of struggle and effort was biased by American viewpoints; it was necessary, he considered, to replace this "symbolism of self-reference" by something objective, by a "symbolism of standards," against which to appraise all peoples and nations, American no less than any others. The methods of content analysis, he implied, could achieve something of the kind.

With the general intent of this I am in full agreement. The principles, however, need careful consideration lest the magic of words lead us to overlook the practical matters. The symbolization to which Lerner is referring is a two-step matter. The key themes have first to be grasped, after which the creative writers, poets, artists, directors, musicians, editors, and all the full array of the mass media can be involved in their daily propagation. One should observe that in the U.S.S.R. all the resources of creative writers, the press, and others are at the service of the state; in comparison the American government has a mere pittance to deploy and there is no guarantee that given key symbols the mass media would use them.

It is in this framework that I conceive of Q-studies in this area of concern. The methodological problems are solved — Lerner can now be given a "symbolization of standards," and genuine science in the place of dogma and metaphor. But the communication difficulties remain, and I have no illusions about their vastness. What can be offered fits well into existing organizations, such as the advertising profession, which is undoubtedly growing in research stature in genuine directions. The methods also easily fit mass communication as it is organized in the U.S.S.R. But in a free society with a free press and free mass communication, and with controversial matters at issue in all political and ideological fields, the situation is wholly different. At the very least it surely calls for a Council of Mass Communication at which the free leaders of the mass media can sit down together to see what might be done for the public good.

CONCLUSION

The concepts of peace, security, safety, and relaxation upon which Western Europe was initially motivated after the ravages of two world wars could well have been found with Q-method, as they were by content analysis. Instead, Europe was given the symbols of effort, preparation for war, and achievement. These are all merely subsumptions, however, of prior conditions. There is little evidence that contrary manipulated symbols, concepts, or themes could have changed the course of any history. Yet, if our principles mean anything, they have reference to a public orientation in politics as they have to a consumer orientation in advertising. What people need and want can be found by methods I am here suggesting, and these needs and wants can be realistic enough. Who can say that what Europe needed was not relaxation rather than effort? The interconnections of economics and international politics are highly complex. I can only say, again, that we can now probe into the public mind and recommend the symbols suited to its needs.

APPENDIX
Q-SAMPLE ($n = 54$) ON DEMOCRATIC PRINCIPLES

ADAPTED FROM MCKEON (88)

1. A single party that could foster special methods for insuring the popularity and autonomous character of decisions taken by the government — by methods of information, discussion and constant occupation of the people with political, welfare, etc., work — could be democratic.
2. A process of restriction, which is nevertheless far removed from censorship and intolerance, is practiced in any democracy.
3. Only when actions hostile to democracy, that is, to public and private autonomy, become *dangerous* to it, does democracy with good reason defend itself.
4. In the ideal democracy there will probably be no parties at all — instead, the people will elect the persons best fitted to govern; and each of these will vote according to his convictions.
5. Democracy consists of a combination of compromise, discussion, and toleration, and the doing away with class privilege.

6. Democracy is government by discussion — controversial matters are discussed, a common consensus is reached, or, if not, approximated to by the vote of the majority.

7. What is needed in the world is rational and comprehensive information about all affairs, without misleading suggestions . . . not solemn promises, but clear and rational arguments.

8. Ideally, what the world wants is political democracy with no social injustice, and social democracy with freedom and human dignity.

9. Democracy must tolerate dissentient *opinions*, provided that it reserves the right to oppose or suppress *action* hostile to its existence.

10. The great factor making for optimism about the world is the progress of science as it applies to social affairs, national and international.

11. Ideological controversies are never assuaged — like the controversy over evolution, they are dropped because one alternative does what it claimed; there are few direct conversions on the mere logical merits of an issue.

12. No organization can leave out of account the strange kind of beings laid on it to organize; their requirements are always irritating to the technocratic mind.

13. Democracy consists, first and foremost, in the acquisition of understanding, in the most scientific possible detailed study, *of the concrete present* — the real, daily life of peoples.

14. Democracy is a continual process, and we cannot foresee its end in any conceivable future.

15. The final goal of democracy is the extension of the rights, duties, benefits, enjoyed now only by some, to the whole of mankind — to each human being as a human being and because he is a human being.

16. Raising standards of living, education, culture, will necessarily lead to man's common dignity being achieved; it is the democratic faith.

17. At present there are opposing ideologies, but we may hope for a synthesis, a coming together of opposing ideologies (rather than the suppression of one ideology by another).

18. In democracy there must be a frank recognition that ordinary people can exercise *control* over a government, but cannot itself govern.

19. A genuine science of society now exists; it will inevitably command general assent for the same reason that modern physics commands general assent — i.e., because it is most probably true.

20. There is a present general underlying tendency toward a certain unification of the world, but the way is blocked by groups of nations with different ideologies.

21. Man has a persistent desire to *be* somebody; he has an urge for

self-assertion, which will seek an outlet in any setting, even one devoid of economic challenges.

22. Management of collective farms, co-operatives, local housing, etc., is real, simple democracy; the more of this there is, the more vigorous and flourishing is the democracy likely to be.

23. The primary meaning of democracy is government by people who are freely chosen by and responsible to the governed.

24. Self-realization of the individual is the natural result of a democratic way.

25. The ideal is to teach the *whole* of the population the art of administration — by encouraging popular participation in the functions of state, business, the economy, education, welfare.

26. Communism, liberalism, and Western democracy are all based on a common arsenal of values, with a common heritage — although it is exploited for different ends.

27. Democracy is organized suspicion; it is the citizen against authorities and bureaucrats — everything that controls and limits power is democratic.

28. Where the majority rules, it is certain that, but for stupidity and ignorance, the interests of the majority will prevail. There is no evidence that consistently, or over a long period, the minority has ruled in the interests of the majority.

29. We hold these truths to be self-evident, that all men are created equal. . . .

30. In a democracy citizens are treated not only as equals, but as different. It is a good thing for people to disagree. Unanimity is usually suspect.

31. In a democracy there must be a constant effort made to maximum equalization of all liberties for all citizens — political, social, cultural, educational, economic, etc.; the aim is maximum satisfaction of *needs*, not merely equal suffrage rights.

32. The great factor making for optimism about the sanity of the world is technology — it encompasses all nations, all strata of populations and all conditions of life.

33. It is inconceivable that there should be unanimity with regard to ideas about social welfare or affairs of state among all members of a society; the facts of history, background, experience and temperament are bound to influence different individuals in different ways.

34. Society as we see it, by and large all over the world, is characterized by poverty, ignorance, weariness, cruelty, loneliness, with periodic depressions and wars.

35. Successful functioning of a democracy depends on harmony between the living convictions of the governed and decisions of the

governors. This harmony is not necessarily realized by modern party systems. There are probably better methods than the party system for arriving at harmony.

36. Democracy ideally is noble, just, charitable, humanistic, caring for the individual.

37. The tendency is for dictatorships ultimately to become democracies in full harmony with the ideal democratic pattern.

38. Democracy is talked about, as is politics, by a *vocabulary*; people are articulate, can *talk* democracy and politics without really knowing what is going on. It is a "game," with its own rules and vocabulary, but the people do not really know what is happening.

39. The central feature in democracy is human dignity in every individual — to see man not as an object of social science, but as a subject of self-realization, whose dignity comes to its own way only insofar as he collaborates with his fellow men, on an equal basis, toward his own welfare.

40. The freedom of individuals is in no respect the work of individuals; it is a collective product — one is truly free only when all others around one are equally free.

41. Every democracy tolerates only those opinions that uphold the social order on which that democracy is based.

42. Man will always compete. What we have to do is to eliminate the more *destructive* forms of competition, and to turn competitive urges into socially acceptable channels.

43. It is not impossible that, at a particular time, one man, standing alone, may be the true representative of a people or of all peoples.

44. Freedom of speech, press, assembly and the secret ballot, trial by jury, etc., are *instruments* for maintaining democracy; they are not implied, however, in what *democracy means*.

45. Democracy does not mean government in the *interest* of the people; it means government by persons chosen by and responsible to the governed.

46. In an ideal democracy discussion and criticism will continue, but there will be full agreement on common aims and no division of peoples into class interests.

47. In a democracy the governed govern themselves, benefiting each and all.

48. The spirit of tolerance and recognition of the rights of other people to form and express their own opinions is one of the great democratic virtues.

49. Democracy is directed to the economic well-being and supremacy of the ordinary man. His welfare comes first.

50. All evidence goes to show that all normal human beings have, to a

preponderant degree, "common" needs — the determination of these is a scientific problem and not one for the "press," or "parties," or the like.

51. A form of government is democratic insofar as the people can exercise an effective influence on the decisions of government.

52. Nothing gives a greater sense of freedom and creative activity than acceptance of one's station and its duties. It is division of mind ar᷉ uncertainty about one's objectives that cause hesitation and a sense of frustration.

53. Discussion, rather than voting, is the essence of the democratic principle.

54. What is important in a democracy is that its people should have an interest in public affairs, a readiness to think about them critically and a sense of personal responsibility for the decisions made.

9

How Nations See Each Other

The study by Buchanan and Cantril (14) entitled *How Nations See Each Other*, was undertaken for UNESCO; it deserves attention as being in line with our own objectives. The study was instituted in 1947 but took six years to complete. It was an inquiry into the distinctive character of the various national cultures to see what influences could be brought to bear upon them toward better international understanding and amelioration of aggressive nationalism. Observers felt that modern methods for bringing about changes in mental attitudes — developed in education, political science, psychology, and sociology — might have some contributions to make in these worthy international directions. The study was regarded as of a pilot nature, even though samples of 1,000 were taken in each of fourteen nations (none, however, from behind the Iron Curtain). A questionnaire translated into the various languages was used. For each country the responses to the questionnaire were analyzed in relation to age, educational level, sex, and income level. Several conclusions were reached, for example, that the concept of "social class" is meaningful to all people and that the poorer the class, the more lacking in "fellow feelings" are the people in it. In matters of social character the only result that emerged, apparently, was that some people are optimists and others fatalists, the former believing that human nature is perfectible and the latter that wars are inevitable because people are warlike by nature. The prescription offered to UNESCO by the authors for amelioration of international feelings (that is, as they put the matter, "to make each individual a citizen of the world") was to give people security (food and work), to give all a sense of their interdependence, to improve communication facilities all over the world, and to give everyone opportunities to act in the common interest.

The conclusions are impeccable, but one could have recommended them without six years of study. They are surely counsels of perfection, seen from the high attics of the academic mind, *dolce far niente*, sweetly doing nothing.

One cannot forbear making a methodological point about such a study, nor can I miss the opportunity to look at the study from the standpoint of how one would go about giving advice to UNESCO concerning what could be done to reduce international tensions. The methodological matter is dealt with first.

STRONG INFERENCE

It is axiomatic for us that science deals with explanations rather than with facts. In the case of the Buchanan-Cantril study, which provided facts in abundance, the difficulty was of a contrary sort — they did not grasp an important fact but lost it among the wealth of relatively unimportant data that they so patiently collected. Their study dealt with 12,775 individuals from nine nations under careful sampling conditions. I propose to study nine persons only and reach a result missed in the large-scale study, not because it was not there but because the questionnaire method precluded it. Yet it is a really significant fact, providing a key communication concept for UNESCO. The result is reached in terms of two methodological advances: one the use of strong inference and the other a comparative step overlooked in questionnaires.

First, with respect to strong inference (a term used by Pratt [108] which is particularly appropriate to our method): Pratt remarks that the fields of molecular biology and high-energy physics are making headline discoveries at a fast rate, not because of the richness of the areas or of the diligency of the scientists, but because those involved have learned to provide alternative hypotheses, to devise crucial experiments, and to do so expeditiously with clear results. Nowhere is there a simple deduction which is tested, as is the case in numerous papers published currently in psychological and sociological journals. Instead, there are alternatives and crucial experiments performed almost in one day, which set out not so much to prove hypotheses as to disprove them. Pratt calls the method one of multiple hypotheses, contrasting it with current procedures which he derides as "The Eternal Surveyor," "The Never Finished," or "The Frozen Method." He reminds us that Roentgen, eight weeks after discovering X-rays, had identified seventeen of their major properties, one experiment rapidly following another. Similarly for the UNESCO project, what was required was a method to reach (in a matter of weeks) results which had theoretical as well as practical importance.

Next is the comparative operation to interject into the Buchanan-Cantril questionnaire. In all questionnaires the respondent answers each question separately; the data are then examined either for each question separately or in the form of contingency tables showing how data for one question relates to those of another. What can never be reached, however, is the respondent's judgment about the relative importance of the various questions to him. Asking this question may bring to light interesting facts, very quickly made available, that data for the separate questions cannot possibly supply. Both of the above steps are taken care of in Q-method; P-samples provide hypotheses for strong inference and Q-sorts the comparative judgment missed altogether by the questionnaire technique.

These matters are illustrated for the Buchanan-Cantril study, as follows. The questions in their questionnaire (14, p. 126) are made into a Q-sample.

The questionnaire has five categories of questions: position in the class structure of one's country, degree of personal security, attitudes to other nations, stereotypical opinions about foreigners, and perceptions about human nature and national character in general. These are covered by the following Q-sample design:

Effects	Levels			No.
A, Involvement	(a) Self	(b) Society		2
B, Motives	(c) Security	(d) Status	(e) Stereotype	3

The Q-sample was composed to fit this factorial design. This replaced the questionnaire for our purposes, covering it indeed more comprehensively and systematically. Examples of the statements involved in our Q-sample (of size $n = 30$) are as follows:

1. All nations are basically alike in character.
2. Ours is essentially a classless society.
3. There should be a world government able to control the laws made by each country.
4. Materially, we are doing pretty well as individuals in this country.
5. I feel friendly to all foreign peoples.
6. Ours is a freedom-loving nation.

7. Everyone is free here to make his own place in society — there is equality of opportunity.
8. The United Nations should have its own military forces.
9. You can plan ahead in this country and feel confident in the future.
10. I feel there is little in common between myself and people anywhere who are not of my social class.

For a P-sample I took nine subjects, as follows:

1. American husband (No. 1)
2. His wife
3. American husband (No. 2)
4. His wife
5. European husband
6. His wife
7. American secretary (female, divorced)
8. American male youth, age 20
9. American female youth, age 17

The multiple hypotheses to be tested quickly concern all those involved in the above factorial design — for example, that effects A and B are significant, under various conditions, such that in social character $A > B$, and $be > ae$ (for details about such hypotheses one is referred to Stephenson [147]). But more particularly I argued that among educated Americans, men and women are likely to have very different perceptions of the matters involved in the Q-sample design, and I considered that if husbands and their wives were put in the same matrix this could be subjected to a crucial and clean-cut test. Moreover, if Americans have ideas quite different from those of Europeans in the matters at issue, as one might suppose, the inclusion of an Englishman and his English wife, both very English, would test this particular proposition. I next needed a few people, Americans, male and female who are not married (or without partners) in the matrix — whence variables 7, 8, and 9 above. The hypothesis is that the females will be on one factor, and the males on another. Moreover, the reasons for this will be not merely the different attitudes at issue, but dynamic factors (defenses), as the various scores given to the statements of the Q-sample would indicate.

All of this allows accumulative inference free play, and strong inductive inference — as soon as Q-sorts are performed and factors isolated.

I asked each person to perform a Q-sort to represent his or her views of the matters involved, with the results given in Table 1.

Only two factors appear, in sharp focus (centroid method). One is obviously on the men and the other on the women; the English are on neither (significance can be set at 0.55).

TABLE 1
FACTOR-LOADINGS OF FACTORS F, M, FOR Q-SAMPLE
OF 30 BUCHANAN-CANTRIL STATEMENTS
(Decimal Points Omitted)

	Loading	
Variable	Factor F	Factor M
1. American husband (1)	24	59
2. His wife	75	13
3. American husband (2)	13	55
4. His wife	57	−20
5. English husband	15	18
6. His wife	14	−32
7. American secretary (F)	60	00
8. American youth (M)	30	81
9. American youth (F)	75	13

The main point, at once, is this complete (uncorrelated) difference between the men and women, matched for primary affiliation (as far as the husbands and wives are concerned). No such sex difference emerged from the Buchanan-Cantril study because, with so much data in hand "dimension by dimension," there was nothing in the methodology to determine their relative importance. No one ever asked the subjects to say which question mattered most to them. By so simple an omission, which occurs every time a questionnaire is applied, in countless studies, the broadest inductions are bypassed altogether. The most important discovery that Buchanan and Cantril ought to have made, but did not, was that there is a profound difference in attitude of mind between comparably educated men and women about these international matters.

I was unaware at the time that Gillespie and Allport (39) had undertaken a study with an objective paralleling that of Buchanan and Cantril, but conducted on foreign students in this country, using an autobiographical approach and a questionnaire. The students were asked to project into the future, by writing an autobiography on "from now to 2000 A.D." Qualitative analysis suggested at once that sex differences were "of special significance." The women students showed a greater desire for autonomy (as well they might), more desire for travel, for greater self-expression outside the home; they were fearful of family misfortunes. The men had economic worries, but expected a higher standard of income than their parents; they had greater aspirations than women for leadership; and they endorsed trial marriages. In all, data were obtained from 1,819 students, including Americans, New Zealanders, South Africans, Egyptians, Mexicans, French, Germans, Japanese, and Israeli. The authors nevertheless felt that the samples for different nationalities were too small and not likely to be representative "of their countries as a whole." They had, they said, tested no hypotheses; they were interested only in trends, "not in statistical data"; the trends observed were said to be congruent with other data, even if they were not statistically significant themselves.

I make no such apologies. My data are for nine subjects only, and they are in agreement with such trends as are above described. The important point is that out of all the inductive possibilities at issue, for concepts covering everything involved in either the Buchanan-Cantril or the Gillespie-Allport questionnaires or techniques, the sex difference is predominant. This is so for American subjects among their own kind. The same applies, however, for English subjects among English, and French among French, obtained for similar small P-sets I used in later studies. The factors for the different nationalities may be different, as for the Americans and English (variables 5 and 6 in the table of factor loadings are on neither factor F or M, but, put along with Q-sorts performed by other English persons, factors appear which are particular to the English); however, again the sex difference is dominant. My method calls for just such assemblages of data, on a quick study-by-study basis, dealing stepwise and intensively with inductive inference.

Of course one may want to repeat any such simple probe with new subjects. But that would be secondary to the main purpose, which is to deal more and more intensively with the real matters at issue.

Interpretation leads to the conclusion that factor F, thoroughly feminine as it is, involves an underlying insecurity (as Gillespie and Allport had already suggested), whereas M is defensive about hostilities and aggression; it is not difficult to see that the men are defensive about military matters — they deny their own aggressiveness unnecessarily forcefully. The two factors are in agreement that the United Nations should have its own forces and that we in America are doing pretty well as individuals. They agree that we can be characterized as practical, progressive, somewhat materialistic, and that mankind today is improving his lot all over the world. On the negative side there is agreement that ours is *not* essentially a classless society; it is *not* true that we have nothing in common with others of other classes; it is also *not* true that our national characteristics are fixtures; and it is denied that a weakening of traditional standards is required if ever we are to reach freedom — though this is said with some misgivings.

The statements distinguishing F from M, primarily, are shown in Table 2.

TABLE 2

Statement	Score on Factor	
	F	M
National forces should be replaced by United Nations forces.	+4	−3
World peace is possible.	+4	+1
There should be a world government able to control the laws made by each country.	+3	−2
We are all created equal, e.g., with an equal opportunity to succeed in life, if we make the effort.	+2	−1

It will be said, of course, that these are merely witness to the impracticality of the women. The main point as far as the United Nations and UNESCO is concerned, however, is the ready acceptance, in idealized form no doubt, of international forces and the expectancy of (as well as commitment, therefore, to) peace.

The statements most discriminative for factor M are shown in Table 3.

TABLE 3

Statement	Score on Factor	
	F	M
This country offers a greater measure of social equality than any other.	0	+4
People everywhere are more alike than different.	−1	+3
This country offers everyone the best chance of leading the kind of life you want to lead.	+2	+3
My own social class level has been reached because of my upbringing.	0	+2

These attest to the American achieving society rather than to anything on the international level.

But I need not go into matters more intensively. Given the resources made available to Buchanan and Cantril, I would have constructed a more comprehensive sample and would have penetrated intensively with it using various P-samples in the different countries. The conclusion would have been to the effect that women have a commitment to peace, men do not. This we can say from a handful of small P-sample studies made here and in Britain. My advice to UNESCO would have been, therefore, to the effect that it might look seriously at the women of the world for commitments to peace.

The key communication concept of a woman's commitment to peace would require creative treatment such as we have been suggesting in these chapters. I am sure that Buchanan and Cantril missed an opportunity to point to a simple fact that among more educated people women have a friendlier attitude to peace than men, and that this theme, sharpened by modern methods of mass communication, offered most to UNESCO in its project for the amelioration of world tensions.

10

The Happy Alienated Worker

Our more specific studies begin with a problem discussed by Riesman (115) concerning the place of leisure in modern industrial nations. Rather than use Riesman's discussion, however, I again demonstrate strong inference and Q-methodology by considering a study by Mac-Andrew (82) on job satisfaction. It may seem a long way from this to mass communication, but the result is worth a journey. The general question has been raised, for example, by industrial psychologists, whether work should be made interesting for workers or whether work is intrinsically something by which to earn a living, the better to live one's real life at golfing, fishing, or other leisure pursuits. For my part, again, I see the mass media as the great garners of gossip, suitable for conversation, banter, and jokes inside the factory walls. But some play is noble, and I shall look at that later.

WORK VERSUS PLAY

I have tried to sharpen the difference between work, as communication-pain, and play, as communication-pleasure. Nowhere is it more essential to make the distinction clear than it is in theory and research about the images that have to be developed, in modernizing as well as modern nations, about work on the one hand and play on the other. The Puritan ethic is nowhere shown to be more vindicative than in the sanctimonious injunction that work is to be worshipped and is everyone's salvation. Lest anyone become lazy or get something for nothing, sanctimony keeps the unemployed at bare subsistence level and the poor at less. Even today, few in the United States think of indigency as a chronic social disease; instead it is widely held to indicate a character weakness.

There is scarcely any topic as voluminously worked over, to so little effect, as that of dissatisfactions and morale in industry. Haire (42), in the *Handbook of Social Psychology*, has to say of a review of studies on job satisfaction that the field is chaotic: "There is probably no other field in which there are so many publications as there are under the general heading of *morale* . . . [but] in spite of this, it is difficult to say what is meant by morale. . . . there is little to be learned from the summary" (p. 1118).

The problem concerns the vast movement away from self-employment to employee status in modern societies, of men working for nationalized industries or for corporations — all very different from the Jeffersonian dream of a citizenry of small and independent farmers attending Grange meetings, such as Rhea Foster Dulles (25) describes. In 1940 fully 40 per cent of all employees were office workers, compared with 12 per cent in 1870. And although automation and new electronic equipment are digging deep into such work, it is not at the expense of office workers — more, rather than fewer, are needed to feed the speeding machines. Modern industry calls less for skills formed by long apprenticeship and more for application of button-pushing, requiring little training but much "knack."

There are many who would like to restore the happier days of craftsmanship, when men loved their work. These are the radical utopians, like Gandhi, whose prescription for a New India was a restoration of husbandry, the weaver and his cottage spindle — "craft idiocy" it has been called. Marx and Engels, in *German Ideology*, did not of course discuss alienation but only capitalist exploitation; workers, they argued, are tied to their jobs and must remain so if they want to keep their means of livelihood. In a communist society they would be free to work at one job today and another tomorrow, since society governs production — so, as Marx put it, one might be fisherman in the morning, farmer in the afternoon, and art critic after dinner, "just as one has a mind," without ever becoming a fisherman, farmer, or critic. This is already in process of achievement in the United States, for not only is there much "moonlighting" but it is predicted that the present generation of young people will change *occupations* (not just jobs) seven times in their lifetime.

Mayo (84, 85) sought to restore the ego-involvement of a worker in his work by explaining its over-all purposes; however trivial the job, one could learn to see how important it is in the final objectives of an industry. Thus a management and personnel elite was developed to adjust the worker to his job by doses of background information, production charts, and collaboration in understanding between employees and employers. Human relations were to be the cure-all. Mayo dismissed the problem of the downgrading of skill, since by a suitable plaster of human relations laid upon however tedious a job, one could "grease the skids," make the worker "solidaire with his work" — not vis-à-vis his peers, group, or others but by the logic of *understanding* his factory, office, and industry. The evidence is clear that it did not work; the more one tried to improve morale this way, the lower it dropped.

Riesman (115), instead, accepted the downgrading of work as an unavoidable nuisance. He suggested making work as short in time and as sweet in dollars as possible, and to make alienation complete. Automation would be maximized; work itself would become impersonal — a mere standing beside a switch for a few hours each day, four days a week. Workers would come to life outside the factories and offices in activities into which they could throw themselves wholeheartedly. One could become sportsman, creative artist, scholar, plain leisure-lover, hobbyist, a "do-it-yourself" fan, or the like, as one willed, "just as one had a mind." The changing role of "play" in modern societies is thus exemplified anew; in inner-direction the worker took recreation to offset fatigue and to fit himself the better for work again, but the new conception is very different — one now "plays" to develop one's capacities, to become competent in the art of living, really to enjoy leisure creatively if one has a mind to do so.

Riesman has no doubt changed his mind somewhat, for in fact it seems that people relate to work in diverse ways, depending on the type of work, the region of the country, the conditions of the economy, and the ecology of the population. The other-directed suburbanite is now working so hard at so-called leisure pursuits — minding the children, lawns, dogs, and electrical equipment of the home — that he finds work a recreation, if not a joy. Women have the same experience; many like the peer-group company they have at work, as a great relief from the never ending demands of rearing a family. They are respected more overtly at work. Again if one asks people what they would do if a four-day week were instituted, housewives are apt to say, "Heaven forbid!" They have enough of their husbands as it is. Studies have shown that in Florida men seek an extra job; in Seattle they will build a new house; only in New Jersey might they go fishing, hunting, or golfing. We see, in any case, that work of a trivial kind can become play, in the sense that it involves communication-pleasure — in a word, the gossip of the day, the *company* at work.

MacANDREW'S STUDY

MacAndrew (82) set about studying the various theories of Mayo, Riesman, and others, using Q-method and some strong inductive inference for the purpose. His Q-sample was composed so as to embrace these various viewpoints and job satisfactions, with the following balanced design:

Effects	Levels	No.
A, Work climate	(*a*) Informal-personalized (*b*) Formal (*c*) Ambiguous	3
B, Gratification	(*d*) Socio-economic status (*e*) Work per se (*f*) On-job status (*g*) Aspiration (*h*) Interpersonal relations (*i*) Security (*j*) Independence (*k*) Objective working conditions	8

There are $3 \times 8 = 24$ combinations of these levels of the effects A, B. MacAndrew's Q-sample had 72 statements, 3 of each of the 24 combinations. The statements were culled, however, from the literature and from his own extensive reading, rather than from his experimental subjects. They were statements of the following kind:

(*ad*) You really have a chance to meet the right kind of people here.

(*bd*) Knowing I'm part of a large company like this makes me feel pretty important.

(*cd*) I can live quite comfortably and enjoy my leisure time on what I make here.

(*ae*) I get a real feeling of "pride and accomplishment" from the work I do.

(*be*) At 4:40 I can completely forget about the job until the next morning. I don't have to "take the job home with me."

(*ae*) You can learn a great deal on this job.

(*af*) If you've done a good job, you can be sure of getting credit for it.

(*bf*) The procedures are set up so that if you have a real complaint, you can be sure of a fair hearing.

(*cf*) Long service really means something here.

(*ag*) You can get ahead if you know your stuff and really work hard.

(*bg*) If you stay here long enough, you can be sure of ending up in a good job.

(*cg*) There are always plenty of good jobs opening up here.

(*ah*) I really like the people I work with.

(*bh*) Everything here is so automatic that you don't have to worry about what kind of a mood everyone is in.

. . . and so on, for each of the 24 combinations of the design.

MacAndrew's study was with 23 subjects who worked in the main office of one of the country's largest corporations. A large building housed two thousand employees, all of the one corporation — twelve elevators took them to their respective floors and back again at the end of the day's work. A coffee shop, in which the more privileged employees passed some time, occupied part of the main lobby. MacAndrew was free to choose his subjects in any of the innumerable departments. He selected them with an eye to the variety of their work tasks and official classifications so as to have subjects widely inclusive of these, rather than to rely on random sampling. The P-set was as follows:

	No.	Sex	Average Age	Present Employment in Years
Supervisors	3	M	39	10
Junior supervisors	5	M	35	8
Secretaries	6	F	30	6
Clerks	9	F	29	4

They were called upon by MacAndrew during a stay in the office of some weeks, to provide three Q-sorts, with the following conditions of instruction:

Q-sort I: What is *true* and most *important* about your present job?

Q-sort II: What you would *most* want to be true, in order for your job to be as satisfying as it possibly can be. (That is, it may or may not be true of your job; and the changes should be *realistic*.)

Q-sort III: What you would *most* want in the *best* job you can imagine for yourself.

The conditions of instruction take the employees from a description of present condition, to realistic changes, and then to ideal conditions. It is a measure of Q-method's versatility that it can move easily into ideals in this manner; it was a weakness in Mayo and Riesman that what people ideally want and what they recognize as realistically possible are left unquestioned. I propose, therefore, to look at the data MacAndrew provides in this connection, that is, to see what employees feel along this axis from existing to ideal conditions.

The factor data are fully reported by MacAndrew; here it is sufficient to give his interpretations for the major factors.

The factors for supervisors are different from those for office clerks and secretaries. The supervisors wanted to give meaning to their current work, to work fully in it, and to find their real rewards in it: their major factors, for Q-sorts I, II, and III, respectively, call for the following interpretations:

(Existing): They regard their work as a challenge, of crucial importance in their lives, affording them prestige, and recognition from their employers. The Q-array was distinctly *work-oriented*.

(Realistic
changes): The factor stressed work-task gratifications; and recognition from employers, with pay, was obviously important to them.

(Ideal): This called for work to be interesting, enjoyable, self-expressive; pride in accomplishment was stressed; they wanted a maximum of responsibility, and free play for their independent judgment.

Notice that as we pass from present to ideal we move from the hardness and obduracy of work to a wish for self-expression and enjoyment. The inner-direction of the existing condition is manifest, and the factors are thoroughly work-oriented. Nowhere is there (to quote MacAndrew) "even the faintest glimmer of a human relations orientation." There were plenty of statements in the Q-sample which could have been used to represent insights into the human relations aspect of work, in one way or another, if anything of the kind was on the minds of the supervisors. There is a note of dissatisfaction, indeed, in the first two factors above; the *ideal* alone expresses a yearning for or pride in accomplishment. Their present work clearly does not allow the supervisors to make independent judgments.

Among the secretaries and clerks a very different picture appears. They fall into two types, each along the axis from Q-sort I to Q-sort III. One runs approximately as follows:

(Existing): Most thought that their work was interesting and rewarding; the pay and fringe benefits were good and the job secure.

They felt that their colleagues, and the bosses, were all a decent lot. The factor clearly indicated a sort of contentment or acceptance of the status quo.

(Realistic change): In this factor a more *dependent* strain appears — naturally they would like bosses who are easy to get on with and not aloof, who showed concern for them and told them what to do.

(Ideal): The ideal conditions were, for this factor, a relaxed, unchallinging job now. Work is regarded as a necessary evil, transitory, giving the employee money and *time* for the full exposition of his or her leisure.

Thus, if one is content and is asked to say what would better the conditions, any shift is not toward better "human relations" — on the contrary, it is toward more of the same dependency, and, *ideally*, not even that matters so much as what a pay check can do to make life more interesting outside the office.

The other line of factors, again for office personnel and secretaries but not supervisors, proceeds as follows:

(Existing): This factor stressed the *sociability* of the work; and at first sight this may seem to be indicative of a need for a solution to alienation. However, the same subjects thought little about their work; the work-task was not rewarding — nor did they feel that increased effort is the royal road to more pay. They felt, indeed, frustrated; their efforts, they felt, went unrewarded. Clearly, *sociability* was a rationalization, a vicarious matter — it wasn't serving to make work more palatable. If you can't find any interest or reward in work, then it was felt you'll find it in the people around you.

(Realistic change): This factor emphasized pay and convenience (e.g., short distance from work); they felt that if their work was boring (as it was) they should always be free to get away from it. The present job was as good as one could expect, however, and therefore at weekends one could get away on motoring, boating, or the like activities. This factor was called, by MacAndrew, a true vignette of the alienated adjusted worker.

(Ideal): The factor in this case indicated that they did not see their job as a potential way of life, even ideally; rather, it made possible some of the pleasures, and the things money can buy. The saliency is toward life outside the office. In no way does the factor indicate any "human relations" attitude.

The Mayo position therefore fares very badly as a proposed remedy for alienation. Only one factor gave saliency to human relations, and that was vicarious, something to make work bearable rather than anything integrated into it. Moreover, when called upon to say what could be a realistic improvement, or an ideal job, the employees drop even this concession to sociability — they are dominantly leisure-oriented. In stressing "human relations" Mayo and those who followed his counsel overlooked the question of what workers might regard as realistic changes and also what they would like ideally. Moreover, what is actually at issue, when it looks like sociability, is suspect — a little look under the carpet shows the dust and dirt of dissatisfactions. Mayo indeed reversed the causal relations at issue. Low morale leads to expressions of saliency about human relations (without mending anything vis-à-vis work); adding "human relations" to the workers' lot would be calculated, one may be sure, to lower morale. All these conclusions follow in the wake of the strong inductive inference brought to bear upon this set of only 23 subjects.

MacAndrew's study is important in several respects. It indicates how one can set about studying these broad philosophies of industry. It indicated, at the time, how right Riesman was to welcome alienation. But, the "meaning" of work clearly depends on the work. There is, after all, a difference between the work of the manager and the clerk, as between the florist and the carpenter. The supervisors, in this study, were at the top of their backyard heap; they were no doubt pushing hard for a bigger heap next door. In such circumstances it is reasonable to expect a strong work-orientation.

Thus, the suggestion is that, apart from any question of differences in the ambitions of men in the first place, the attitude adopted about one's job is dependent upon the job — not that work-oriented men succeed and leisure-loving ones do not. If you do not succeed, then with a reasonable pay check and time on your hands you become rather more pleasure-loving, or more content, and ultimately an adjusted alienated worker.

We should note also the relation of the factors to Riesman's typology. The supervisors appear as inner-directed, the clerks and secretaries more as other-directed. But there appear to be at least two types of other-directed, one with a dependent relationship and the other adjusted. The two are very different. Even here, however, with added security it is likely that the dependent other-directed will veer toward adjustment; if so, this would point once more to the interactional nature of social character.

Not only does social character vary with one's movement into a new part of the country, as Heberle suggested (45), but in MacAndrew's study we have a glimpse into the fact that it varies with one's place in the industrial hierarchy.

THEORY OF JOB SATISFACTION AND MASS COMMUNICATION

I would proceed from this study to accept as normal the adjusted alienated worker. To make his work more tolerable requires, instead of the rationalizations of a Mayo, the simple suggestion that at work people can *converse*. There are jealousies, gossip, rivalries, conflicts, competition, and much else to occupy the alienated worker at work, or on his way to work, or at lunch with his or her fellows. It is the function of the mass media, and of mass communication, to give him something interesting to talk about in these circumstances. Mention was made earlier of the study by Matthews (81) of the popular London *Mirror*, a morning newspaper which can be read in ten minutes on the way to work in a bus or commuter train and which provides workers in Britain with their conversation piece for the day. On a Monday it may be the football pool, on a Tuesday some scandal in high places, on Wednesday the latest train robbery. The ease with which people talk in this way is a better indicator of morale, it would seem to me, than anything that concerns work itself. But this is in inverse relation to responsibility. The gossip of the bosses at cocktails and lunch, however, is of the same warmly human brand of communication-pleasure.

Moreover, the ease with which we are now able to measure people for their Riesmanian or other type of direction is due to the readiness with which people converse about these everyday matters of gossip, of ordinary aspirations, of anybody's commonplace ideas. It is because these are on the tip of everyone's tongue, as common parlance, as something people accept without question, that their measurement along Q lines is facilitated. Thus, MacAndrew was easily able to measure much of Riesman's typology, from the inner-direction of the supervisors to the other-direction of the nonsupervisory personnel.

There is much to be said therefore for a morning newspaper, brief and to the point, as the London *Mirror* is. The American newspaper, entirely at the call of advertising revenue, takes an hour to peruse; while this is admirable for commuters from Connecticut or New Jersey who sit patiently in trains for so long a time that the *Wall Street Journal* and the *New York Times* serve excellently to provide conversation for the day, this is not the case for millions who drive to work by car each morning. The car radio, in this case, has the job of giving workers everywhere something of the kind — and there are a few bright spots of the kind in radio. Interview material I have gathered in the Chicago area suggests that a morning commentator, with a humorous touch, is not unwelcome. His job, in a sanely helpful world, would be to give the worker something to talk about for the rest of the day, whenever there is a coffee break or a time to chat. Our thesis fits neatly, of course, into Simmel's scheme — such general conversation is pure play.

Thus, I do not conclude that while at work one should not play. On the contrary. Ideally I would prefer to see people working short hours and few days (since not all can hold responsible jobs) and they should be allowed to chatter endlessly, if they wish, while the machines do the work. Outside working hours, however, there is a *need* to play. I see this not as escapist or puerile or anxiety-reducing, but as thought about in relation to a country's ideals, its goals, and its higher values. This is taken care of by legend and myth, as of a Kennedy, or a Great American Society. It is taken care of, as well, by modern paperback publications, recordings of music, and the like — the market for these has grown enormously, filling a void. Alienated people need to be reminded of ideals, even when it is clear these are never likely to be realized for themselves.

What is important about leisure pursuits in a modern nation, when the problems of work have been solved and poverty eliminated, is to see them in relation to their potentiality for creating culture — not in the sense of being affected or scholarly, but as a way of life suitable to the times. Bridge-playing, for example, is a sterile exercise in itself; though it passes the time and keeps one up with the local gossip, it is in itself useless for culture. People now appreciate art, music, and literature more, but it is often merely self-consciousness and not genuinely playful. Games in the United States are in essence professionalized and thus lose their genuine play elements. Football is a spectacle and big business — not play, as soccer or cricket is in English schools and colleges *sans* coach, bands, and ticket offices. The United States, however, has its genuine play in other directions — an excellent example is boating, where a noble spirit may be fostered as people genuinely play at sailing and boating.

What is necessary, it seems, is a certain idealism, a certain nobility, dignity, or style in play. Television's most popular programs, the ubiquitous Westerns, keep a place in the hearts of people for the open spaces and frontier days, and this is good play. Murder mysteries, like bridge, pass the time, but are scarcely conducive to genuine play and therefore to cultural development.

11

Ludenic Theory
of Newsreading

In modern societies newspapers serve many functions; they give news about happenings in the world, both serious and sensational (62). Motivation research undertaken for a leading American newspaper, *The Detroit Free Press* (55), suggested that people feel lost and anxious without a newspaper because, otherwise, they would not know what is going on in the world and, fearing the worst, they are reassured to read each day that everything is well. Janowitz (57) observed that a community newspaper not only supplies information for parents grappling with problems of rearing children but is supportive of the parents' way of life — the newspaper has to support the housewife, for example, as she sees herself. If she thinks of herself as good, intelligent, doing a good job, this has to be reflected for her in the newspaper.

The earlier theorists, however, were more apt to draw attention to a less functional aspect of newsreading. Cooley (17) remarked on the strange behavior of a man who would "sit down to his breakfast table, and, instead of conversing with his wife and children, hold before his face a screen on which is inscribed a world-wide gossip." Newspapers ought to have been bulletins for "news," for the interchange of ideas (through letters, reports of speeches, etc.) and in the final analysis a binding force, integrating public opinion in relation to deeper human values; they had become, instead, "mostly organized gossip." News, Cooley remarked, is copious — like gossip, "occupying without exciting the mind." One has to concentrate to read a book but not to read a newspaper. He complained that news is unreliable, like gossip; yet, like gossip, it encourages a sense of belonging to a community. Even so, it is the antithesis of literature and of spirituality. Nor does a newspaper deal very seriously with serious problems; the important news of today is old and forgotten tomorrow.

The truth is that newspapers are a bit of everything to a bit of everybody, and everything said about them applies in some degree. These is more to say, however, in theoretical respects. In democratic countries news is written from the "human interest" angle, the focus being on the intimacies of private lives, more especially of any public or popular figure. This puts the individual in the position of a confidant, Helen Hughes (51) argued, reflecting inner experience; and is not this, she continues, an essential ingredient of change in a free society? The emphasis is on human, consumer interests. It is very different in Russia, where the citizen is not allowed these intimacies; the news is dedicated to the state. Instead of expanding the human interests, the press in the U.S.S.R. is involved in contracting them, fearful perhaps of what might happen if people there could speculate unreservedly about what goes on in the world. The news in Russia, in short, rests on state production interests. The theory that "human interests" provide the pivot about which change occurs in a free society should be compared with the obvious fact that most people in our societies hold opinions about many current issues and are capable of discussing them; there is a distinct growth of self-consciousness in this respect, an awareness that one holds this or that opinion and that others have different opinions. This is not true of underprivileged peoples, for example, in India (122). Many in the world have not achieved a degree of self which permits discussions about current issues. Hughes's point is that the "personalizing" of the news, to emphasize its human interests, is necessary to the healthy growth of sound citizens in a free society.

Other theories are of more particular psychological interest. Schramm (127), an acknowledged expert on mass communication, is author of the theory that newsreading is governed by Freud's pleasure principle; some people read news for immediate gratification, whereas others are more reality-oriented and prepare themselves for good news in the future by reading the bad news of today. This we have already examined in detail in chapter 4. Kay (61) proposes that the conscious (and sometimes unconscious) motive for newsreading is "to obtain new information, either because that information will be applied toward the solution of a problem, or because it evokes images that are different from images already stored in the reader's memory." He adds that if a reader knew beforehand what is in a newspaper there would be no reason to read it. But it seems to us that people read most avidly what they already know about; they go to a football match, then read about it in a newspaper and are doubly delighted if they see it rerun on television or made the feature sports story of a national magazine. What needs explaining is why people read about the same things over and over. Kay has also proposed (61) that newsreading is essentially *abreactive*: people build up tensions because of everyday pressures and frustrations; newsreading serves to relieve these, much as opening a valve reduces pressure in a boiler.

There is no dearth of theory, therefore, about newsreading. Our own application of play theory to newsreading is perhaps best regarded as supra-ordinate to any of the above; it encompasses that of Hughes and develops that of Schramm. It is more fundamental and at the same time keeps newspapers and newsreading in place as adjuncts to community culture. Before discussing it I need to introduce an old concept, that of *apperception*, so that there can be no doubt about the fact that I regard newsreading as an active process — not merely a passive one of having news thrown at one to read willy-nilly.

APPERCEPTION

Apperception is an old concept of systematic psychology (151). A homely example serves best to introduce it: a young baseball fan, out for a walk, will pick up stones to hit and a stick to use as a bat; his date, a student of botany, will see instead a purple helleborine or other rare flower on the same pathway. The boy does not notice the flowers and the girl does not see the sticks and stones. Such is apperception. It is a readiness to perceive this or that in relation to prior systems of interest. (The principle of preselection is subsumed under the concept of apperception.)

Both boy and girl are capable of seeing everything, and both probably notice in common the pleasant grass, the shady woods, and the common flowers, all diffusely, without special interest or attention, like background music as one drives a car. Or, each could switch attention at will and become richly cognizant of the scenery — provided that the beauty of the countryside is a topic of interest for them. There are, unhappily, many who never can perceive such beauty; a man with economic interests might see the scenery, instead, as a housing venture, five houses to an acre. The concept of apperception involves the assumption that the individual is a complex of interests, all active and vibrant, with feelers out all the time under appropriate conditions, ready to receive instantly whatever ties in with a prior interest. So the girl and boy alike will miss both helleborine and an actual baseball bat lying on the roadway as they walk arm-in-arm in formal dress on their way to a dance.

Otherwise, people do not notice what is all around them, except when great novelty or loudness obtrudes. A loud shot of a gun will of course gain anyone's attention. But novelty is more likely to be rejected or feared rather than accepted or liked. Trouble comes in mass communication theory when all people are conceived as blank minds, each a *tabula rasa*, and all messages are thought of as obtruding noises that no one can fail to hear. The contrary is the case; people are complexes of apperceptive masses, and mass communications are best conceived as "blends" or "mixes" pretty well matched to audience apperceptiveness.

The critics who stress the dysfunctional character of mass communication (who think that "its morality sinks to that of its most brutal and primitive members, its taste to that of the least sensitive and most ignorant" [83]) are unaware of the apperceptiveness of the public and of the diffusiveness of much of the mass media content.

PLAY THEORY OF NEWSREADING

Newspaper reading, subjectively regarded, has all the earmarks of play. One reads one thing at one moment, and another at the next moment, with no relation between them. Reading a newspaper is voluntary, that is, it is not a task or duty. It is not related to the person's everyday life; it is a temporary interlude, satisfying in itself and ending there. The commuter trains in New York City are full of men who sit, two by two, each absorbed in his own newspaper, all deadly silent. The reader is in a sense disinterested in what he is reading; he might look at stock exchange prices to see how his recent purchase of shares is faring, but normally what he reads about is entirely outside the immediate satisfactions of his needs or specific interests. Yet the reading creates a certain order, as in a child's playing, a brief grasp of the reader's own world. It casts a light spell upon the person — not of rapture, but of deep absorption. It involves the reader in direct self-identification; the person projects himself into the news as a storyteller does in any TAT situation (93). Who indeed has not imagined himself being more effective about a situation than others, who have blundered (making mistakes *we* would not have made)? One surrounds one's newspaper with an air of mystery (10). Who has not claimed that his newspaper is better than any other? The self, indeed, is everywhere in the reading, down to the smallest detail.

Who has not caught glimpses of his own incomparable good sense, his more accurate appraisal of affairs, as he reads a paper?

What is missing in earlier studies of mass communication in general, and of newsreading in the present case, is a realization that communication is carried on in play. The communication situation is not one in which information is passed from a communication source to a receiver; it is one in which the individual plays with communication.

More sophisticated newsreading takes on the character of a formal game rather than of pure fantasy (142). People may read a paper from the back page forward; others follow a sequence, more or less regular, from headlines to comics, sports, and thence to editorials. These are only loosely maintained "rules," but a newspaper can foster or hinder such play. In the London *Times* everything has its proper place. The *Wall Street Journal* is similarly consistent in its makeup, as is a news magazine like *Time*. But how different are many modern newspapers, where novelty replaces regularity! Most people on picking up a weekly magazine like *Life* or *Look* first skim or scan it, skipping from page to page, looking at the pictures first, examining the headlines and captions; nothing is read thoroughly. Only later, if they return to the magazine, or if a feature article has attracted them, do they settle down to serious reading. The initial and usual interaction is one of "milling" around, as people do aimlessly and yet pleasantly at a fair, a shopping center, or at the seaside promenade. All of this is "pure play attitude."

Popular newspapers and homogenized news magazines like *Life* or *Look* encourage the "pure play" attitude. More developed newspapers such as the *New York Times* and magazines like *Time* permit of a game element, that is, of regularity, order, and perspective in the reading. A newspaper or magazine, to fit a theory of *developed* newsreading, should induce and encourage such regularity, orderliness, and sensitive contemplation. The editor has to make his newspaper interesting; for some readers this can be achieved by primitive play conditions, which are characterized more by a scattering of the mind than by any well-developed absorption. Sophisticated newsreading is contemplative rather than scatterbrained. I have written elsewhere (142) about this ludenic theory of newsreading.

Newsreading as play is not mentioned anywhere in the writings of the experts on mass communication — so, indeed, the Greeks portrayed their gods playing, but had no God of Play. Play was too much with them to be seen objectively and personified. And so, perhaps, it has been with the social scientists who have undertaken to study newsreading.

Q-FACTOR MODEL FOR THE THEORY

Following the methodology outlined in chapter 2, it is a simple matter to test the ludenic theory from the subjective standpoint.

First, the writings on newsreading by Cooley, Kingsbury and Hart, Schramm, Berelson, Janowitz, Kay, and others provide a ready source of self-referent statements on the newsreading XYZ situation. From a collection of these a Q-sample is composed, in the present case as a random set. A Q-sample so arrived at is as follows:

Q-SAMPLE NR

1. Newspapers have fine appreciation, good judgment.
2. Newspapers are enjoyable to read.
3. It's a bit of a chore to read a newspaper.
4. They are for relaxation.
5. Newspapers seek reality.
6. They are for passing the time.
7. Papers are marked by restraint, caution.
8. While you read a paper it is absorbing.
9. Newspapers serve for the interchange of ideas.
10. Newspapers are sensational.
11. They give a correct picture of the world.
12. They are concerned a lot with the doings of the rich.
13. They are often biased.
14. Newspapers have sound scientific judgment.
15. It's a habit — you miss reading the paper.
16. Newspapers have social consciousness.
17. They are associated with the enjoyment of leisure.
18. News is about the same every day.
19. Newspapers dig below the surface of the news.
20. They raise essential questions about society.
21. You forget the news quickly; it is difficult to remember what was in yesterday's paper.
22. They perform an indispensable service for the government.
23. They are an interlude in the day.
24. They are marked by seriousness.
25. Newspapers are critically reflective.
26. Newspapers exaggerate; they are out for display.
27. Newspapers relieve and reassure you.

28. They are frivolous on the whole.
29. Newspapers today are cultured.
30. Newspapers are imaginative, in the sense of telling about princes, kings, etc.
31. They deal with superficial emotion.
32. Everything is taken seriously by newspapers.
33. Newspapers have educational aspirations — they are trying to educate the public.
34. Newspapers are trying to raise cultural standards.
35. Their content is copious rather than discerning.
36. Newspapers give you a philosophy of life.
37. They give the interesting rather than the important.
38. They never come to grips with things.

It will be observed that the statements are not in self-referent form. This is for the sake of simplicity and so that the subject, performing a Q-sort with them, can attach his own self-reference to them — saying, for example, that in *his* opinion a newspaper or newsreading is this or that. Thus, there are irate gentlemen, surely, who become very hot under the collar about statements 12, 18, 26, 31, 35, and 38, and whose strong feelings would be reflected in their Q-sorts.

STUDIES WITH THIS Q-SAMPLE

It will be noticed that the Q-sample has no formal factorial design; I present it as a reminder that it is not essential to structure Q-samples. It consists of central concepts about newspapers held by authorities who have studied or written about journalism, from Cooley to Schramm. Yet each is only someone's opinion. I could find few key concepts in the literature about play involvement and, therefore, added some for myself — they are statements 2, 8, 15, 17, 18, and 23. The Q-sample is implicitly structured, therefore, with many statements nonludenic and others ludenic in import.

The Q-sample has been used in several studies. I propose to consider one here to illustrate certain contingencies that have to be faced in all Q-studies. The Q-factor model is for college students, graduates and undergraduates, men and women. The factor scores are in Table 1.

There are two factors, A and B, but each is bipolar; that is, some students are negatively loaded on the factors, so that their Q-sorts are in the reverse order of those in Table 1. The negative for A (call it C) is the same factor array as that for A, with all the signs changed. Similarly the negative for B (call it D) is the same as B with all signs changed.

The student P-samples can be of any mixture of men or women; they tell us little, in the *XYZ* situation, except that students are not apt to be very avid or regular readers of newspapers. They have little leisure for it and sometimes cannot afford a regular subscription. Married students, in campus quarters, tend to pass around a newspaper. One can expect them to be defensive; they may say, in the Q-sort, what they would like to be ideally, rather than what they really are. The truth, however, will out and in being defensive a person exaggerates or distorts things in his Q-sorting and gives himself away to the interpreter.

TABLE 1
Q-FACTOR MODEL FOR NEWSREADING BY STUDENTS,
$n = 38$ STATEMENTS (Q-SAMPLE NR)

Statement	Factor* A	Factor* B	Statement	Factor* A	Factor* B
1	−1	1	20	1	1
2	5	2	21	0	−1
3	−3	−1	22	2	4
4	2	−1	23	2	−1
5	−2	5	24	−1	0
6	1	−3	25	−1	0
7	−4	0	26	0	−2
8	4	0	27	−5	1
9	3	4	28	−3	−3
10	0	−2	29	−3	0
11	−2	2	30	0	−4
12	0	−2	31	1	−4
13	3	−2	32	−4	2
14	−2	2	33	1	5
15	5	1	34	−1	2
16	2	3	35	3	−1
17	4	1	36	−5	0
18	−2	−5	37	1	−3
19	0	3	38	−1	−5

*The factors are bipolar (differences greater than 3 across factors are significant).

In line with our practice the model is made available for anyone to examine and to interpret, having the above in mind. Here I give my own interpretation. Factor A is genuinely ludenic, its students skillful newsreaders; factor B adopts an idealized view of newspapers, but rarely reads any — they are covering up, a little ashamed of their negligence vis-à-vis newsreading. The reverse of A (C) used the Q-sample to project anxiety — they are anxious readers. The reverse of B (D) are aggressive, anti-newspaper students, who think newspapers are sensational, trivial, and the like.

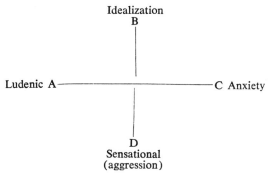

Only the ludenic factor, A, it seems to me, is being "truthful"; that is, the Q-sort bears a direct relation to what the person really feels, to his real inner "state of mind" about newspapers and, by inference, to newsreading. The statements to which he gives most significance concern the enjoyment of newsreading (2), its habitual and absorbing character (15, 8), its association with leisure (17). But the factor is realistic, agreeing that news is often biased (13) and copious rather than discerning (35). In these respects the factor is very different from B, and from C and D as well. For factor A all that concerns the outer world of events, in the Q-sample, is kept in place, subordinate to acceptance of the newsreading as *enjoyable*. What is at issue is not that these individuals have a happy disposition, placing pleasure before duty or enjoyment before seriousness; rather, they truly reflect what a newspaper means to them. The young students of factor A are already self-absorbed in newsreading; they have caught the newsreading habit; and yet they retain their identity about reality — they are aware that newspapers are not all that truth requires.

Factor B makes a paragon of every virtue out of newspapers. They are said to seek reality (5), to have educational aspirations (33), to perform an indispensable service for the government (22), to have social consciousness (16) and the like. The suggestion is that newspapers are solid, virtuous organs, doing a thorough job of educating the public.

Whereas A was subjective (a reflection of one's enjoyment, absorption, etc.), B is objective, concerned with the supposed social and public functions of newspapers. Factor A is concerned about the newsreading as *he* experiences it. B is making judgments about the functions of newspapers as such in public respects. Thus B gives little significance to newspapers as sources of relaxation and leisure. That a newspaper is absorbing is given a zero score by B — it does not appear to matter to B, which is a sure sign that these students do not read newspapers much.

Factor B is what some students suppose that newspapers *should* be like, rather than an account of what the same students could give as a "real" account of their views on newspapers and newsreading. Actually, they have little time for newsreading and have formed no ludenic newsreading skills.

The students negatively loaded on factor B (called D) indicate a viewpoint which is the opposite of that for B; the individual (D) says that he thinks of newspapers as sensational, frivolous, superficial, never coming to grips with things, exaggerative, that they are merely for passing the time, and so on, and that they in no way educate or inform the public, having no social consciousness or social purpose. Clearly it is a sour, anti-newspaper attitude. There is no indication that they enjoy a newspaper, or indeed that they read one. As students will, they are no doubt being somewhat facetious; certainly they are being aggressive. But that some students regard newspapers negatively is certain. They have not made a beginning with newsreading enjoyment and they would not be able to enjoy even sensational news if it were put before them.

There are students who give the reverse of factor A as their Q-sort, which we designate as C. These consider that newspapers give you a philosophy of life, and relieve and reassure you. Newspapers, they assert, are marked by restraint and take things seriously; they cannot but seek reality, with sound judgment; they cannot fail to come to grips with things. But all of this is false; the same students say that it is "a chore to read a newspaper" (statement 3), which scarcely squares with their opinion that newspapers are reassuring and that they are marked with restraint and so on. Closer examination indicates that the students are ashamed; they really never read a newspaper and have no real views about them. They try to guess, however, what the right answers should be and produce a Q-sort which, though coherent and self-consistent in its parts, is nevertheless quite false. They are anxious, and usually are young women students.

DISCUSSION

The Q-sample is a very simple one, and yet every statement in it comes from writings of authorities in the field, expressing their key journalistic concepts. It is comprehensive, and this explains why the factor configurations are so straightforward. It is not our purpose to discuss student newsreading, however, but to indicate through this factor model that we rarely reach factors without intrusion of dynamic influences such as the negatives C and D illustrate, as well as B itself. The defensiveness of C, the idealization of B, the negativisim of D are all to be expected and are plain enough to be seen by the interpreter who keeps in mind the P-sample conditions. It is a worthwhile exercise to construct the two Q-sorts for Table 1 to see how neatly, and precisely, they cover the four spokes of the above figure. Factor axis BD is objective in attitude, whereas AC is personal and subjective. We mention these finer points to indicate something of the precision, in the logical as well as the psychological sense, of the matters grasped by Q-sorting.

NEWSREADING TYPES

Q-audiences have been defined for the wider public in a number of studies, using different Q-samples, by Danbury (21), Ross (119), Cornetta (18), Crumley (19), and Stephenson (142). Three broad factors appear for the XYZ situation of readers (X), social conditions (Y), and the "news" (Z), no matter what Q-sample[1] is employed to represent it. Projected on the general public, we must suppose that this is segmented into three Q-audiences, which we designate M, N, and P, respectively. They are as follows:

M are *mature* newsreaders; they give high saliency to ludenic items in their Q-sort descriptions of their own newsreading. Newsreading for them is thoroughly habituated, absorbing, enjoyable, an interlude in the day, self-enhancing. The individuals are apt to be wide-ranging in their interests, with a "mix" of community, national, and international news. Newsreading is not merely entertaining for them.

N are *non-pleasure* readers, sometimes essentially non-readers, who have no awareness of newsreading as absorbing, enjoyable, or the like. Rather, it is purely utilitarian (for *sales*, etc.), or regarded as sinful, wasteful, and so on.

P are *pleasure* readers, who are apt to think of newsreading as entertainment, "to pass the time," and so on. Their newsreading is "pure play" — whereas that for M is a "game" in theoretical respects.

How many people there are of these types can only be conjectured. The number of mature readers (M) is probably not less than the num-

---

[1] Provided it represents the XYZ newsreading situation. Reference can be made to the studies by Cornetta, Ross, Crumley, and others mentioned above for such Q-samples.

ber of college-educated persons in the United States. City dwellers are likely to be more M and P, and less N. People who live in rural areas and in poor areas of cities are likely to be largely N. Clearly M are likely to be educated people, with wider interests than N or P. But many professional people may be type N, because of a narrowing of their interests in business, law, medicine, and the like. Most typically, N are moralizers, who think newspapers are sinful. They would like newspapers to change their ways — "to become more educational, more truthful." Such wishes, often made about television programs as well, have little substance except in the Puritan ethic; individuals, however, do read specialized "news" — for example, in religious magazines or in relation to their own professions.

The Q-audiences, M, N, and P, make good sense in relation to what is suspected about the newsreading public. It is hard for anyone who has not attended college to be a mature (M) reader. But some teenagers are already headed for M in their high schools, so that college education is not a sufficient cause. Careful study shows that M tend to be liberal in political viewpoint — liberal in the sense that a President Kennedy was and a Governor Rockefeller is — notwithstanding the different political faiths at issue; basically they have introjected the belief that peoples are interdependent. They already tolerate the rest of the world. P, on the contrary, is very much a creature of the current mass media at its spectacular, sensational, sports, gossip, and human interest levels — it is the *mass* audience in the usual meaning of the term. N are the vast *a*political, *a*social, local-interested groups, out of which the P-type mass no doubt forms. Given to extreme views, in which sin, guilt, and (oddly enough) modern technological skills strangely intermingle, N are essentially uneducated individuals. But one can find doctors and professors of the type, who are scarcely aware of what is going on in the world and yet who are prepared to be highly vocal, narrowminded, and moralistic about what they imagine is happening in it.

CONCLUSION

At its best, newsreading is a great skill with which the reader creates his own order, commanding his own grasp of things in the world. There is an air of mystery and ritual about it; it is deeply absorbing, almost trancelike. It is not just a joke to say, as many a housewife has, that her husband loses himself in his newspaper. Yet the core of it has been overlooked by the theorists. What was never explained was its intrinsic enjoyment, which we explain as communication-pleasure, in Szasz's term. The old idea in psychology was that pleasure is the steam released when needs or tensions are reduced. Schramm's theory, and Kay's, is based on this conception. In communication-pleasure there is merely an interchange of attitudes; but the self gains in self-enhancing, self-supporting directions. The self is enlarged. In the ludenic trance, so to speak, the person can thrust forward a little for himself, to self-stride. Many a youthful reader, in adolescence or early manhood, must have taken on a new commitment that was born in newsreading. So it is with great editors who have sought freedom for man, or who have been in the forefront of revolt; none had any thought of material gain, profit, or prizes for himself.

Communication-pleasure, like the bloom on a peach, may seem a very thin covering indeed for the lush fruit of newsreading and newspapers. But there are few opportunities left to us in which we can go into retreat, as we do within a newspaper, there to talk to ourselves and to practice the arts of self-designing. Behind the pages there are moments when we seize upon things in an authentic making of self — we become committed to this or that in ludenic newsreading. This is without thought of gain and serves no function but to give enjoyment; but there is still the possibility that, at moments, in true leisure, one finds something for oneself. Reading is well recognized as a place for this self-projection. H. G. Wells caught it in Mr. Polly, who though beaten down in the darkness and emptiness of his life could still grope toward a delight, somewhere, in the printed word. And Mr. Polly was surely Mr. Wells himself. Something of this excitement and release, Larrabee and Meyersohn (69) and others have suggested, characterized the spread of reading among our forefathers. So it is, at times, in the reading of great newspapers today.

12

Khrushchev's Visit to the United States

To illustrate the application of my theory to the "news" I select one historical event, which was handled very competently by the press — Khrushchev's visit to the United States in 1959. At the time world affairs were a cause for serious concern. There was much tension about international affairs. New countries in the dozens were being formed out of collapsing colonial empires. Khrushchev's visit was particularly notable and is supposed to have had a profound effect upon him, whatever it had upon us.

Much of America in 1959 was strongly anti-Soviet. The news about Russia, sparse as it was, was biased. As Kriesberg (66) had shown, from 1918 to 1946 the *New York Times* had overlooked news favorable to the Soviets and had given headline treatment to news unfavorable to it. This was done in a hundred small ways. Let there be one crooked Russian, and his character would be regarded as typical of all. Unwarranted headlines, loaded adjectives, questionable sources of information — in such petty ways the picture was built of evil and hate. Contrariwise, anything favoring the United States was accentuated, with Pollyanna-like devotion. This is not to say the *Times* was deliberately distorting the news; it was merely giving its audience what it wanted to hear, and what the *Times* editorial staff wanted to hear as well. It is our responsibility in communication research to remind the editors, however, that in such circumstances they are playing a game, and that every now and then it might help to change the play a little.

Thus, the Khrushchev visit offered an opportunity to see what the XYZ condition was at that time, where X is the American public, Z the communication it had accepted about the United States–U.S.S.R. relations, and Y the media involved. We require a Q-factor model to permit us to be theoretical about the situation.

Following our usual procedure, intensive interviews were conducted with 36 individuals, chosen to fit the P-sample of Table 1. The interview plan called for discussion of the respondents' television-viewing and news-reading habits, after which the visit of Khrushchev, then under way, was reviewed with special reference to any recent program on television showing Khrushchev's progress through the country. The subjects were encouraged to talk freely.

TABLE 1
P-SAMPLE FOR STUDIES OF KHRUSHCHEV'S VISIT

Effects	Levels	No.
I, Political allegiance	(a) Democrat (b) Independent (c) Republican	3
II, Sex	(d) Male (e) Female	2
III, Age	(f) 20–30 years (g) 30–60 years	2
IV, Socio-economic level	(h) White-collar (i) Blue-shirt (j) Professional	3

(Combinations $3 \times 2 \times 2 \times 3 = 36$)

The P-sample assumes that political allegiance, age, socio-economic conditions, and sex are likely to offer broad differences in views about Khrushchev's visit. The liberal democrat is supposed to be softer on communism, older people more rigidly opposed to coexistence, professionals more open-minded than blue-shirt workers, and women more peace-loving. The P-sample represents such hypotheses.

From the interview material a Q-population was collected, inspection of which suggested Table 2 as the design for Q-sample construction. A

TABLE 2
Q-SAMPLE DESIGN FOR KHRUSHCHEV'S VISIT

Effects	Levels			No.
V, Valency	(a) Pro	(b) Con	(c) Others	3
VI, Involvement	(d) Visit	(e) Policies	(f) Khrushchev's personality	3

(Combinations $3 \times 3 = 9$)

Q-sample of size $n = 72$ was put together, for eight replications of the design.

The following statements afford an idea of the statements involved in the Q-sample:

1. Khrushchev is locked in a cage of communistic economic doctrine.
2. I think Khrushchev is very charming — after all he is leader of 200 million Russians.
3. People have been able to watch for themselves. I think Khrushchev has gained some respect here.
4. I can understand Khrushchev and respect him.
5. In my opinion the American public is curious and suspicious about Khrushchev.
6. Mrs. Khrushchev's quietness and motherliness is doing a good job for Russia.
7. Khrushchev is a shrewd man, who knows what he wants.
8. It seems to me that our policy should be for coexistence.
9. Khrushchev's visit is a question of peace or war, a question of the life or death of people.
10. The longer we wait, the less chance we have of winning a war with Russia.
11. Democratic capitalism can take the measure of communism anytime.
12. Khrushchev is overrated.

The Q-sample generated five main factors, A to E, briefly designated as follows:

A. Peaceful women
B. Pollyanna men
C. Fatalists
D. Men of firm conscience
E. The fearful

A better description of each is given below:

A are mainly women, who favor coexistence and are hopeful of eventual disarmament. This goes with greater acceptance of Russia, Khrushchev, and, also, with more awareness that we might profit by taking another look at ourselves.

B are largely male, and strongly anti-Russian, in the Pollyanna-manner of the early *New York Times*. They are all for the ingroup, all against the outgroup. There is no need to look at ourselves, no need to take Khrushchev seriously, no need to accept anything that is to his advantage. Thus the factor is against coexistence. But with the odd inconsistency of the shallow-minded, though they trust Khrushchev least of all, they would still utilize every basis for mutual understanding. Pollyanna-hope springs eternal in the ingroup breast.

C are male, nihilistic, self-destructive, fatalistic. They feel that only a war will solve matters and that the longer we wait, the less is our chance of winning. Of course we do not want war, as long as Russia does not push us too hard. But Russia is ahead of us; the press is misleading us; the country is going downhill — and no doubt Eisenhower is a Communist. It is the typical picture of the ultraconservative, blind to facts, who would go to war without knowing why or even understanding its consequences.

D are as strongly anti-Soviet, and most strongly of all assert that conscience is at issue. But they do not deny their own country. They merely reject Khrushchev and his disarmament proposals, without having to support their own ingroup position by external projections — their own conscience is enough to maintain them.

E are fearful, superstitious, feeling that war is very near. Khrushchev is merely trying to impress us. Russia comes into the world in strength, not weakness, and therefore is to be feared.

The interviews conducted with these individuals support these interpretations. But the factors are objective. And can anyone doubt their pertinency? Could one ever accept coexistence without internalizing first, as the women in factor A have done, a willingness to accept others on faith as a bit like ourselves? Can anyone doubt the nihilistic character of C, or its obvious correspondence with ultraconservative extremism? Note its denegation of its own country, its blindness to facts, its acceptance of war almost in a vacuum. Can one deny the fear of E, who could believe that Khrushchev's visit was a matter of life or death for us? As for B and D, both strongly anti-Soviet (as, of course, are C and E as well), the difference is one of self-conscience. B are a product of the *New York Times* Pollyanna game, internalizing very little, but chanting the necessary slogans. D are more self-contained, and in no need of the outgroup-ingroup game to support them.

The model gives us an account of what must be present a millionfold across the country. From the play-theoretical standpoint we see B as genuinely "playful," with ingroup-outgroup agonism truly at work. C, on the contrary, are at war with themselves, rather than against anything else! D are disillusioned and hurt, instead of entering into play. E, being frightened, are running away. Only A remain in a world approximating to things as they really are.

Such are our interpretations.

The example illustrates the methodology in a complex situation, the theoretical discussion of which is made possible not by a remote concept concerning anxiety-reduction or the like (such as Schramm [127] and Kay [61] recommend), but by considering Q-audiences in terms of a variety of theoretical considerations which seem to be in keeping with the complexity of the situation. More detailed study might attest to the underlying anxiety of factor A. But only factor E is manifestly anxious. Again, at deeper levels of concern, factor C's nihilistic attitude must hide serious fears.

IMPLICATIONS FOR COMMUNICATION

International affairs are too complex for the ordinary person to grasp, and they have therefore to be symbolized and made simple and dramatic. The trouble comes only when such symbolization is out of step with what the times require. It seems to me that this had happened in 1959 for factor B of Khrushchev's visit. For decades the *New York Times* played the ingroup-outgroup game of factor B vis-à-vis Russia (66), unaware of the dimensions of the deceit. There can be no question that such a great newspaper must serve to reinforce the prevailing American interests; its news must be keyed to whatever is really good for the country. But its prospective audience is likely to be segmented about great issues, such as our factors A to E illustrate for Khrushchev's visit. For the period 1918–46 perhaps it was in America's interest to play the game of factor B. By 1960 it would have been wiser to play D; and soon, perhaps, A will come into its own.

But even for a Q-audience such as A, one would still have to resort to play. Facts are still very complex, and even A's viewpoint would require expressive symbolization and an ingroup-outgroup dynamism of its own. One saw something of the kind in the 1964 presidential election in Chile, where the Christian Democrats won against Communists and Fascists. President Eduardo Frei said of his party that it "believes that the modern world is in crisis, and that only a complete readjustment of society can save man from materialism and collectivism" (*Time* Magazine, September 18, 1964, p. 48). The ingroup is Christian democracy; the outgroup is materialism and all forms of collectivism, fascist or communist. Frei's talk, it is said, had a sharp appeal for the underprivileged in Chili as well as for Latin America's deeply religious women, rich and poor alike. The women gave Frei some 63 per cent of their votes and won him the election. Thus, I am not advocating any distillation of truth as such, or any idea that a factor like A (though more compassionate than B, C, D, or E) can be put into mass communication as cold fact; on the contrary, it too has to be made agonistic to fit the necessity for sharpening and dramatizing issues and for giving people something to fight *against* as well as *for*. Methods are now available for defining the audiences for mass communication not in general but keyed to particular important issues. The choice is an editor's, to emphasize what he believes is good for his country.

From its earliest days journalism has undoubtedly been concerned with public enlightenment and with political and social reform. Enlightenment in some degree is a consequence of almost any communication. And, as for political and social reform, this is a two-edged sword; newspapers can be supportive of existing political systems or social conditions, or else be in opposition to them. It is hard to conceive of a newspaper in Cuba or Russia in 1964 as other than supportive of the existing political and social systems.

The two functions, of support to ongoing conditions and of opposition, involve much the same principles. In both, the "news" is incidental and the cause important. The Soviet press is not obligated to report current events (56) or to be objective in any such reporting (169). The cause is the main thing. But this is just as true of journalism in an oppositional role — the main thing is the replacement of one cause by another. This applies, of course, to news in our own country as well; what the United States public hears about Cuba is one thing, and what the British press may say about it is likely to be something different. Everyone perhaps understands this, regarding the differences as matters of opinion. It is not necessary to suppose that the press in a country is misleading its public deliberately.

Our theoretical concern, however, is with the "play" involved in these matters. What, indeed, is the press supposed to be doing? In the United States high ideals are placed upon it. It is the responsibility of the press, Ethridge (28) writes, to explain what the issues of the world are to its readers. The 1947 Committee on Freedom of the Press (Ethridge [28]) emphasized this responsibility. The press should give a truthful, comprehensive, and intelligent account of the day's events in a meaningful way; it should be a forum for exchange of sensible comment and criticism, and for projecting opinions and attitudes; it should clarify the goals and values of the society in which we live; and it should reach every member of the society with these wise currents of information, thought, and feeling. These are solid virtues, asserted almost as prerogatives of the press. But scientists have had much the same to say; the cultural anthropologist, for example, concludes that the very complexity of American culture and the intricacy of the relationships at issue between peoples calls for the mass media in general and for newspapers in particular "to illuminate, explain, and dramatize" the meaning of being a man in today's world (38).

There are wide gaps, however, between these ideals on the one hand and press practices on the other.

News in the Western democracies is not so much *important* information as it is something that happened an hour ago. It has to be, first, novel, and well steeped in human interest, thoroughly "personalized." It is certainly very different from the Russian concept of news, which consists of official documents on industrial or production matters and which for weeks may not report things happening in the world today — not necessarily because of censorship but because they are not important in relation to the goals and values of communism.

The mass media are daily involved in vast programs of *representing* events in the world as news, information, and entertainment; and what is represented in newspapers and television programs is symbolical rather than a true statement of what is going on. It is of course difficult for most of us to believe this. *Hard* news is true enough — someone was found gagged at 2:30 A.M. on Princess Street. But two television documentaries on Castro's Cuba — one prepared for the B.B.C. for the British public, and the other for Mr. Huntley's program on N.B.C. — are so different that a man from Mars would never know that they are about the same country. Yet neither the B.B.C. nor N.B.C. is deliberately deceiving its public. It is only that what is everyday conversation in the one country among producers and audiences is not common in the other. The imagery, imputations, beliefs, and sympathies are very different in the two countries. To say that one is more objective than another is perhaps supportable, but it is not the point we wish to consider here.

Thus, the press, even when it deals with news, is veering toward fiction and toward pre-selected interests rather than toward anything that would be called the truth in science.

What, then, can the professional communicator do in circumstances such as I have been describing? How, indeed, does the journalist ever break out of the heavy chains of his own milieu? For myself I can now offer at least an objective appraisal of the Q-audiences at issue about all important national and international affairs. I can point out the good sense of a factor such as A, the defensiveness of D, the harsh agonism of B, the hatreds and fears of C and E. There is perhaps nothing new in these, as viewpoints. The objectivity of their definition, however, is another matter. In practice there is much the professional communicator could do about a viewpoint such as A's, just as there is much an advertiser can do when he is given the theme for a campaign. Normally, however, the journalist editor has only his own good sense to guide him. When there is a sound professional body of communicators, fed by research in the way advertising is supported, then the editor, too, will be able to penetrate myth and see things for what they are.

But he would still have to "play," as we must remind him. Studies, illustrated above for Khrushchev's visit to this country, can indicate what a newsreading public consists of in relation to any *XYZ* situation. The situation vis-à-vis Russia is obviously of great editorial significance, no less than of general political importance. If we look back at the factors of the Khrushchev study, the theoretical implications are quite clear. Factor B probably represented, in 1960 or so, the prevalent viewpoint of men in this country; the *New York Times* had been reinforcing it for thirty years, even at the highest elite level. Factor D is probably taking over now, in 1966, at the same level. But the feminine factor, A, is often neglected. Who cares about a woman's view? Yet it was that of an Eleanor Roosevelt, as it is today of a Pauline Frederick. Might not editors pay it more respect — not as truth, but as play which requires its own symbols, its own rules, its own imagery, its own alertness to the social character at issue?

13

The Army-McCarthy Hearings

The famous television broadcasts of the Army-McCarthy hearings in 1954 provide the next application of the theory. Robert Browning's masterpiece *The Ring and the Book* describes a murder as related by various witnesses. Each saw it differently. Anything one has to say about the Army-McCarthy hearings is likely to play the same trick upon us. The hearings were broadcast to vast and entranced audiences. For some the concern was with Communists in high places in the federal government; for others there was a trampling on civil liberties; others saw the Army taking revenge on a senator who had humiliated one of its members; and still others merely seemed to enjoy the spectacle of important people "nipping" at one another in public. All of these aspects of the hearings have some truth; but none is of interest to us until the hearings are looked at in play-theoretical terms.

The Army-McCarthy hearings were of course real events. Broadcast on television they could become instead drama, not merely in a manner of speaking but drama as *Oedipus Rex* is drama. It is this possibility at which we now look. What has to be explained about the hearings, it is suggested, is not due to their interest for any reasons concerned with real events but their *fascination*, stemming from subjective sources. The concern is with our tendency to re-create for ourselves an imaginary world of human beings which personify deeper wishes. The first English plays had such characters as Toil, Hunger, Poverty, Discord, Envy, and Deceit, strange creatures of fixed form which a peasant could abreact upon with excitement. McCarthy engendered such a fixed form: a man of Wrath — devouring imaginary Communists, joyless, sardonic — with whom thousands of relatively undeveloped people identified.

McCARTHYISM

McCarthyism was a political phenomenon of high significance in the early 1950's. For nearly five years McCarthy captured the headlines by making accusations about communism and Communists in high places in the government. The press, caught in the same fantasies, gave McCarthy top treatment; a story on McCarthy appeared nearly every day for these years, and almost anything he said got into every newspaper in the country. For McCarthy, any association with communism was branded as near treason. McCarthy's Permanent Investigating Subcommittee in the Senate was a Star Chamber in which Americans were "accused, judged and convicted" for crimes ready-made for them by its principal investigator. Yet as we look back now it is arguable, as de Antonio and Talbot (22) suggest, whether McCarthy in fact exposed a single Communist.

What has to be explained is more than the mere depth of public interest in McCarthy and his accusations. De Antonio suggests that the mood of the times carried McCarthy along. People were deeply suspicious about communism and were ready to believe him. Soviet espionage was undoubtedly active, and indeed effective, and it was said that communism had a place in the thinking of many an American. It was not treasonable, however, to be a Communist or to have been one in the past, although few thought of this. But it cannot be denied that the cold war, the icy conflict with the U.S.S.R., was of serious concern to Americans. Even so, this is not a sufficient explanation of why so many gave McCarthy such a strong place in their own feelings.

G. D. WIEBE'S STUDY

I am not about to argue the history-changing magnitude of the hearings but only their entertainment value, which I look at in terms of an important study, made shortly after the hearings had ended, by Wiebe, psychologist for the Columbia Broadcasting System. His study (165) of the hearings follows my own procedures up to a point: he undertook 46 open-ended interviews, 23 in Maine and 23 in Kansas, six weeks after the completion of the hearings. The respondents were asked (1) to think back to *before* the hearings, to say what they felt then about Senator McCarthy and his work; then (2) to say how they feel about it *now*. If a change in feeling was expressed, they were asked (3) what changed their views; and if their feelings were unchanged, they were asked (4), "As you look back to the hearings, what comes to your mind as the most outstanding or important thing that happened?"

Wiebe had hypothesized that the respondents would be concerned about the civil rights — that it is wrong to assume guilt until innocence is proved; that assuming guilt by association is wrong; that freedom of speech should not be encroached upon; that no one man should sit simultaneously as prosecutor, judge, and jury; and the like. He found to his surprise that respondents did not talk about such values, either directly or indirectly. As a second guess, Wiebe thought that perhaps many of the senator's followers would turn against him because he was attacking highly respected figures; again no rejection of the kind occurred. The data for the respondents were congruent with the results of a Gallup poll taken at the same time, showing that 36 per cent of the respondents still favored McCarthy after the hearings, compared with 38 per cent before the hearings — an insignificant shift. The beliefs at issue were apparently fixed and unchangeable.

Nonplussed, Wiebe put his data aside, and then returned to it two years later to examine the interviews without preconceptions for their "actual value themes." His analysis now indicated that all the respondents of course opposed communism. But there were also many value judgments interspersed through the material which indicated that respondents were thinking of McCarthy as a "lone hero." The most unexpected theme was that McCarthy was *right*; he was perceived as selfless, dedicated, sincere, courageous, sticking to his convictions, blameless, fighting alone against distractors, a David against an army of Goliaths. Wiebe concluded that the respondents were playing out their early super-ego formations, by reintrojecting (as they had done as children) the "lone hero" as a great father figure, powerful, feared, and yet to be respected.

That is, fantasy was at issue, not reality. The respondents were subjectively reliving the super-ego formations of their culture. They learn in childhood that it is "sinful to go against father," and "sinful also of others to pick on him"; it is wrong to be "weak," wrong to "waste time," wrong to "prattle, carry tales." Few children in our culture, Wiebe argued, are assumed to be innocent by their parents until proved guilty; few enjoy freedom of speech. Most children are punished for, or warned against, associating with others disapproved of by their parents. This is the complex that they introject and upon which super-ego formations are originally based. The reactions to the Army-McCarthy hearings were therefore played out, Wiebe concluded, in terms of these primitive formations.

The respondents did not perceive the hearings as a basis for coming to any decision or consensus about the Army and McCarthy, but "regarded the hearings as events requiring moral justification in terms of preconceived decisions" (165, p. 500).

Civil liberty calls for something quite different. Wiebe concluded that our society does not provide for introjection of freedom at an early age, with the consequence that perhaps only 5 per cent of the American public has any real sense of what encroachment on civil rights means as a threat to liberty.

One can see, therefore, in such terms why the hearings were drama; McCarthy conjured up an imaginary man of wrath, feared, but admired, in a half-world of joyless and archaic conscience.

Questions can be raised about the substantiality of the facts upon which Wiebe depended. I do not doubt the small sample or the interviewing. But one might wonder how far the data were mere trifles, mere hints dropped by one woman, a bit picked up from another, and really without much substance. When a woman says "it is wrong to lie," to "tell tales," to "pick on a person," are these not mere habits of speech, rather than indicators of deeply rooted belief? It is easy to object that Wiebe jumped too readily from such minor details to the deep super-ego formations he believed to be at issue.

APPLICATION OF Q-METHOD

Q-method can be applied to Wiebe's thesis to see how far his conclusions are substantiated.

In 1960, when I first looked at Wiebe's study, six years had elapsed since McCarthy had left the stage. Even so it seemed worthwhile to repeat his study with housewives; there were indications that many still firmly believed in McCarthy and, although the excitement had died down, results of interest were likely.

For my purpose a Q-sample was composed from statements gathered from preliminary interviews with housewives, to cover the following balanced design:

Effects	Levels				No.
A, Domain	(a) McCarthy's personality	(b) The hearings	(c) Civil liberties	(d) Archaic conscience	4
B, Valency	(e) Positive		(f) Negative		2

Levels *a, b,* and *d* were suggested by the content of the preliminary interviews following Wiebe. But as no woman had mentioned civil rights or responsibilities in the interviews, statements for *c* had to be invented.

I composed a sample ($n = 40$) for the above design; typical of its opinions are the following:

1. Events have proved that McCarthy was right.
2. The hearings were a waste of everyone's time.
3. It is a threat to our liberties to assume guilt by association.
4. It was wrong to put obstacles in his way.
5. He was a sick man, and should be forgiven — he tried his best.
6. He was attacking respected figures, such as General Marshall.
7. McCarthy didn't believe that it was wrong to require a man to testify against himself.
8. The fact that he was censured by the Senate probably broke his heart.
9. It is wrong to be "weak" in the face of the communistic penetration in high places.
10. Censuring by the Senate was too slight a punishment for all the cruel treatment he meted out to others.

With this Q-sample in hand I conducted interviews in Kansas, much as Wiebe had done six years earlier, for a P-sample of 2×2 design (age, above and below 30; and socio-economic level, blue-shirt and white-collar families, respectively). Wiebe had not indicated any differences for Maine compared with Kansas, and where archaic belief systems are at issue none is to be anticipated; it was sufficient, therefore, to interview women in Kansas.

The interview plan followed Wiebe's, adapted to suit the lapse of six years; at the conclusion of the open-ended interviewing, each housewife performed a Q-sort to represent her over-all views about the hearings.

The interviews contain a great deal of information relative to levels *a, b, d* (as had been the case for the preliminary interviewing), but again nothing about *c,* the matter of civil rights. Otherwise my own qualitative analysis suggested, contrary to Wiebe, that the women had some quite definite conclusions and a consensus. They were sympathetic to McCarthy's purpose to rid high places of Communists; many felt, however, that he had gone about it the wrong way. These same women felt that the hearings had discredited McCarthy (showing him as overambitious, publicity-seeking, even malicious and vicious), but had not weakened his case for vigilance about communism.

The Q-sample generated four factors, A, B, C, D, which can be given the following labels:

A. Women of good sense
B. Archaic thinkers
C. The self-righteous woman
D. The non-involved

Details about each are given below.

Factor A

Factor A cut across age and socio-economic differences, though larger P-sets would probably show a preponderance of white-collar housewives.

There was no mention of civil liberties in any of the interviews for these women (undertaken prior to the Q-sorting). All condemned McCarthy for his conduct at the hearings, but all agreed that McCarthy did some good in making people aware of the infiltration of communism in high places in the government. "Somebody had to get the communists out of the government"; "he *did* uncover some key communists"; "he was a worthy public servant because he made us aware of the enemy within"; "he did *some* good because he made people think of communism and its dangers" — and indeed "we ought to have more people like him to show up communists." Such are typical statements, spontaneously given in the course of interviewing these women of factor A.

All, however, were sure "he went too far," and none liked the way he behaved to witnesses at the hearings. He was seen as ambitious and ruthless — "he didn't care who he hurt"; "he got everyone against him"; his methods of questioning were unfair, "even dishonest, to discredit people." Many felt that though there might have been something in his probes before the hearings, after seeing him in action, "he was putting on a show" and everyone lost faith in him. Besides, some of his testimony "was fixed." The hearings, it was clear, had exposed McCarthy; some of the women were disgusted at the way he treated witnesses — "he badgered . . . intimidated them. . . . His attacks on them were vicious and malicious."

"I'd give him credit," one woman said, "for standing up to his convictions and being brave enough to stand up to people whether right or wrong." "Some people," said another, "said he was fearless and courageous, that he had the nerve to buck public opinion — but he was like most politicians, just out to make a name for himself." In almost all cases the women say that "he had a good idea," but "went about it the wrong way."

The Q-sort for this factor gives highest saliency, however, to statements mentioning civil liberties. Correspondingly, the archaic conscience statements are strongly denied.

Statements scoring positively attack McCarthy's personality, but other statements scoring as high accepted it as a fact that McCarthy made people in the country aware of the Communist danger.

At the negative end of the Q-sort, McCarthy is denied as being fearless, dedicated, sick, or a lonely figure.

Obviously, acceptance of civil liberty conceptions goes along with denial of the archaic conscience statements; there is denunciation of McCarthyism without denying, however, that communism was McCarthy's just target.

The factor is testimony to a certain forthrightness and involvement. How else could such a type react, except by recognizing "communist dangers" when it was *de rigeur* to do so? But they had judged McCarthy's conduct at the hearings for themselves and found it wanting; they were fully cognizant of the overriding importance of civil liberties, giving the key statements on these the highest scores of all. These, of course, are legalistic concepts (that it is a threat to liberties to assume guilt by association, to assume guilt until a man is proved innocent, and to act simultaneously as prosecutor, judge, and jury); it is asking too much to expect housewives to have such ideas in mind for everyday discourse. The Q-sample, however, puts the ideas into their heads, and then they deal with them very adequately. They recognize justice and liberty even though they have probably never talked about it before for themselves. Many of Wiebe's housewives in Maine and Kansas must have been such women of firmness and good sense; interviewing alone could never have elicited the saliency for them of civil liberty which the Q-sorting brings clearly to light.

FACTOR B

This factor also cuts across age and socio-economic level, from a poor Negro woman to a teacher with a B.S.E. degree. Typical of the factor is the former, who says during her interview that politics "is something I haven't paid much attention to as I should — government and such; being of a minority group, I have other problems to think of." She had seen some of the hearings sessions, her recollections continuing as follows:

> "It keeps sticking in my mind he was a Democrat."
>
> "But he passed on since, didn't he?"
>
> "He brought out things I never heard of before."
>
> "He paid attention to people's feelings — he appeared sincere."
>
> "He stood alone — wasn't given support by others; he should have been."
>
> "He had a fair procedure" (at the hearings).
>
> "I can't remember that he changed me much. I put most of my trust in the Lord. Most of my help comes from above."
>
> "He was prosecuting an Army dentist, and it seems to me they gave him promotion that wasn't earned. He had been associated with communists, but they never proved it."
>
> "Our leaders should be alarmed. . . . none of them says what he really stands for. McCarthy would say what he thought — I got that impression of him."

The factor supports Wiebe's thesis of the archaic character of the thinking of such individuals, and it is difficult to believe that college-educated women are of this kind. McCarthy was seen as a dedicated man, pursuing a good cause, making the country aware of the dangers of communism. He stuck to his convictions; he was attacking communism, not making a name or money for himself. Freedom of speech was freedom for McCarthy to speak his mind. All of these are given highest scores for positive saliency. Statements concerning civil rights are given slightly positive scores, but the indication is that the values attached to them were the reverse of those intended by us: the women feel that it was *right* to assume guilt until a man is proved innocent; it was *right* for McCarthy to act as prosecutor, judge, and jury all in one. Anything critical of McCarthy was attributed to sickness. That Eisenhower and others considered McCarthy had gone too far was, so to speak, "too bad." The cardinal fact for these women was that it was wrong to be weak in the face of communism. McCarthy's views were those, it was felt, of every thinking American; he found Communists; he had no failings. The women took very seriously any statement mentioning sin or doing wrong.

FACTOR C

McCarthy was seen by this type as sincere, but a fanatic. As one said, "I saw much in him that was objectionable, but felt he was fighting desperately for what he believed and would use anything to win." He was sincere in trying to find Communists in high places. But he was also all out for the limelight; he had a perfect formula, one said, for getting the headlines. Contrasted with McCarthy's cruelty was the dignity of Lawyer Welch, who "upgraded the entire affair and kept it from being a cheap show of sensationalism." The censure was seen as hurting McCarthy; the "trial" ruined him.

The scores given to statements on civil liberties showed little or no educated awareness of the significance of these concepts. Human drama was at issue, not civil rights. They could identify with the dignity of Welch, but they more than half-admired McCarthy. One feels that they had indeed admired him in the past; it was wrong to put obstacles in his way; the hearings were a waste of time; he was clever. But reason also said he was cruel, aroused suspicion, and disrespected the law and dignity of the Senate. Anything in the way of fantasy about a lonely hero is thus deeply hidden or rejected, and the statements concerned indeed attest to this — they are given lowest scores (highest negative) as though in over-denial for the earlier beliefs of these self-righteous women, beliefs which we can guess are still there, hidden by overcompensation.

Factor D

This, for middle-class housewives at ease with their world, mothers who are bent on smiling, is a factor cutting across age. They were little involved, really, in the McCarthy situation and still take an unemotional, somewhat detached view of it. Little was remembered of the hearings, except that "there was a young man, a private in the Army and all the benefits he had received through Senator McCarthy. . . . He had all privileges, was allowed out on passes, had his hotel bills paid. . . . The whole thing was in the news all over, and all the accusing. . . . The Senator was accusing many people in the Army of being communists. . . . The Senator would give information on them to the reporters."

The factor agrees that McCarthy made the country aware of the Communist danger, but he wanted to be in the limelight. He stuck to his convictions, was fearless, a dedicated and determined man, and clever, pursuing a good cause; but if there was Communist penetration it could have been dealt with in other ways.

But he was not unscrupulous or cruel; nor was he a threat to our liberties. He found some Communists. He was not dishonest, nor yet a great man, nor sick. Nor did he really disrespect the law and the dignity of the Senate.

The civil liberties statements showed judgment against McCarthy, but they saw nothing in McCarthyism that was a threat to our liberties. McCarthy, in short, had his good points but was a troublemaker, trying to get his name into the limelight; no doubt the Army needed "cleaning up," but it could have been done "in a much quieter way."

There is indifference; the attitude is therefore unemotional. It shows, however, at least some awareness of civil liberties in the Q-sort which did not appear in the interviews. In some respects the type is like A, but is benign, warm to everyone, even to McCarthy.

DISCUSSION

These findings make good sense, and are clearly substantial. Everyone agreed that communism was a threat and everyone remembered the hearings.

Some were disturbed at McCarthy's methods (A), whereas others took them more calmly (D); both of these factors had an awareness of civil liberties, which Wiebe missed. There is a difference, of course, between what people are able to recall spontaneously in interviews and what they can remember if they are given a reminder about it; the Q-sample provided such a reminder. Wiebe's conclusion that only 5 per cent of the adult population was likely to have internalized the softer values about civil rights and responsibilities therefore is considerably in error. Our own estimate would be that many more have the softer introjections. They do not talk freely about these liberties, but there is an awareness of them nonetheless.

Factors B and C are in line, however, with Wiebe's main thesis. These, especially B, have the harsher super-ego values, which see Wrath moving on the stage as a "lonely hero," fearless, with everyone else against him. Reason, in the case of C, pours doubt upon this; but feeling is another matter, and C is not far away from the kind of personalization that characterizes B's view of McCarthy. Not only are civil rights not internalized, their very opposites are introjected, as factor B indicated.

EXPLANATON OF THE FASCINATION AS SUBJECTIVE PLAY

We can only guess what went on in the minds of these viewers. But there is now a typology to be speculative about; we can look at matters in play-theory terms.

Hamlet, acted on a stage, is a play; every manner of expert, from Plato and Aristotle to Freud, has offered an explanation of the fascination of such plays. Most, following Aristotle, consider tragedies and poetry to be "more philosophical and serious" (79) than the real history of persons and events. If we want to regard the hearings as drama, it must be reasonable to suppose that what was involved was subjective, rather than anything in the "reality" of the situation. That is, if the real events offer no satisfactory explanation of the admitted fascination that the hearings had for the women, we are left in a stronger position to accept an explanation in terms of feelings "more philosophical and serious" than meet the eye.

Consider then, factor A, who saw McCarthy fighting fearlessly for a good cause, but going about it the wrong way. The real event at issue, for these women, was whatever was true about Communist infiltration; somehow any theory that concern about this was "deeply philosophical" for these women does not ring true. Similarly for factor D: they were little involved in the situation, and could not even be indignant about McCarthyism. It is unlikely that they were avid viewers of the hearings; but if they were, it is again hard to believe that any real events, other than the humanity of Welch and the villainy of McCarthy, could have spurred their viewing interest.

For type B the real events scarcely mattered at all — "Politics," as our Negro woman said, "is something I haven't paid much attention to." Instead, a man was seen who spoke the truth, as the gospel speaks it, and was sincere, considerate of others, who stood alone, with everyone against him, who stood up fearlessly for his principles. Type C, at heart, felt this way, too.

It is simple enough to suppose that each type, viewing the hearings, lives out his own emotions. For type B it is a precept for morality — to speak the truth fearlessly, even if everyone is against you. This is philosophical and sincere enough. For types A, B, and D there was an arousal of inner conflict, it would seem, of a right way to do things as against a wrong way; but it is hard to think that this explains the fascination for these types.

Real life is no doubt drab for most people, and it is only reasonable to suppose that fantasy reached out into more exciting possibilities. One doubts whether a single viewer of the hearings, however, felt that she was indulging in such fantasy. All, on the other hand, could have attested to a certain similarity of interest common to everyone; everybody had some interest in the events, and many had deep involvement. But this is only consequential upon the hearings, and it is nothing to which the fascination with the hearings can be attributed. Also, if one believes that the events altered history, as de Antonio and Talbot (22) do, none of our housewives was cognizant of it.

Whatever possible explanation is sought, nothing applies except that pertaining to factor B. For these women a conscious assertion of morality is obvious, of a primitive, serious, truly "philosophical" kind. How ironical that moral values should fasten upon base real events! For types A, C, and D we are forced to conclude that unconscious influences were at work. There is, as Hemingway would have agreed, a certain "tragic beauty" (79) in bullfights. *Hamlet* and all the great tragedies influence us, the psychoanalysts say, because the Oedipus complex is their main theme and content. There can be no doubt either that the death of an *Urvater* (149) arouses primitive feelings in us all, producing great art as well as outpourings of profound pity, remorse, and deeper feelings. Bartlett (6) describes how primitive comradeship, under conditions of stress, can arouse feelings of which few could have felt themselves capable. Great art has followed the death of primitive father figures throughout history, from the days of the Roman *Saturnalia* to recent requiems. Leonard Bernstein's *Kaddish*, though not necessarily great music, is an example of the impulse to re-create the depths of feeling and sense of tragic loss at the death of John F. Kennedy. Can there by any doubt about the primitive feeling aroused the wide world over at the death of the President? Can it be explained in any better way than as an unconscious *Urvater* phenomenon? And in explaining it this way, does it not ennoble the impulse? The tragedy grasps for us a feeling more philosophical and serious than any real events could mediate.

So it is with attendance at a play. The play re-creates at best something with which we are familiar in a primitive sense. We sit before the stage, as the housewives probably sat at moments before the television screen, with a sense of magical re-creation, an experience or feeling evocative of deeper moralities.

The Army-McCarthy hearings, insofar as they interested people, did so no doubt for many reasons besides the one to which I here draw attention. Undoubtedly some viewers got vicarious pleasure at seeing important people discomfited and humiliated; some were alarmed at McCarthy's incursions into civil freedoms; others were engrossed in the unfolding human interest stories; others had no real involvement in the hearings as such. But in addition to any such, and supra-ordinate to them, was a degree of fascination with the hearings and a corresponding blindness to reality that few could see for themselves. For type B it was all the reality they knew. For the others the same explanation accounts for the fascination. The magic was Wrath, pounding out points of order on the stage, re-created everyday, and reintrojected as in every archaic and primitive experience. A play on a stage has the same magical introjecting significance for a person as playing house has for a child; the hearings were drama, serious and philosophical, for millions who were unaware of it. And all, in our opinion, were the better for it and remain so six years later.

14

Study of Wants and Needs

The empirical work of this book continues here with one study in the field of advertising (wants) and another in the area of public opinion (needs). The former is in the province of convergent selectivity and the other is a matter of social controls. The play elements are clear. A beginning is made with convergent selectivity.

A Study of Utility Images

Utility images have been described in detail elsewhere (143). It is generally felt that utility companies have a poor image across the country — women do not think highly of them. What, then, might advertising do to remedy matters, to give the utilities a better image?

We begin with housewives, who are likely to have various feelings, ideas, prejudices, and so on concerning utilities and the respective merits of gas and electricity for cooking, heating, and other uses. They have had experiences with appliances and service, and no doubt have seen many advertisements, billboards, and the like about appliances and utilities. Interviews with housewives provided material for a Q-sample, typical statements from which are as follows:

1. There should be competition in public utilities so that prices would be cheaper to the consumer.
2. I pay my utility bills just like the next guy, but other than that, I hardly ever think about it.
3. Cost is the most important thing to me. I would rather pay a little less and get less service.

4. The utilities concentrate on supplying new areas before taking care of the older ones.
5. Peak loads really aren't anybody's fault. You just have to live with them.
6. Some people fail to take into account that utilities have expenses, too, just like any other business.
7. The adequacy of the supply is the most important thing to me.

The Q-factor model for this Q-sample shows two factors, F_1 and F_2, which were interpreted as follows:

> F_1 represents women who express friendly feelings (have a positive regard) for utilities as corporations; they expect good service, and are prepared to pay for it. They are interested enough to want to learn more about utilities, by visits to plants, by hearing more about what happens to utility finances, and so on. They also favor advertising undertaken by utilities.
>
> F_2 represents women who are not negative so much as apparently indifferent to utilities — they couldn't, as they say, care less; they don't care who owns them, as long as they get good service. But advertising is strongly resisted, far more evocatively and emotionally than seems warranted by the expressions, otherwise, of indifference to utilities. One therefore suspects their assumed indifference.

The "market" is segmented, from a motivational standpoint, into housewives not only with a positive attitude about utility companies but with an urgency to learn more about their functions and possibilities, and into others whose apparent indifference to utilities masks a great deal of negative feelings, probably of a vicarious nature.

What, then, of the images? F_1 suggests a friendliness to utilities in a corporate sense, with little that is personal to themselves as housewives. F_2 suggests an image of good service to the housewife, and indifference to utilities in a corporate sense. The self is vicariously involved in F_1, and more genuine to the situation in F_2. F_1 is supported by the individual's own good will; F_2 depends only on services provided or expected. F_1 women, being self-important, want to feel about utilities with business or economic imagery; F_2 housewives, being self-sufficient, want to do so with service imagery.

There is nothing in the factors indicative of a negative image about utilities, such as the industry was concerned about. Rather, there is a favorable sort of *economic man* acceptance of the industry among F_1 women, and, implicitly, acceptance of service as its real purpose among

F_2 women. The latter are not precluded from F_1, however; it is simply not given the housewifely significance that it might have.

Up to this point I have said little about the Y of the XYZ situations under study. The involvement of "social mechanisms" (Y) in Q-samples comes about by their homologous representation, using slogans, advertising themes, artwork, or the like as Q-sample material. A Q-sample drawn from advertising themes for the utilities would contain, for example, items of the following kind:

> Miracles of Modern Gas.
> Serve better meals for less.
> Weather hot or cold, it's springtime indoors.
> Saving you money is my job — use gas.
> The *lightest* bill your postman carries!
> No woman wants to stay home on the Range.
> Every bit you buy burns.
> For service beyond the mains.
> Make every meal a masterpiece.
> All your dreams come true the electric way.

Such themes have been "worked over," perhaps for months, in the copy-writing departments of advertising agencies; all suggest facilitating mechanisms and benefits. They are better than housewives can conjure up for themselves in interviews; yet they could represent the ideas or feelings they would like to have expressed, had they the expressive gifts commensurate with their feelings. Thus, a suitable Q-sample of advertising copy themes for a particular XYZ complex can be strongly expressive of motives, fancies, and wishes. Four-color artwork of modern magazine ads and stills from colored or black-and-white commercials, or from movies, are also useful for Q-samples.

From a Q-sample composed of copy themes, along with that already studied and from which factors F_1 and F_2 emerged, I was able to decide what a suitable theme for national promotion of utility companies could be. There is first the problem of expanding an already receptive friendliness toward utilities as corporations for a large segment of the public, represented by factor F_1. The other problem is to alleviate matters vis-à-vis F_2, who are violently opposed to advertising but unconcerned about utilities. The utility industries could with reason, perhaps, ask the advertising profession to put its own public image in order. But that would still leave unsolved the total lack of an image about utilities as corporations for a segment of the public, represented by F_2. The problem thus becomes one of providing a newborn image for F_2 which is compatible with some enrichment or development of the friendliness of F_1. We observe, however, that F_2 is friendly to any idea of service.

What our study recommended, therefore, was a central theme of the friendliness and neighborliness of utility companies. The image to project, I suggested, was that of a friendly neighbor, experienced, willing to help out, willing to teach anyone else what she knows — not merely in serving you, but in being your neighbor, always ready for a chat, always available to help when needed. One does not promote material gains, price, benefits, savings, bringing out the beauty of your home, "new life for tired kitchens," trading-up, making every meal a masterpiece, the "miracles of modern gas," "meeting tomorrow's needs today," or anything of the kind. The image has to be of a universal, broad nature, such as this of neighborliness.

We need go no further in this direction, except to note that the utilities have not, as yet, projected such an image. But we see again how themes evolve from the methodology.

IMAGERY FOR PUBLIC MEDICINE

The other example comes from a study within the purview of public opinion (141). It began by asking what is the image people have of public medicine and public health services, but it ended by considering an ethical question about the public good; that is, what is good for the public. We have public education, public libraries, public health services, but no public medicine. Yet it seems a good thing to use public funds to help build hospitals, to care for the needy, to solve the problems of polio, cancer, and the like — for *our* good, even if we suffer from none of these afflictions. It seems good that the state should help the unemployed and the small farmers, but of course also good that federal subsidies should maintain the railroads, airlines, highways, hospitals, and many large businesses. It is good for everyone to accept some regulation in the sale of drugs, the purity and control of water supplies, sanitation, banks, use of roads, utilities, and commerce. Behind all of this outpouring of good will there must lie, of course, an economic system — in the United States a system of stupendous wealth. In poor countries the needs may be the same, but the means are not available for their sustenance.

It is of interest to study the XYZ situation as a matter of public opinion. This results in the discovery of attitudes about public health and medicine which require explanation in terms of deeper belief systems, such as underlie all our values. But we shall have to try to influence people, nevertheless, and shall try to do so as a matter of convergent selectivity by bypassing the values and beliefs so brought to light. Unless we know what the latter are, we do not know what to stay away from in our search for key themes, slogans, or imagery.

That advertising "works" in the medical area is obvious. It does very well for the patent medicine industry. Upwards of 40 per cent of an urban population may habitually take vitamin pills, tonics, tranquilizers, and the like without a medical prescription, testifying to the effects of mass communication perhaps more than to any sound diffusion of medical knowledge.

How, then, are we to study communication in this area of concern? The medical profession itself is interested in its store of information (I); the retrieval of this from its vast libraries (L) or comparable sources is vital to it; transmission to physicians (P), individually and from one to another, is of crucial importance; its flow to the sick (S) and those who care for them — nurses, attendants, families, and others — is no less important; and its movement, as well, down into the minds and actions of the general public (A) — all of this complex information system is at issue. We call it ILPSA, the ongoing information system, schematically considered. Computers are busy in the I and L components; special librarians and medical writers are busy too at various parts of the system; and medical teachers are everywhere within it. The complexities of such an information system are attested to in Orr's (97) symposium report.

Our concern here is in none of this, but in what the persons affected feel about it all — considered as matters of opinion. The ongoing information system (ILPSA) should be concerned with scientifically proved fact. We shall look instead into the opinions (O), attitudes of mind (M), and inner beliefs (B) — the OMB — of everyone involved in the ILPSA information system. The OMB is what motivates the ILPSA system, serving not only to give it its values but also its headaches in the form of resistances, frictions, and controversial issues. OMB is where the "noise" is, as well as the driving force of the information system as a whole. Thus, the controversy about socialized medicine is a matter of opinion, reaching into deep beliefs.

I have used two Q-samples. One was based on interviews with members of the general public gathered in the usual way. The other was taken from a set of lectures by Dr. Alan Gregg (41), entitled *Challenges to Contemporary Medicine*. I frequently abstract a book in this way to study a man's ideas about an *XYZ* situation. Dr. Gregg was a notable medical educator, a man who idealized medicine hoping one day to see it as Great Medicine, where doctors would be housed in efficient hospitals, dispensing the best possible medical care to everyone. He was an early advocate of prepayment medical plans, which his profession so strongly resisted. I argued that Dr. Gregg could speak with authority on the matters at issue, and that his views could be used to validate any empirical views of the lay and medical publics, against his, Dr. Gregg's, considered judgment.

One can understand the tenor of the Q-sample taken from Dr. Gregg's work by the following few statements from it:

1. In medicine, the poor get the leavings — they don't get the very best of treatment.
2. Specialization in the medical profession has run wild; it used to be doctor-nurse-orderly. . . . Now there are scores of specialists, and one never sees a general doctor any more.
3. The cost of medical care is increasing beyond all reason.
4. Fortunately, some of us have enjoyed good health all our lives.
5. Disease is a matter of chance — you can do little about it.
6. Modern man can have life more abundantly by making full use of modern medical science.
7. Our health insurance plans are too timid; the time has come for us all to pay more for future services.

The Q-model provided five factors, A to E, to which I added a Q-sort to represent Dr. Gregg's viewpoint; if Dr. Gregg had been alive he could scarcely have done other than give this Q-sort (F). The factors can be referred to briefly as follows:

A. Bitter-enders
B. Friends of the medical profession
C. Foreigners
D. Well-to-do liberals
E. Housewives
F. Dr. Alan Gregg's viewpoint

As one should expect, B and F correlate (0.50); otherwise, the factors are uncorrelated. P-samples show that A individuals tend to be from lower-income and rural groups; that B includes doctors, nurses, and people friendly to the medical profession; that C is for people from English-speaking countries (England, Australia, Canada, India); that D are upper-middle-class, well-to-do persons of a liberal turn of mind; and that E are housewives, who come more intimately into contact with public health services and home nursing because of the needs of their children.

The factors represent different attitudes about the *XYZ* situation. Since none correlates with any other, none of the Americans has a viewpoint corresponding to "socialized medicine" (which is what factor C believes in). D is friendly to *public* medicine for the poor and aged, believing that the country is wealthy enough to afford it.

None of the factors (except B and C) had as salient motives concerning medicine as they had for food, clothing, housing, employment, education, and the like, concerns of one's daily living. The public (whether A, D, or E) does not conceive of medical matters, including medical expenses, as on the same level of commitment or expectancy as they do food, clothes, education, a job, and so on.

But when chronically ill persons are Q-sorted the situation is very different. A different set of factors emerges, which we designate I, II, III. By chronicity we mean polio victims, heart cases, cancer patients, the aged, and the indigent, all of whom know out of their own, often dire, experience what it is to suffer, to be deprived and incapacitated. All accept socialized medicine, or any help that can be given to them. Yet factor I proclaims his or her independence; they would indeed like to be able to pay their own bills — only the threat of being ruined makes them willing to accept public help freely. Factor II accepts help, too, but out of a sense of the interdependence of people — that all should help one another. Factor III is chiefly for the poor, the indigent, and they are highly dependent — where else could they get help, they cry, if not from the state or federal sources?

We have several different attitudes, then, but A, B, E, and I are subserved by the same beliefs, briefly indicated by the term "independence" — a rugged independence and self-sufficiency with little regard for anyone else. These are all strongly opposed to socialized medicine, except I (who is so in principle but not in practice). Attitudes D and II are subserved by a softer, nicer super-ego structure of the kind that characterizes a liberal-humanitarian, who sees that people are interdependent and that government involvement in modern complex societies is not only inevitable, but good. These accept a measure of "socialized medicine," II completely so in the form of *public* medicine. Factors C and III are dependent at bottom, though much of C will veer no doubt toward D and II as well. The poor and insecure, individually or nationally, are glad for any help they can get from any source.

This, all too briefly, gives some of our results for studies of the OMB for medicine and public health. They suggest causes other than any deriving from the ongoing information systems concerning public health and medicine (ILPSA). Instead, nonscience *values* are everywhere dominant. The self in no way obtrudes; rather there are deeply internalized beliefs, structures of the kind dealt with in ego-psychology — such as we have discussed in more detail in chapter 13 with Wiebe's study of the Army-McCarthy hearings.

What should be emphasized, also, is the low level of motivation about medical matters for the lay public compared with its daily drives for food, clothing, work and so on — all of which are booming in the American affluent and achieving society. There is a demand for the latter, but little for medicine except, of course, among the sick. One should recognize what is happening in this connection (for food, clothing, and the like) under the influence of advertising. The influence is not merely on the growing economy but also on values, which are allowing people to enjoy what they can now so readily buy (107). That the public has ideas about public health and medicine is clear, but A, C, D, and E are scarcely well informed about the matters and A, C, and D are less than friendly to the medical profession. The public has by no means internalized important beliefs which permit it to accept wide measures of public medicine, even preventative and creative medicine; it scarcely realizes that chronic illness is a family catastrophe in the same degree that floods, earthquakes, and hurricanes are community disasters. There is nothing emotive to support these concepts. Thus the indigent are not seen as sick social creatures but as weak-willed. It is very easy to motivate women to slim for advertised beauty but it is not so easily accomplished for health reasons. Millions smoke cigarettes, in spite of cancer. Only the chronically ill know what it is to be motivated in medical and health matters.

We shall now return to consider mass communication in connection with the above. Any head-on promotion of a controversial matter has little ultimate effect (63), serving largely to reinforce existing beliefs. From the data provided in my studies, however, I found one or two statements in the Q-samples which were acceptable to all the attitudes A, B, C, D, E, I, II, and III — they were (*a*) the idea of a family doctor, a person deeply revered by all alike — even by B, and (*b*) the idea that doctors and nurses in this country are well trained professionally (though little interested in you as a person). Now family doctors, as visiting doctors, are a thing of the past; doctors expect you to go to their hospitals or private clinics for treatment. Visiting nurses, however, are likely to become increasingly important for medical care. The thought at once occurs to one, therefore, that modern medicine might do worse than to promote, as a key theme, the idea that the modern nurse serves you as "your family nurse," who is "sent to you from your family doctor," or who is "like a family doctor." The concept has reference to a visiting nurse who acts as communicator between doctor and patient, who is able to recognize symptoms, who can encourage early medical attention in the family, who can teach sound care and health practices in the home, and so on.

Now, therefore, we have reached over from deeper needs to noncontroversial images. One could build up an image of the visiting nurse as a modern Florence Nightingale. The popular idea is that she was a saintly woman, whose devotion to troops in the Crimean War established the nursing profession. Florence Nightingale was in fact a brilliant, temperamental, energetic woman, and elegant, witty, fascinating, and much else — if we are to judge by Woodham-Smith (168). The advertiser could do well by her, as could the medical profession, to provide a new image of a new Lady of the Lamp — an electric lamp and a lady in white nylon, who is technically highly proficient, elegant, and quite a woman.

Again, however, the prescription is for *all* communication from the profession to the public; as for Chrysler's famous theme, so here too, the concern is with a prescription for continuity of purpose — in this case to focus attention on nursing as of high significance for the public good, and, through that, to public medicine generally, to influence people as a matter of convergent selectivity, so bypassing the internalized ego-structures which support the quarrels and ideological struggles with which the topic of public medicine has been plagued.

15

Play Theory of
Mass Communication
Broadly Considered

Finally, I turn back to repeat some opening thoughts and to add what seems necessary to complete my theory.

We have throughout been occupied with basic methodological matters. An examination of Stouffer's work (150) gave us an opportunity to be critical (in chapter 2) of the hypothetico-deductive method when it is used to explain empirical data without regard to alternative theories. We might remember here some remarks of Popper (106), from *The Logic of Scientific Discovery*:

> I now feel that I should have emphasized in this place a view which can be found elsewhere in the book. . . . I mean the view that observations, and even more so observation statements and statements of experimental results, are always *interpretations* of the facts observed; that they are interpretations in the light of theories. This is one of the main reasons why it is always deceptively easy to find verifications of a theory, and why we have to adopt a highly critical attitude towards our theories if we do not wish to argue in circles [p. 107].

It is indeed deceptively easy to verify a theory, as Stouffer did, with as large a sample as anyone could wish. I adopt the less formal abductive basis for my work, though the methodology is sophisticated and precise.

Anyone with an eye to systematic science will wonder about our typological conceptions. I have in fact shown elsewhere that Q represents Weber's methodology and takes it much further along scientific lines (140). The concern in Weber's day was with *verstehen* (understanding), and there are social thinkers today (e.g., von Hayek, 158) who maintain that an unbridgeable gulf separates physical from social sciences in this respect. The methods of natural science are external and analytic. Those of social science — in the *verstehen* tradition — are understood by "reliving" in one's own experience whatever is under study until one grasps its significance. Social and historical scholars therefore have direct, immediate, subjective contact with their subject matter, whereas in the natural sciences instrumentation mediates between the scientist's thinking and the objects of his study.

My proposal is that Q-sorts represent understandings in social or historical study. Hempel (47) observes that sociologists who have discussed "ideal" typology (from Weber [163] to Merton [89] or Sorokin [134]), have been involved in logic-of-science respects merely with properties of classes, a matter of archaic Aristotelian logic. They have never reached a developed methodology in which relations between types and quantitative assessments are at the heart of matters. Hempel indicated what he thought would be necessary for typology in the social sciences to merit scientific consideration; he distinguished three forms of types, namely, *classes, extremes,* and *abstract models.* I *model* a person's understanding as a Q-sort; classes are reached, but from operations and not from any a priori definition of types. Extremes are involved, but only as the Q-sorts of highest factor loadings for a class and therefore, in principle, epitomizing a class to the degree of the observed loadings. What is categorical in Hempel's logic is operational in Q-method. This is not to say that I recommend to sociologists that they proceed, like Weber, to cogitate and to adumbrate "ideal" types; in such a case each social scientist would merely be Q-sorting himself to grasp the essences of things. It is surely more important to begin with the understandings of everyone and in this way to grasp a genuine typology for situations. This is what Q-methodology achieves. When we ask a person to represent his attitude of mind as a Q-sort, genuine understandings are at issue, measured for the first time in social science.

FORMAL STATEMENT OF THE THEORY

This methodology applies to the theory of play in mass communication. Up to this point, I have not given a formal statement of the theory in terms of its axioms, definitions, postulates, and theorems, because doing so suggests a logic-tight system when nothing of the kind is true. But it is useful to have such a statement available for review purposes, and this is provided below under the headings of Principles, Postulates, and Pragmatics.

PRINCIPLES

1. The subjective standpoint is axiomatic in my theory. The concept of *self*, of apperception, and all else indicative of an active mind is taken for granted.

2. Two matters of definition follow from this: they concern self-referent statements and attitudes of mind. Self-referent statements are synthetic propositions and are the "bits" of our science. Attitudes of mind are modes of subjective behavior. (It is not difficult to show how far a person's attitude of mind corresponds to overt behavior relevant to it — a matter for pragmatics.)

3. The postulates of the theory concern culture, social control, convergent selectivity, play, work, communication-pain, communication-pleasure, primitive communication, beliefs, and so on.

None of these is axiomatic. The postulates are not analytic propositions, capable of precise definition. All instead are synthetic complexes with excess meaning. Theorems or hypotheses cannot be derived from them in any logical manner.

4. The current fashion in social science is to test deductions which have been previously derived from analytic postulates. In that case operations serve merely to test hypotheses. I require operations to do much more; they must derive hypotheses for us *de novo*.

The pragmatics for this involve a complicated metatheory of factors, with Q-sorts, Q-samples, P-samples, Q-audience segmentation, Q-factor models, and so on, in due place.

(The Stouffer study was used in chapter 2 to illustrate the above principles. Stouffer used polling to test certain deductions from an analytic postulatory set. I used factors, instead, to reach new hypotheses.)

POSTULATES

The reminder is given (see principle 3) that our postulates are not subject to precise analytic definition. The following provide the basic meanings in our play theory of mass communication.

1. Play is distinguishable from work.

Play is disinterested, self-sufficient, an interlude from work. It brings no material gain. (Prizes are for show; amateurs play for fun, professionals for money.)

Work is not disinterested, is not an interlude in the day for most people. It produces goods, services or ideas, etc., by application of effort for a purpose.

2. Much work and play is subject to *social control*, and some, instead, is a matter of *convergent selectivity*.

Social control is the way in which cultures function from the standpoint of involuntary, categorical imperatives. (It is said that everyone must work, that idleness is sinful, that work is a duty and one's salvation, and so on.) Social control induces conformity, consensus, and established custom or is an outcome of such cultural conditions.

Convergent selectivity is relative freedom from social control, tending toward individuality of choice in behavior. The behavior is more voluntary. Convergencies may be chaotic, as in a gold rush; or they may be ecstatic, as in mountain-climbing. All are directed toward individuality and self-existence.

3. Work and play which are subject to social control are supported by inner *belief systems*, that is, latent or inner beliefs of individuals, formed by childish introjections and early internalizations in primary group (home) situations. One's religious, political, economic, and other important values and beliefs are fixed early in life and are thereafter largely immutable.

Conditions of convergent selectivity are of a more superficial nature and concern fads, manners, fashions, taste, and the like. Moral and ethical sanctions are largely bypassed; no *issues* are involved, no deep controversies, but only more or less acceptable differences in taste or minor matters of opinion.

4. Public opinion is subject to social control; advertising, drama, art, and so on involve convergent selectivity.

5. The self is differently involved in conditions of social control and convergent selectivity.

I distinguish *self* from *ego*. The former is overtly attitudinal, and the latter a matter of mental structure.

Self-attitudes are developed largely in interactions under social control. (The boy who wins a prize at school adds to his self-stature thereby, and almost all that we are in selfhood respects is given to us in relation to social controls.) But the self so put upon us is to a degree false — a façade only. The person has to be what custom or status demands of him.

Convergent selectivity is an opportunity for the individual to exist for himself. Such existence is experienced as enjoyment, contentment, serenity, or the like. Certain free aspects of self are possible outcomes of convergent play.

The mass media, plays, art, and the theater generally offer opportunities for convergent selectivity. The self so involved is enhanced. There is an increase of self-awareness — typical, for example, of the mountain climber. There is no gain in social or material respects but much gain in one's self-existence.

6. Characteristic of work (and socially controlled play) is *communication-pain*; convergent selectivity is qualified instead by *communication-pleasure*.

These are concepts, though in many cases actual pain and enjoyment may be overtly experienced by the person or observed in him by an onlooker.

Communication-pain is a command for work and action, for effort and production; education, the development of skills, and so on all may entail hard work and are subject to communication-pain. In attendance upon communication-pain there is always a certain negation of self-existence.

Communication-pleasure is enjoyment, contentment, serenity, delight, such as is characteristic of entertainment, art, drama, conversation, sociability, and the like. In attendance upon it is a certain enhancement of self-existence.

7. Ordinary life would be impossible without *communication*, in school, church, business, on the farm, and so on. "The act of communication is part of the living function of society" (126, p. 35). It is important, however, to distinguish between that part of communication supporting social control and that part of it offering opportunities to convergent selectivity.

The former relates to all social institutions, such as school, home, church, law court, regiment, factory, farm. Convergency is evident in mass communication and in much of art, drama, and literature. Communication in conditions of social control is a "mover" in national and individual development: it informs a nation of its work, its five-year plans; it teaches literacy and technology; it develops industry and extends markets. Further, it is involved in all urbanization, industrialization, and educational growth.

Mass communication, literature, drama, and the like serve instead for sociability and self-existence. These are vehicles for communication-pleasure — directly in the enjoyment they enjoin, and indirectly in the social conversations they support.

8. Convergent communication, being communication-pleasure, serves mainly as a "fill" in mass communication. The "important" communication concerns social control matters. The "fill" serves to maintain status quo positions, since it serves no "work" purposes. It pleases, entertains, and projects fashions and fads. It is basically aesthetical, and amoral, a-ethical. Its function is not to relieve anxieties but to increase the sum total of self-existing possibilities.

(The "human interest slant" given to popular "news" puts the reader in the position of a confidant, reflecting inner-experience, inducing reverie about himself and so on — all pointed toward more *existence* for oneself.)

9. Culture develops in play, and play enters into social control and convergent selectivity situations alike.

But the play in religious practices, the armed forces, the law courts, in diplomacy, professional practices, is always more or less subject to internalized belief systems; deeply held values, loyalties, needs, and ethical matters are everywhere evident.

The play in convergent selective situations is at best indifferent to such values, needs, and beliefs.

10. There are correspondences between *social character* and social control and convergency. Traditional and inner-directed forms of social character, such as Riesman (116) describes, are formed in relation to social controls. Other-direction, instead, is fashioned more by convergent selectivity; it is characterized by communication-pleasure.

11. The mass media, in much that pertains to social control as well as convergent selectivity, I do not communicate truth or reality but only a semblance of it — of a fictional, representational, or charismatic character. Reaching the truth is a matter for science, technology, reason, and *work*. Charisma, imagery, and fiction are characteristic of convergencies.

But this is not to be despised. On the contrary, reality is so complex that its symbolical representation is essential to give it meanings that ordinary people can appreciate. Politics is conversation about freedom, democracy, liberty, fundamental rights, and the like — issues which need bear little relation to ongoing real conditions or legislative actions. But all these can be good fun, that is, good communication-pleasure.

12. Most important in the above connection is the use of significant symbols, charismatic leadership, and expressions of national character. These have been regarded as suppressive, as means whereby an elite

maintains its power over the masses. I look at them, instead, as conditions under which people can find enjoyment in sociable conversations and communication-pleasure.

13. Fantasy is not mainly escapist, substitutive, wishful, neurotic, or the like. It can be genuine communication-pleasure, a matter quite overlooked by inner-directed Freud. (I have not so far considered this postulate, but do so on pages 200–202 below.)

14. The concept of *primitive communication* is important as being nearer to communication-pleasure in its symbolical representations.

The above postulates are what Stouffer might have called "preliminary speculations." They serve not merely to explain facts, however, but to tell the investigator what to look for.

It remains to say what is empirical in the theory, and the following points are important.

PRAGMATICS

1. Areas of study are defined as XYZ interactions where X is the person, Y the mediating social or other facilitating mechanisms, and Z the communication.

2. *Opinion*, *attitude*, and *belief* are operationally defined as concerned principally with conditions of social control.

This is the domain of *public opinion*, for which I have provided a new basis of measurement (138).

Opinions are self-referent statements put into Q-statement form. Attitudes are aggregates of such opinions, modeled by Q-sorts. Factors are proof that such attitudes are to that degree held in common by different persons, that is, evidence that consistent attitudes of mind are at issue. Attitudes so conceived are not constructs to account for consistencies in behavior, but are merely models of subjective states of mind.

Q-factors are explained in terms of belief systems. Needs, with ethical and moral constraints behind them, are strongly in evidence in any interpretation of factors deriving from socially controlled conditions.

3. *Notions*, *wants*, and *images* are defined as primarily involved in conditions of convergent selectivity.

Notions, like opinions, are self-referent statements put into Q-statement form. Wants and images are aggregates of such notions, modeled by Q-sorts. Factors are proof of common wants and images.

4. Q-factors are explained in self-theoretical terms for conditions of convergent selectivity rather than in relation to deeper belief systems.

5. Audiences are operationally defined by Q-factors, that is, by the subjects themselves in a particular *XYZ* situation. They are not socio-economic or other logical categorizations of populations. The definition applies to both social control (public opinion) and convergent selectivity. So defined, such audiences are called Q-audiences.

6. The population for any *XYZ* situation is therefore apt to be segmented, each Q-factor representing a different segment.

The determination of the segmentation for a given *XYZ* situation is the primary empirical step in all Q-studies. The significance of the segmentation depends upon the comprehensiveness of the Q-sample and the representatives of the P-samples used. Q-samples ordinarily cover an area of discourse on a wide basis; P-samples normally insure that all important "interests" are involved.

7. The most important practical outcome from Q-study is a specification of significant themes or symbols to guide communication in an *XYZ* situation. Others concern the specification of facilitators (*Y*).

Thus, in advertising, a product is given an "image" which is congruent with existing wants. In politics an "image" can be fashioned which is pertinent to movements, issues, or controversies. Creative writers, artists, and directors of plays, documentaries, and movies can be advised about existing wants and needs.

The pragmatics consist of deriving themes from Q-samples, from what matters to the Q-audiences concerned. One seeks to fit imagery, themes, and symbols to suit the motives of Q-audiences. One can use the term "motive," as in "motivation research," because of the axiomatic principle that the concern is with apperceptive conditions (*see* principle 1).

Previous study of significant symbols and communication themes has been by way of content analysis, usually in relation to Lasswell's principles (70) in which distinctions are drawn between symbols of *fact*, *demand*, and *expectancy*. I have had little to say of these principles, but of their importance there can be no doubt.

8. Q-method solves the problem of measuring social and national character and for studying the component Q-audiences of cultures in general.

This completes the formal statement. It lacks only some indication of the theorems which derive from a theory. In this complex area these are legion, but in accordance with the basic abductive method none is likely to be a logical derivation from the theory, since I have no analytic postulates in the system. The method generates hypotheses by way of its factor analysis.

It is very natural that communication theorists should turn to modern technology for their ideas instead of to abstract factors. They see their problems in *information*, in its machinery, its diffusions, and the like. But what is really important in communication theory?

Schramm (126) has the following to say about communication in newly developing nations:

> Each . . . has a great shortage of teachers. Each . . . has a broad educational task — children to be put into school, adults to be taught to read and count, farmers to be taught how to produce more from the soil, housewives to be taught better hygienic practices, workers to be taught the skills of technology, public servants to be taught the duties and responsibilities and privileges of citizenship at a time critical for their country. But in almost none of the countries is there much development along these lines. . . . in other words, the coast is clear. The planning can begin afresh [p. 50].

No one can doubt the good intentions in Schramm's declamation. But it is all about work, unleavened by any conception of play. Information theory likewise is all about work and not about fun. It seems to us that any dispassionate regard of communication, in its broadest context of both social control and convergent selectivity, must see that play is of primary importance in it.

In the above exposition of my theory I have therefore left information theory and technology to take care of themselves, as they are well able to do. The urgent problems are not in these directions or in studying how mass communications diffuse into a society or in what comes first, industrialization or mass communication. The problems of immediate importance concern the myths of man. And this is not with any idea of replacing unreason by an age of reason but to understand myths for the sake of communication-pleasure. I propose, therefore, to end my efforts here with a reminder that the study of a country's drama, art, movies, entertainment, and literature — all the popular and humanistic arts — is of first importance in every theoretical respect. Because of my methodological and general interests, notably to differentiate between social control and convergent selectivity, I have given scant attention to what, after all, is the basic concern. This has not been without some misgivings and regrets — because the area of study is congenial to me, is richly reward-ing in empirical respects, and is entirely untouched by methods such as I am here advancing. But that there will be many Q-studies in the future in the area of the arts is certain.

Let us look, then, in conclusion, at the popular and humanistic arts from the play-theory point of view.

THE RAPE OF THE LOCK

We can scarcely do better than to turn to Pope's classic, *The Rape of the Lock*, for an application of play theory to the humanities. According to Hyman (54) this *divertissement* invites comparison with Homer, the Bible, and the works of Dante, Milton, and Shakespeare. Yet nineteenth-century critics thought it trivial. The poem had its origins in a tiny scan-dal — Lord Petre had cut off a lock of Miss Arabella Fermor's hair, refused to return it, and bad feeling erupted between the two families. Pope wrote a brief poem to make a jest of it all and to try to bring the families together — according to Addison it was "a delicious little thing." Pope later enlarged it into his masterpiece, intending it for the amusement of a few young ladies. It describes an elaborate, sensual toilet of the heroine, suffused with the glows of a film in technicolor, with super-natural asides. The precious lock of hair is lost in a wild free-for-all battle between the sexes, *beaux* and *belles*, in which the wildest female emotions appear in orgiastic beauty; the lock reappears in the heavens as Belinda's Comet with a hairy tail — the heroine is thus immortalized.

A tiny incident is taken by Pope and embroidered with imagery rivaling Shakespeare's. Freudian interpretations make hay with the poem — in psychoanalytic terms it is obviously a spectacular symbolic defloration. Some literary experts attach a more serious, metaphysical significance to the poem. Others see the hand of a Marxist ideologist behind it, de-nouncing the waste and profligacy of capitalists and the bourgeoisie.

No doubt all this can be projected upon the poem, metaphysical, Freudian, Marxian, and the rest. But I would agree instead with Hyman that the poem is largely unadulterated *fun*. The tiny incident, absurd, yet so serious, and the heroine so gently loved in the cutting of a lock of her hair — what matter if nasty minds are at work about it? The incident is trivial, but the human delight is enormous; the poet mocks the one, but symbolizes its significance for the human being by putting it in the sky as a comet. Thus, writes Hyman: "Pope must affirm the incident of the rape of the lock as important to show its ultimate significance. He must see whole heavens and earth in a lock of hair to tell us something serious and important about the small spot we live in" (54, p. 10).

Instead of dull Marx, nasty Freud, or ponderous metaphysician, all dealing with problems in the real world, Pope gives us a poem to play with in the mind, with joy, wit, fun, delight, freedom, rapture, fancy, ecstasy, and a bit of naughtiness, all in step in unalloyed fantasy.

This is subjective play, regarded as pure communication-pleasure. Pope wrote with no thought of hurt or gain, with no wish for vicarious sexual experience, and without rancor, satire, or metaphysical quibbling; he was having fun, as a child has when it plays. If we are so minded, and so open to joy, reading the poem gives us the selfsame satisfactions. And this is the core of our theory.

FREUD'S THEORY

But Pope's poem is an example of fantasy at its greatest, its most highly developed form. To understand fantasy more systematically we must turn to Freud's paper, "The Relation of the Poet to Daydreaming" (34). This is our postulate 13 (p. 196 above).

In his paper Freud remarks that the poet arouses in us emotions (and imagery) of which, it seemed, we were incapable; sweeter far, indeed, is the song unsung. Freud asks how this comes about.

He provides an answer in relation to play. The child at play, Freud writes, is like a poet; both "rearrange things" in their worlds "to suit them better." Both child and poet distinguish between the real world of painful emotions, frustrations, hurts, and obduracies, and the play world, where these real-world fears and hurts are transmuted into humor, pleasure, and delightful wish-fulfillment. Play is escape from what goes on painfully in the real world. That something of the kind occurs is certain. But Freud overlooked the other half of fantasy, which "rearranges" not only things but the self to suit itself better. The self may grow, develop, and restructure itself in daydreaming and fantasy. The emotions that we did not realize we were capable of, the very things that Freud set out to explain, are an intimation of a growing self, of rearranging within oneself, rather than transmogrifications of painful experiences. Freud saw only mental sickness in daydreaming. The child wants to feel "grown-up," and thus plays. The adult gives up such playing, he thinks, but may daydream instead. We all create fantasies, as long as we live; but, for Freud, the more "normal" we are the less daydreaming we do. I would rather say that the more we *work* and live by work, in Freud's inner-directed world, the less we have time for daydreams. But by the same token the development of self is likely to have stopped when we lose ourselves in work.

Thus, Freud argued that happy, adjusted people never make fantasies; only the unsatisfied daydream. Ambitious wishes, expressed in fantasy, exalt the person; erotic wishes no doubt gratify him vicariously. Almost mechanically, in Freud's theory, if a person daydreams too much or over-luxuriously, neurosis is the outcome. This, again, is to confuse a poet having much fantasy and a clear selfhood with a neurotic, having as much fantasy but little self.

Nor does Freud concern himself in fact with poetry. He refers, instead, to writers of cheap romances, novels, and popular stories. What he says of these is basic, however, to the *projective* techniques; the Thematic Apperception Test (93) is fundamentally based upon it. These "common" novels all have a hero with whom readers are able to identify. The hero is His Majesty the Ego, that is, a projection of the reader himself. Most psychological novels are written "from within"; the author writes as though he were the hero — from inside his soul. Contrariwise, in cheap novels the hero is a nonentity; everything happens to him — he is shipwrecked, beaten, sick, drowned, lost, wins a fortune and the fair lady, and scarcely once is he described as a person as such. The easier it is then, in such a case, for anyone to project upon the story — anyone can put himself in the hero's role without a jarring note, since the hero is without a face. Voltaire's *Candide* is such a story, its hero being anything one wishes to project upon him.

In a creative work, therefore, the author or artist puts us in a position in which we can deploy and enjoy our own daydreams without, as Freud said, reproach or shame. This is undoubtedly the key to much that concerns us in any theory of mass communication. But there are three rather different aspects to consider — one is the realm of identification with heroes, to which reference has just been made (and this is undoubtedly the realm of much in advertising, television, novels, and the like); another has deeper origins, in legends, myth, fairy stories, and high drama; and another is sublimated. There can be no question that myths, legends, fairy tales, and the like are vestiges of archaic wishes — the "age-long dreams of young humanity." But equally so, the beauty of Pope's *The Rape of the Lock* is young humanity dreaming a new conception, developing a sublime experience and creating in the process a self that will never be quite the same again. This, if anywhere, is where the individual can exist for himself.

MASS CULTURE

It is worth looking back for a few moments at scholarly efforts to bring a measure of understanding into the arts.

Aristotle held that we go to the theater to release or relieve our emotions — a purgation, catharsis, rather than a purification of one's emotions. The epic, lyric, and comedy were meant to purge us of aggressiveness, malice, and licentiousness, to relieve our anxieties and to restore us to a happy normalcy. The theater and movies, and mass communication generally, are still regarded by some authorities as cathartic in this way; anxieties and emotions built up during one's day-by-day living are assuaged, purged, or relieved by entertainment. But Aristotle also taught that the theater and entertainment can make man active, can purify as well as purge. In Elizabethan literature, likewise, Sir Philip Sidney could say that man is made finer when the theater's emotions are added to the finer human qualities.

Plato attributed great power to drama and music; a new style of music, he averred, could upset a state. The poet Fletcher is often quoted to the same effect: "If a man were permitted to make all the ballads, he need not care who should make the laws of a nation." Happily, nothing is as simple as this. Yet music, drama, and art, whether high or low, make one *feel* something; the experience itself is worth studying. The feelings may be richer and wider than any we have in real life, but they are not otherwise different from them. If we ask a scholarly person what influenced him most in his life, he is indeed apt to say *books*: "No real person has influenced me as much," writes Lucas (79), "as my reading of Homer . . . Ronsard, Montaigne, Johnson, Morris, Ibsen, and Hardy." He continues: "Real life is often drab; it is only natural (in spite of prigs pursing their lips at 'Escapism') to seek wider and richer experiences in fantasy. And even if our real life is not drab, it remains brief and limited. What more natural, or more rational, than to wish to travel like Odysseus among other ways of living?" (p. 275). This viewpoint is much like my own; subjective experience, like a piano, has to be practiced if one is to be skilled in what it offers in communication-pleasure.

The modern critic, however, believes that mass communication is subjugating the masses by a "phantasmagoria of world-wide social security — which asks for no more than to be served with things needed for reproduction" (83). The classicist Eliot (26) and Ortega y Gasset (98) would try to improve matters by instituting authoritarian orders and aristocratic controls. MacDonald would rely, instead, on an avant-garde elite with a Joyce or Stravinsky to spearhead the movement toward better mass communication. Gilbert Seldes (129), as I observed earlier, saw people everywhere in this country as in a desperate state of alienation. All want companionship, Seldes suggested, but the mass media answer the need with reveries, daydreams, and childish fables, distracting the masses from their real needs. Nothing is done to inform the public of its perils and of the real needs of the world. In my view mass communication is better understood, instead, as being manipulated subjectively by its audiences, who thoroughly enjoy what they are being offered for the first time in man's history. The media are not oppressing or manipulating their audiences. Nor should they make work of what should be pleasure. The charge that mass communication is sensational or the like is also not proved. People may have to see something of the sordidness and crudities of life in order to be free individuals and self-respecting selves. I would have liked to report for Seldes a comparative study of playgoers at the staging of *Hamlet* and TV watchers enjoying "Bonanza" to illustrate how latent beliefs and communication-pleasure mediate in the individual's enjoyment of these forms of entertainment. The underlying importance of archaic forms of thinking was sufficiently indicated, however, in the study of the Army-McCarthy hearings; analogous forms appear, one knows, as one watches *Hamlet*, or as one follows this or that episodic hero in "Bonanza." We do of course need better studies of the communication-pleasure that is possible for the playgoer at the theater, for the watcher before a television set, for the reader of a novel, and for all users of the mass media.

PLAY THEORY AND ADVERTISING

I have said all too little about advertising, except to see its connections with convergent selectivity rather than with the formation of opinions. This has too long been overlooked. Advertising has been blamed for social effects that belong, instead, to the contrary principles of social control.

Klapper (63) ignored advertising in his work on the effects of mass communication; his findings, he says, do not apply to advertising. He apparently felt that the methods of persuasion reviewed by him were not the same as those used by advertisers. The methods of persuasion imply or state explicitly that *rational* discussion of the communication is somehow involved. This ignores the obvious dependency of communication upon social mechanisms, on the Y of our principle of XYZ interaction.

The important paper in this area of concern is Wiebe's (166), in which he considers why television can sell soap but not, it seems, citizenship. The reason lies in the part played by mediating mechanisms in advertising; in between the advertisement (Z) on the one hand and the consumer (X) who reads it there are the facilitating factors (Y) of supermarkets, shopping habits, and the ready availability of spending money which make it relatively easy for a consumer to be "sold" a new brand of soap. It is the absence of such mediating institutions that makes it very difficult for a society to "sell" citizenship.

Hovland (49), an early worker in the field of communication, also overlooked the importance of mediating mechanisms. He noticed that communication, where effective, is not memorized but accepted. One does not memorize an advertisement (though slogans are so remembered, especially by young children) so much as one acts upon it under appropriate conditions. One is persuaded, according to Hovland, by way of incentives, based on either rational support for the communication or because of "motivational factors." Thus the vain woman (a motivational factor) is persuaded to buy Camay soap, instead of Lifebuoy as hitherto, because of the promise of beauty implied in the promotion of the former. At the conclusion of many years devoted to such work Hovland admitted, however, that he should have started at the outset to study internalization (which he felt was at the bottom of accepting a communication), and to probe into opinion change in situations of conflict. It was left to Festinger (31) to develop theory and research into the latter, as cognitive dissonance. Festinger's work, though important, lacks any operational treatment of one of the key postulates of his theory, namely, that embraced by the "cognitive" concept.

Advertising theory is not well developed, but evidence is mounting that the key to acceptance of communication is the degree to which a person can readily identify with it (20). Nothing as deeply psychological as internalization is at issue. A blue-shirt worker dislikes an advertisement for a Hathaway shirt which shows a well-dressed man-about-town, patch on eye — it "makes no sense" to him because he cannot see himself in such a sophisticated setting. A picture of a cheap beer, with some Fritos at hand, appeals to him enormously because he can put himself readily into the picture, identifying with it.

Conclusion

We have touched upon play theory, as *paideia*, in the above excursions into a vast region of cultural concern. If we look again at our definition of play, we see its many attributes of pretense, disinterestedness, seriousness (but not *really* serious), and its voluntary character. We play in different ways, with pure play and fantasy, or more formally. Subjective play involves all ways of playing, in interwoven complexity.

There can be no doubt that what we are as individuals is fashioned by social factors, the deepest effects being in childhood, and made permanent by constant reinforcement throughout life. These, for everything held dear to civilization, are all rooted in play — whether the concern is with law, illness, religion, politics, art, or customs generally. The beliefs supporting these, however, are not necessarily in tune with the rapidly changing times — and nothing that mass communication can do can alter them. But by way of developing new wants, images, and new forms of social character, much might still be done to offset these early fixities where they are contraindicated in a society, and this presents mass communication with its opportunities. Its more careful regard should serve two purposes. It should suggest how best to maximize the communication-pleasure in the world. It should also show how far autonomy for the individual can be achieved in spite of the weight of social controls against him.

With respect to the first, it is not a matter of flooding the media with more and more fun, more sex, more comics; as I define communication-pleasure (as crucial to entertainment and enjoyment) culture is at issue and not mere laughter or sensuality. I would like to see more play, rather than less, but play directed to cultures which fit the times. The study of entertainment is not an inquiry into trivialities, a mere *dolce far niente*. I am not asking that comics be made funnier, or movies more spectacular. On the contrary, I merely look for conditions under which people can have communication-pleasure. It is easy enough in the case of high culture. Poetry and drama, everyone will agree, provide experiences which are richer than real life, and yet are of the same stuff and metal. The humanist is puzzled, as Lucas (79) was, to find no moral purpose in Shakespeare's plays; I suspect that Shakespeare, prince of entertainers, knew the ground rules of communication-pleasure very well. But what, even among the elite, is the purpose of such delight? Even with them, it seems to me, fantasy can encourage a liberation of the human spirit. It may be very little, but it is worth the experience. At least a number of modern novelists have had a glimpse of it. Nathalie Sarraute, for example, probes into "inner life" (as she calls it) in the intimacies of family life — the home, for her, is a catastrophic place, with no redeeming qualities of love or generosity. If this is enjoyed in the reading, suggesting that life holds almost nothing in it, what is the enjoyment? Is it merely a vicarious pleasure in the degradation and morbidity of a decadent family? From a communication-pleasure standpoint, instead, it may be existence for oneself.

But what of low culture? People of every sort seem to enjoy television. "Low" culture is to be regarded as the "normalizer" of manners and popular taste; it develops wants and images and molds social character. It is characterized by absence of involvement in deeper belief systems and socially controlled internalized values. Somewhere in such entertainment, we must suppose, there are moments of self-enhancement, of self-existence, a breakthrough into communication-pleasure. True enough, there will be moments of vicarious pleasure of feasting one's eyes upon lust, murder, and malignity. But in many a sociable moment, with a quick smile or quip, the television watcher is learning to exist for himself. Be it ever so little — "a crocus not yet open" — this is where the focus has to be in mass communication. I have merely opened the door to the possibilities.

With respect to individuality, everyone talks of it, but here I see the self as central to all else. It has to be admitted that one's selfhood is fashioned very largely by social controls. But subjective play is in a more secret place, and there is at least an opportunity for growth of the self in relation to it. Communication-pleasure is always self-enhancing, and this gives us hope for the future of entertainment. Thus, from a consideration of subjective play we find ourselves involved in elaborations upon convergent selectivity, and from these we reach into existential psychology. And is it not agreed in existentialism (125) that one should *exist* before one becomes petrified by social forms? From a mass society of really existing individuals one might indeed find new forms of society arising.

This, however, is the author dreaming. Enough has been said to ask for far more serious regard of play, and not of information, as the primary concern of any communication theory.

Bibliography

1. Adorno, T., *et al. The Authoritarian Personality.* New York: Harper, 1950.
2. Allen, F. L. *Only Yesterday.* New York: Harper, 1931.
3. Allport, G. W. "Attitudes," *Handbook of Social Psychology*, pp. 798–844. Worcester: Clark University Press, 1935.
4. Almond, G. A., and Verba, S. *The Civic Culture: Political Attitudes and Democracy in Five Nations.* Princeton: Princeton University Press, 1963.
5. Ayar, A., *et al. Studies in Communication.* London: Secker & Warburg, 1955.
6. Bartlett, F. C. *Psychology and Primitive Culture.* Cambridge: Cambridge University Press, 1923.
7. Bauer, R. A., "The Obstinate Audience," *American Psychologist,* XIX (1964), 319–27.
8. Benitez, J. "The U.S., Cuba, and Latin America." Occasional paper, Center for the Study of Democratic Institutions, New York, 1961.
9. Berelson, B. "The State of Communication Research," *Public Opinion Quarterly,* XXIII (1959), 1–5.
10. ———. "What Missing the Newspaper Means." In W. Schramm, (ed.), *The Process and Effects of Mass Communication.* Urbana: University of Illinois Press, 1960.
11. ———, Lazarsfeld, P. F., and McPhee, W. N. *Voting: A Study of Opinion Formation in a Presidential Campaign.* Chicago: University of Chicago Press, 1937.
12. Blumer, H. "Collective Behavior." In A. M. Lee (ed.), *New Outline of the Principles of Sociology.* New York: Barnes & Noble, 1946.

13. ———. "The Crowd, the Public, and the Mass." In W. Schramm (ed.), *The Process and Effects of Mass Communication*. Urbana: University of Illinois Press, 1955.

14. Buchanan, W., and Cantril, H. *How Nations See Each Other*. Urbana: University of Illinois Press, 1953.

15. Caillois, R. *Man, Play, and Games*. Glencoe, Ill.: Free Press, 1961.

16. Cherry, Colin. *On Human Communication*. New York: Wiley, 1957.

17. Cooley, C. H. *Human Nature and the Social Order*. New York: Scribner's, 1922.

18. Cornetta, A. M. "A Study of Ego-Involvement in Newsreading." Master's thesis, University of Missouri, 1962.

19. Crumley, Wilma. "Newsreading Behavior and Anxiety." Master's thesis, University of Missouri, 1963.

20. Cummings, Ernestine (Tena). "A General Theory of How Ads Influence Consumers." Ph.D. dissertation, University of Missouri, 1965.

21. Danbury, Thomas. "A Comparative Study of Newspaper Readers." Master's thesis, University of Missouri, 1961.

22. de Antonio, E., and Talbot, D. *Point of Order*. New York: Norton, 1964.

23. Deutschmann, P. J. "The Mass Media in an Underdeveloped Village," *Journalism Quarterly*, XL (1963), 27–35.

24. ———, and Borda, O. F. "Communication in an Andean Village." Paper read at the Association for Education in Journalism, Chapel Hill, August, 1962.

25. Dulles, Rhea Foster. *America Learns To Play: A History of Popular Recreation, 1607–1940*. New York: Appleton-Century, 1940.

26. Eliot, T. S. *Christianity and Culture*. New York: Harcourt, 1940.

27. Erikson, E. H. *Childhood and Society*. New York: Norton, 1950.

28. Ethridge, M. *The Press: An Interview with D. McDonald*. New York: Fund for the Republic, 1961.

29. Fairbairn, W. R. D. *Psychoanalytic Studies of Personality*. London: Tavistock, 1952.

30. Fenichel, O. *The Psychoanalytic Theory of Neurosis*. New York: Norton, 1945.

31. Festinger, L. *A Theory of Cognitive Dissonance*. Evanston, Ill.: Row, Peterson, 1957.

32. Fisher, R. A. *Statistical Methods for Research Workers*. London: Oliver & Boyd, 1930.

33. Freud, S. "Formulations Regarding the Two Principles in Mental Functioning." In *Collected Papers*, Vol. IV, chap. 1. London: Hogarth Press, 1925.

34. ———. "The Relation of the Poet to Daydreaming" (1908). In *Collected Papers*, Vol. IV, chap. 9. London: Hogarth Press, 1925.

35. Frey, F. W. "Political Development, Power, and Communications in Turkey." In L. W. Pye (ed.), *Communications and Political Development,* chap. 17. Princeton: Princeton University Press, 1963.

36. Galbraith, J. K. *The Affluent Society.* Boston: Houghton Mifflin, 1958.

37. Galton, Sir Francis. *Natural Inheritance.* London: Macmillan, 1894.

38. Gerbner, G. "The Individual in a Mass Culture," *Saturday Review,* June 18, 1960.

39. Gillespie, J. M., and Allport, G. W. *Youth's Outlook on the Future.* New York: Doubleday, 1955.

40. Girard, A. "The First Opinion Research in Uruguay and Chile," *Public Opinion Quarterly,* XXII (Fall, 1958), 251.

41. Gregg, A. *Challenges to Contemporary Medicine.* New York: Columbia University Press, 1956.

42. Haire, Mason. "Industrial Social Psychology." In G. Lindzey (ed.), *Handbook of Social Psychology,* Vol. II, chap. 29. Cambridge, Mass.: Addison-Wesley, 1954.

43. Hardy, F., *et al. Grierson on Documentary.* New York: Harcourt, Brace, 1947.

44. Harman, H. H. *Modern Factor Analysis.* Chicago: University of Chicago Press, 1960.

45. Heberle, R. "A Note on Riesman's *The Lonely Crowd,*" *American Journal of Sociology,* XLII (1956), 34–36.

46. ———. *Social Movements: An Introduction to Political Sociology.* New York: Appleton-Century-Crofts, 1951.

47. Hempel, C. G. *Symposium: Problems of Concept and Theory Formation in the Social Sciences.* Philadelphia: University of Pennsylvania Press, 1952.

48. Henry, W. E. *The Analysis of Fantasy.* New York: Wiley, 1956.

49. Hovland, C. I., *et al. Communication and Persuasion.* New Haven: Yale University Press, 1953.

50. Hsu, F. L. K. *Americans and Chinese.* New York: Schuman, 1953.

51. Hughes, H. McGill. *Human Interest Stories and Democracy.* Chicago: University of Chicago Press, 1937.

52. Huizinga, J. *Homo ludens.* Paperback edition. Boston: Beacon Press, 1950.

53. Hyman, H. "Mass Media and Political Socialization: The Role of Patterns of Communication." In L. W. Pye (ed.), *Communications and Political Development,* chap. 8. Princeton: Princeton University Press, 1963.

54. Hyman, S. E. "The Rape of the Lock." In *Poetry and Criticism: Four Revolutions in Literary Taste.* New York: Atheneum, 1961.

55. Hyshka, D. "Motivation Research Looks at Detroit Newspapers," Detroit Free Press Pamphlet, 1955.

56. Inkeles, A. *Public Opinion in Soviet Russia.* Cambridge, Mass.: Harvard University Press, 1951.

57. Janowitz, M. *The Community Press in an Urban Setting.* Glencoe, Ill.: Free Press, 1952.

58. Katz, D., and Lazarsfeld, P. F. *Personal Influence.* Glencoe: Free Press, 1955.

59. Katz, E., and Foulkes, D. "On the Use of the Mass Media as Escape: Clarification of a Concept," *Public Opinion Quarterly,* XXVI (1962), 377–88.

60. Kaufmann, F. *Methodology of the Social Sciences.* London: Oxford University Press, 1944.

61. Kay, H. "Toward an Understanding of Newsreading Behavior." Master's thesis, Stanford University, 1953. Also, *Journalism Quarterly,* XXXI (1954), 15–32.

62. Kingsbury, S. M., and Hart, H. *Newspapers and the News.* New York: Putnam, 1937.

63. Klapper, J. T. *The Effects of Mass Communication.* Glencoe, Ill.: Free Press, 1961.

64. Klein, M. *Developments in Psychoanalysis, 1921–1945.* London: Hogarth, 1948.

65. Kluckhohn, C. "Common Humanity and Diverse Cultures." In D. Lerner (ed.), *The Human Meaning of the Social Sciences.* New York: World, 1959.

66. Kriesberg, M. "Soviet News in the New York *Times,*" *Public Opinion Quarterly,* XII (1946–47), 540.

67. Langer, S. K. *Philosophy in a New Key.* New York: American Library of World Literature, 1951.

68. LaPiere, R. T. *A Theory of Social Control.* New York: McGraw-Hill, 1954.

69. Larrabee, E., and Meyersohn, R. *Mass Leisure.* Glencoe, Ill.: Free Press, 1958.

70. Lasswell, H. D. *World Politics and Personal Insecurity.* New York: Whittlesey, 1935.

71. Lazarsfeld, P. F., and Kendall, P. L. "Problems of Survey Analysis." In Lazarsfeld and Merton (eds.), *Continuities in Social Research.* Glencoe, Ill.: Free Press, 1950.

72. Lazarsfeld, P. F., and Merton, R. K. "Mass Communication, Popular Taste and Organized Social Action." In W. Schramm (ed.), *Mass Communications.* Urbana: University of Illinois Press, 1949.

73. Lerner, D. "Editor's Introduction — On Modernizing Areas," *Public Opinion Quarterly,* XXII (Fall, 1958), 217.

74. ———. "International Conditions and Communications Content: The Case of Neutralism," *Public Opinion Quarterly,* XVI (1952), 681–88.

75. ————. *The Passing of Traditional Society*. Glencoe, Ill.: Free Press, 1962.

76. ————. "Toward a Communication Theory of Modernization." In L. W. Pye (ed.), *Communications and Political Development*. Princeton: Princeton University Press, 1963.

77. Lindsay, A. D. *The Modern Democratic State*. New York: Oxford University Press, 1943.

78. Lipset, S. M., and Lowenthal, L. (eds.). *Culture and Social Character: The Work of David Riesman*. Glencoe, Ill.: Free Press, 1961.

79. Lucas, F. L. *Literature and Psychology*. Ann Arbor: University of Michigan Press, 1957.

80. Marshall, A. *Money, Credit and Commerce*. London: Macmillan, 1923

81. Matthews, T. S. *The Sugar Pill*. New York: Simon & Schuster, 1959.

82. MacAndrew, C. "Alienation and the Office Worker." Ph.D. dissertation University of Chicago, 1955.

83. MacDonald, D. "A Theory of Mass Culture." In B. Rosenberg and D. White (eds.), *Mass Culture: The Popular Arts in America*. Glencoe, Ill.: Free Press, 1957.

84. Mayo, E. *The Human Problems of an Industrial Civilization*. New York: Macmillan, 1933.

85. ————. *The Social Problems of an Industrial Civilization*. Andover, Mass.: Andover Press, 1945.

86. McClelland, D. C. *The Achieving Society*. Princeton: Van Nostrand, 1961.

87. ————. "National Character and Economic Growth in Turkey and Iran." In L. W. Pye (ed.), *Communications and Political Development*, chap. 10. Princeton: Princeton University Press, 1963.

88. McKeon, R., (ed.). *Democracy in a World of Tensions*. Chicago: University of Chicago Press, 1951.

89. Merton, R. K. *Social Theory and Social Structure*. Glencoe, Ill.: Free Press, 1949.

90. Mosel, J. N. "Communication Patterns and Political Socialization in Transitional Thailand." In L. W. Pye (ed.), *Communications and Political Development*, chap. 12. Princeton: Princeton University Press, 1963.

91. Muggeridge, Malcolm. "The Apotheosis of John F. Kennedy," *New York Review of Books*, Vol. III, No. 4 (January 28, 1965).

92. Mumford, L. *The Culture of Cities*. New York: Harcourt, Brace, 1938.

93. Murray, H. A. *Explorations in Personality*. New York: Oxford University Press, 1938.

94. Northrop, F. S. C. *Ideological Differences and World Order*. New Haven: Yale University Press, 1949.

95. Obaid, A. H., and Maritano, N. *An Alliance for Progress*. Minneapolis: Denison, 1963.

96. Oldfield, R. C. *The Psychology of the Interview*. London: Methuen, 1947.
97. Orr, R. H., *et al.* "The Biomedical Information Complex Viewed as a System," *Federation Proceedings*, XXIII (1964), 1133–45.
98. Ortega y Gasset, J. *The Dehumanization of Art*. Translated by H. Weyl. Princeton: Princeton University Press, 1948.
99. Osgood, C. E. *An Alternative to War or Surrender*. Urbana: University of Illinois Press, 1962.
100. Passin, Herbert. "Writer and Journalist in the Transitional Society." In L. W. Pye (ed.), *Communications and Political Development*, chap. 6. Princeton: Princeton University Press, 1963.
101. Pear, T. H. *Voice and Personality*. London: Chapman Hall, 1931.
102. Pearlin, L. "Social and Personal Stress and Escape Television Viewing," *Public Opinion Quarterly*, XXIII (1959), 255–59.
103. Plamenatz, J. P. In R. McKeon (ed.), *Democracy in a World of Tensions*, chap. 25. Chicago: University of Chicago Press, 1951.
104. Plath, D .W. *The After Hours: Modern Japan and the Search for Enjoyment*. Berkeley and Los Angeles: University of California Press, 1964.
105. Pool, I., and Prasad, K. "Indian Student Images of Foreign People," *Public Opinion Quarterly*, XXII (1958–59), 292–304.
106. Popper, K. R. *The Logic of Scientific Discovery*. New York: Basic Books, 1959.
107. Potter, D. M. *People of Plenty: Economic Abundance and the American Character*. Chicago: University of Chicago Press, 1954.
108. Pratt, J. R. "Strong Inference," *Science*, CXLVI (1964), 347–53.
109. Pye, L. W. *Communications and Political Development*. Princeton: Princeton University Press, 1963.
110. Rawlins, M. J. "A Q-methodological Study of Some Effects of a Fictional and Documentary Treatment of a Controversial Issue." Ph.D. dissertation, University of Missouri, 1964. *Dissertation Abstracts*, Vol. XXV, No. II, 1964.
111. Richardson, L. F. *Arms and Insecurity*. Chicago: Quadrangle Books, 1960.
112. ———. *Generalized Foreign Politics*. Cambridge: Cambridge University Press, 1939.
113. ———. *Statistics of Deadly Quarrels*. Chicago: Quadrangle Books, 1960.
114. Riesman, D. *Faces in the Crowd*. New Haven: Yale University Press, 1953.
115. ———. *Individualism Reconsidered*. Glencoe, Ill.: Free Press, 1954.
116. ———, *et al. The Lonely Crowd*. New Haven: Yale University Press, 1960.
117. Rodó, J. E. *Ariel*. Boston: Houghton Mifflin, 1922.

118. Rosenbleuth, A., and Wiener, N. "The Role of Models in Science," *Philosophy of Science*, XXII (1945), 316–21.

119. Ross, Rose. "Comparison of Reward and Value Theories in Newsreading Behavior." Master's thesis, University of Missouri, 1962.

120. Rosten, L. "The Intellectual and the Mass Media," *Daedalus*, LXXXIX, No. 2 (1960), 333–46.

121. Rowse, A. L. *Appeasement: A Study in Political Decline, 1933–39*. New York: Norton, 1961.

122. Rudolph, L., and Rudolph, S. H. "Surveys in India," *Public Opinion Quarterly*, XXII (1958–59), 224–44.

123. Ruesch, J. *Therapeutic Communication*. New York: Norton, 1961.

124. ———, and Bateson, G. *Communication: The Social Matrix of Psychiatry*. New York: Norton, 1951.

125. Sartre, J. P. *Existentialism and Human Existence*. New York: Philosphical Library, 1957.

126. Schramm, W. *Mass Media and National Development*. Stanford: Stanford University Press, 1964.

127. ———. "The Nature of News," *Journalism Quarterly*, XXVI (1949), 259–69.

128. ———. *One Day in the World's Press*. Stanford: Stanford University Press, 1959.

129. Seldes, G. *The Public Arts*. New York: Simon & Schuster, 1956.

130. Shils, E. "Demagogues and Cadres in Political Development of the New States." In L. W. Pye (ed.), *Communications and Political Development*, chap. 4. Princeton: Princeton University Press, 1963.

131. ———. "Mass Society and Its Culture," *Daedalus*, LXXXIX, No. 2 (1960), 288–314.

132. Simmel, G. *The Sociology of George Simmel*. Translated by K. Woett. Glencoe, Ill.: Free Press, 1950.

133. Smith, B. L., and Smith, C. M. *International Communication and Public Opinion*. Princeton: Princeton University Press, 1956.

134. Sorokin, P. *Social and Cultural Dynamics*. New York: American Book, 1937.

135. Spearman, C. *The Abilities of Man*. London: Macmillan, 1927.

136. ———. "Correlations of Sums and Differences," *British Journal of Psychology*, V (1913), 417–26.

137. Stanford Institute for Communication. *Research Scales*. Stanford: Stanford University Press, 1959.

138. Stephenson, W. "Application of Q-method to the Measurement of Public Opinion," *Psychological Record*, XIV (1964), 265–73.

139. ———. "Application of the Thompson Schema to the Current Controversy over Cuba," *Psychological Record*, XIV (1964), 275–90.

140. ———. "Ideal Types," *Psychological Record*, XII (1962), 9–16.

141. ———. *Image of Public Health and Medicine*. Report to Director of Public Health, State of Missouri, Jefferson City, Missouri, May, 1964.

142. ———. "The Ludenic Theory of Newsreading," *Journalism Quarterly*, XLI (1964), 367–74.

143. ———. "Public Images of Public Utilities," *Journal of Advertising Research*, III (1963), 34–39.

144. ———. "Redefinition of Opinion, Attitude and Belief," *Psychological Record* (1965).

145. ———. "Scientific Creed — 1961: The Centrality of Self," *Psychological Record*, XI (1961), 10–18.

146. "Standard Error of Factor Scores," ms., 1965.

147. ———. *The Study of Behavior: Q-technique and Its Methodology*. Chicago: University of Chicago Press, 1953.

148. Sterba, R. A. "Some Psychological Factors in Pictorial Advertising," *Public Opinion Quarterly*, XIV (1950), 475.

149. ———. "The Significance of Theatrical Performance," *Psychoanalytic Quarterly*, VIII (1939), 335–37.

150. Stouffer, S. A. *Social Research To Test Ideas*. (Selected Writings.) Glencoe, Ill.: Free Press, 1962.

151. Stout, G .F. *Analytic Psychology*. 2 vols. London: Macmillan, 1909.

152. Szasz, T. S. *The Myth of Mental Illness*. New York: Hoeber-Harper, 1961.

153. ———. *Pain and Pleasure*. New York: Basic Books, 1957.

154. Tannenbaum, P. H. "The Indexing Process in Communication," *Public Opinion Quarterly*, XIX (1955) 292–302.

155. Toeplitz, K. T. "Mass Culture." Review of an article, No. 34 of *Cultural Review* (Poland). Translated and reprinted in *Atlas*, May, 1963, pp. 307–89.

156. Tönnies, F. *Community and Society*. A translation of *Gemeinschaft und Gesellschaft*, 1887. Lansing: Michigan State University Press, 1957.

157. Toulmin, S. *The Philosophy of Science*. London: Hutchinson, 1953.

158. von Hayek, F. A. *The Counter-Revolution of Science*. Glencoe, Ill.: Free Press, 1950.

159. Walker, H. M. *Studies in the History of Statistical Method*. Baltimore: Williams & Wilkins, 1929.

160. Ward, W. D. "One-tailed Test of Trivia," *Science*, CXLIV (1964), 1089.

161. Warner, W. L., and Henry, W. E. "The Radio Day Time Serial: A Symbolic Analysis," *Genetic Psychological Monographs*, XXXVII (1948), 3–71.

162. Warshow, Robert. *The Immediate Experience*. New York: Doubleday, 1962.

163. Weber, M. *The Methodology of the Social Sciences*. Glencoe, Ill.: Free Press, 1949.

164. Wheelis, A. *Quest for Identity*. New York: Norton, 1958.

165. Wiebe, G. D. "The Army-McCarthy Hearings and the Public Conscience," *Public Opinion Quarterly*, IV (1958–59), 490–502.

166. ———. "Merchandising Commodities and Citizenship on Television," *Public Opinion Quarterly*, XV (1951), 679–91.

167. Wolfenstein, M., and Leites, N. *Movies: A Psychological Study*. Glencoe, Ill.: Free Press, 1950.

168. Woodham-Smith, C. *Florence Nightingale*. New York: McGraw-Hill, 1951.

169. Wright, C. R. *Mass Communication*. New York: Random House, 1959.

170. Yu, F. T. C. "Communications and Politics in Communist China." In L. W. Pye (ed.), *Communications and Political Development*, chap. 16. Princeton: Princeton University Press, 1963.

Index of Names

Subject Index